Colleges on the Brink

Colleges on the Brink

The Case for Financial Exigency

Charles M. Ambrose
Michael T. Nietzel

ROWMAN & LITTLEFIELD
Lanham • Boulder • New York • London

Published by Rowman & Littlefield
An imprint of The Rowman & Littlefield Publishing Group, Inc.
4501 Forbes Boulevard, Suite 200, Lanham, Maryland 20706
www.rowman.com

86-90 Paul Street, London EC2A 4NE, United Kingdom

British Library Cataloguing in Publication Information Available

Library of Congress Cataloging-in-Publication Data

Names: Nietzel, Michael T., author. | Ambrose, Charles M., author.
Title: Colleges on the brink : the case for financial exigency / Michael T. Nietzel, Charles M. Ambrose.
Description: Lanham, Maryland : Rowman & Littlefield, [2023] | Includes bibliographical references and index. | Summary: "The book comprehensively examines financial exigency, including its history and current status in higher education. It includes a case history about how exigency can help restore the financial integrity of economically distressed colleges"— Provided by publisher.
Identifiers: LCCN 2023035466 (print) | LCCN 2023035467 (ebook) | ISBN 9781475873252 (cloth) | ISBN 9781475873269 (paperback) | ISBN 9781475873276 (epub)
Subjects: LCSH: Universities and colleges—United States—Finance. | Education, Higher—United States—Costs. | Universities and colleges—Economic aspects—United States.
Classification: LCC LB2342 .N54 2023 (print) | LCC LB2342 (ebook) | DDC 378.1/06—dc23/eng/20230803
LC record available at https://lccn.loc.gov/2023035466
LC ebook record available at https://lccn.loc.gov/2023035467

♾™ The paper used in this publication meets the minimum requirements of American National Standard for Information Sciences—Permanence of Paper for Printed Library Materials, ANSI/NISO Z39.48-1992.

Contents

Preface

American higher education has had a difficult 21st century. It's gone through a major recession, the most severe economic downturn the nation has seen since the Great Depression; and it's endured the deadly Covid-19 outbreak, the worst pandemic in American history. Between 2017 and the end of 2022, enrollment in American colleges declined by about 1.8 million students, with most of that loss occurring in the wake of the pandemic. Since 2010, overall college enrollment in the United States has decreased by approximately three million students, a slide that's continued despite intense, annual efforts by higher education leaders to turn it around. As of 2021, 40.4 million Americans had attended college but dropped out before earning any degree or other official credential.[1] That kind of attrition is a symptom of a serious underlying problem.

Tuition revenue has plunged at hundreds of colleges and universities, with the losses being most pronounced at community colleges, small, private colleges, and regional public universities. In many states, appropriations for higher education have declined or remain far below adequate levels. At the same time, inflation has surged, and strikes and labor unrest have swept dozens of campuses, causing the cost of college operations to spike. On top of it all, the public's confidence in higher education, its belief in the value of a college degree, has taken a serious blow in recent years. Americans are also drowning in student loan debt, which, as of 2022, stood at more than $1.7 trillion, equal to almost $29,000 per borrower on average. No wonder then that a shrinking percentage of Americans believe that attending college isn't worth it anymore, with millions dropping out or skipping it altogether. A healthy skepticism about the value of college has hardened in the public's mind in recent years into an almost hostile cynicism about higher education in general.

Those numbers, plus a future where the pool of traditional age college students will shrink by as much as 15% within the next decade, constitute a serious threat to the economic viability of many colleges and universities, which are finding that their revenues are no longer able to keep up with expenses, a trend that was exacerbated significantly by the global Covid-19 pandemic. That threat has given rise to a host of grave predictions about the trajectory of American higher education. Questions like "Is this the end of college," "Are we seeing the death of higher education," "Is the death of the university upon us," have become a common, almost received wisdom, despite a lack of historical perspective or current empirical evidence for such grim assessments.

Perhaps most noteworthy among these projections was the claim in 2011 by the late Clayton Christiansen, the originator of the theory of "disruptive innovation," that as many as half of American colleges would go out of business within 10–15 years primarily as a result of competition from online education.[2] Of course, nothing close to that has transpired, but in some ways what ends up having been the disconfirmation of Christiansen's exaggerated predictions may have given a false sense of security to some institutions that their financial futures were more secure than they actually are.

A more sober, realistic assessment of the financial state of colleges and universities was provided by Robert Zemsky and his colleagues in *The College Stress Test*,[3] which was published just before the onset of the pandemic. The authors examined four variables—new student enrollment, net cash price, student retention, and major external funding—to gauge the economic viability of more than 2,800 higher education institutions. That analysis made clear that while college collapses would not be nearly as prevalent as many doomsayers were predicting, about 10% or less of American colleges faced substantial financial risk and another 30% were likely to face struggles in the future. After the pandemic, Zemsky revised the 10% at-risk number to 20%, saying, "I think in the short term, it's not 10% that are in real trouble, it's 20%. That's not to say 20% are going to close. But it ups the possibility. We're now going to have upward of 20% really terrified."[4]

We wrote this book for the colleges and universities that either are facing a substantial risk of economic failure or are entering a period of serious financial struggles. That number is not small, as Zemsky has pointed out, but it's also not the case that American higher education is a burning platform. American colleges are not the next Edsel or Blockbuster on the road to extinction. Their zero hour is not nigh, but neither are they immune to some very troubling market forces that could threaten the survival of many of them.

So, we wanted this book to offer a voice somewhere between the Cassandras who predict the eventual ruination of higher education and the Pollyannas who seem all too content with defending the status quo. We're bearish about the current business model that many colleges are clinging to, but we're bullish about the capacity of institutions to revise and remake that model. That's the balance we wanted to achieve. Eeyore, meet Tigger.

We believe the tools we describe in the ensuing chapters—up to and including the extreme measures associated with declaring financial exigency, which almost inevitably involves the retrenchment of nontenured and tenured faculty—can be used to change the ways colleges spend their money while still maintaining the academic values most institutions want to honor. The fact of the matter is that the business model followed at many colleges is too costly to be sustained much longer. The chase for higher ratings, the decline in the number of students attending college coupled with the enrollment of too many students who never finish their degree, the investment of too much money in programs and activities that don't produce good outcomes, the construction of too many capital projects, the misdirection of financial aid to students who don't need it, and the assumption of far too much institutional debt all spell trouble for a significant number of institutions. Simply put, they will need to change their ways or face serious financial consequences.

In the chapters that follow, we highlight the major financial headwinds now facing American higher education and why those headwinds may be stronger than at earlier points in history. We discuss the concept of financial exigency and several of its close counterparts or "near exigencies" when institutions undergo large-scale reorganization, restructuring, or budget resets to reduce their ongoing expenses. We outline the conditions that give rise to the need for major financial overhauls, and we discuss the steps that need to be taken to maximize the likelihood they will be successful in helping institutions regain their financial health.

Making major changes to the ways that colleges and universities operate is never easy. The status quo has a powerful lobby, including faculty and staff, who often resist changes urged by administrators; students, who typically like things the way they are; alumni, who like to keep things the way they were; governing boards, who don't like bad news; and outside policy makers, who often worry that when a college makes major changes it will mean more unhappy constituents. The result is that inertia often beats initiative. Reforms sit on a shelf or are sent back to the drawing board. Meanwhile, at-risk institutions sink deeper into the red. We discuss the most prevalent forms of resistance to financial restructuring, and we suggest some ways of coping with them.

It's one thing for an institution to survive financial exigency—in fact, most do—but it's another for it to emerge as a better college, one more capable of fulfilling its mission effectively and efficiently. In the final two chapters, we discuss several policies intended to put student success at the forefront of an institution's priorities. Although these policies are recommended in the context of colleges that are in financial jeopardy, their application should, in our view, be much broader. They constitute good educational practices for all kinds of institutions, regardless of their financial standing.

American colleges have proven to be remarkably resilient across the centuries, and we believe, they'll continue to be so. Throughout a largely prosperous history, they've been able to adapt and survive during hard times. In recent years, however, many colleges have found themselves in various states of financial peril, threatened by economic uncertainties, a prolonged stretch of sinking enrollments, a public increasingly doubtful about their value, a global pandemic, and their own tendencies to overbuild and overspend.

The challenge these colleges now face is to build their road back from that perilous position—the brink—and become better colleges that are leaner, more financially stable, and ready to provide the education that students and society need. For those colleges most at risk, the process we discuss in this book—financial exigency—offers one road back, albeit a hard one, but one that we suggest is navigable by the resourceful colleges and universities that remain one of America's greatest assets.

NOTES

1. https://nscresearchcenter.org/some-college-no-credential/

2. Christiansen C. & Eyring, H. J. (2011) *The Innovative University: Changing the DNA of Higher Education From the Inside Out.* New Jersey: Wiley.

3. Zemsky, R. Shaman, S., & Baldridge, S. *The College Stress Test.* Baltimore: Johns Hopkins University Press.

4. https://www.chronicle.com/article/will-coronavirus-close-your-college-for-good/

Acknowledgments

We benefited from the wise advice and assistance of many friends and colleagues in writing this book. They served as thoughtful, careful readers, who caught our mistakes, improved our early drafts, challenged our assumptions, and helped us think more clearly about what we wanted to accomplish. They helped improve the manuscript in countless ways.

Our heartfelt thanks to Nick and Carol Bormann, Dennis Cryder, Ken Dobbins, Tom Harnisch, Paul Kincaid, David Levy, Brian Long, Jamie Merisotis, Rick Staisloff, John Thelin, Carey Thompson, Bunky Wright, and Parker Young for their insights and suggestions on all aspects of the book.

We also want to acknowledge the willingness of our longtime friends Jay Nixon, former governor of Missouri, and Asa Hutchinson, former governor of Arkansas, to share their perspectives on higher education. We thank Jeffrey Scarborough and Quinn Cosgrove—two students of the Missouri Innovation Campus at the University of Central Missouri—for being interviewed about their experiences in that program.

We are appreciative to Andrew Laws, Austin Tatum, Jackson Nell and Ben Connelly of the Huron Consulting Group and Scott Carlson, from *The Chronicle of Higher Education* for their encouragement and support.

We also want to recognize the faculties, staffs, students, and Boards of Trustees at the institutions where we have had the privilege to serve in leadership capacities: Pfeiffer University, the University of Central Missouri, Henderson State University, and the Arkansas State University System (Ambrose), and the University of Kentucky and Missouri State University (Nietzel). We make special mention of the support provided by the ASU System and HSU teams to the exigency process at HSU.

To Sarah Chamberlin, we thank you for your terrific help with the graphics, illustrations, and other creative content. To George Justice, Provost of the University of Tulsa, thank you for making the library resources of the University of Tulsa available to us. And to Megan DeLancey at Rowman &

Littlefield, thank you very much for your careful attention to the manuscript's final preparation.

Chuck Ambrose thanks Kristen Ambrose, who has endured 25 years as a president's wife, along with 11 moves, two kids and grandkids and one financial exigency. Kristen has been Chuck's constant source of support and wisdom, but most importantly, she encouraged him for years to "write a book."

Finally, we want to acknowledge each other. Along with our labor of love for a lifetime of experiences within the academy, we came to develop a long-term friendship based on shared ideas back in the state of Missouri and our shared hopes for colleges that always find ways to become better. We could not imagine a better creative process than the two of us enjoyed from our first conversation about this book in Fort Smith, Arkansas to the countless 6 a.m. phone calls and texts, asking "Did you see this?" or "Can you believe this."

After our collective almost three decades as college presidents, we have had the rare pleasure of watching many friends and colleagues serve their institutions in extraordinary ways. Their care, compassion and sacrifices are unequaled. We also know that the pandemic had torn off many of the Band-Aids that were covering up the financial problems and systematic disparities affecting a large number of colleges. We hope that this book will help a reimagining of colleges that will work for all students and provide a sustainable future for the institutions about which we care so much. We're grateful to be able to write it with each other—two friends who shared many of the same journeys and who are committed to the importance of the policies and strategies we have amplified.

Chapter 1

Colleges On the Brink

American higher education is a remarkable enterprise. It's a big business, with nearly $700 billion in total expenditures made annually by its roughly 4,000 degree-granting institutions. Nationwide, the higher education work-force totals almost 3.5 million people across all institutions, with about 1.5 million faculty[1] and more than 1.9 million staff.[2] Every major American city is home to at least one prominent university, and colleges are spread all across the nation's landscape.

In many communities, especially in small town America, the local college is the area's largest employer, and it's the lifeblood of the region's economy, accounting for a large percentage of retail, travel, and entertainment custom-ers and preparing skilled workers for many high-demand jobs in the area. Those institutions serve as cultural centers and magnets for talent, turning their home communities into what David Staley and Dominic Endicott have called "knowledge towns."[3] Ever since the founding of Harvard in 1636, American colleges and universities have grown in reputation and stature to the point that they are envied worldwide and imitated to some extent by almost every other nation across the globe. In a 2023 evaluation of 1,594 uni-versities in 93 countries and territories by the higher education analyst QS Quacquarelli Symonds, U.S. universities dominated the world rankings based on evaluations of 54 different academic disciplines. The United States had the highest number of top-10 programs (256) of any country, and U.S. universi-ties were rated number one in 32 of the 54 subjects.[4]

American colleges educate our nurses and doctors, our architects and engi-neers, our teachers and journalists. They are home to some of the world's most brilliant minds, its leading scientists, engineers, writers, and historians. They are remarkable engines for economic growth, the places where miracle drugs are discovered, great books are written, and life-changing technologies are invented. They are home to massive libraries, modern laboratories, leading hospitals, beautiful grounds, and yes—goliath stadiums and stunning arenas.

HIGHER EDUCATION HEADWINDS

But American higher education is also facing a number of serious headwinds. It's in the midst of a severe financial challenge, marked by declining enrollments, stock market volatility, spiraling inflation, inadequate state funding, the great disruption from the Covid-19 pandemic, labor strife, and waning public confidence in the value of a college degree. While individually each of these factors is cause for concern, it's their cumulative impact—their additive effect—that spells real trouble and has brought hundreds of colleges to the edge of financial uncertainty and dozens of others to their financial breaking point.

Even at Harvard, the nation's wealthiest university, concerns about the nation's financial future are shaking confidence that higher education will be able to survive this period of turmoil. In a 2023 interview shortly before his retirement, Thomas J. Hollister, Harvard's Vice President for Finance and Chief Financial Officer, warned that Harvard needs to be "very cautious" in its financial management as it confronts an increasingly uncertain future. Citing an array of economic challenges, including record-high inflation levels, rising interest rates, recent bank failures, and stock market volatility, Hollister called these challenges a "quadruple whammy," that would affect Harvard's financial results in the coming years.[5]

All sectors of higher education—public and private, two-year and four-year, for-profit schools and nonprofit institutions—are facing financial challenges, but small, private colleges, regional public universities and community colleges have borne the brunt of the problems. For many of them, the financial future looks more bleak than it has in a long time. They are what we call colleges on the brink.

We wrote this book specifically for those colleges. In the chapters that follow, we describe how colleges can step back from that brink and avoid financial collapse. We discuss how they can restructure to achieve a more economically secure future. Although we focus on the use of financial exigency, perhaps the most extreme measure any college can employ to right the fiscal ship, we also cover related management strategies that have been used as substitutes for exigency. Even for relatively wealthy institutions where declaring a financial exigency is extremely unlikely, many of the tools we describe can be used to avoid the serious financial crises that have overtaken many colleges and universities with surprising speed.

THE ENROLLMENT SLIDE

According to estimates from the National Student Clearinghouse Research Center, in the five years between 2017 and 2022, total enrollment at degree-granting institutions, counting both undergraduate and graduate students, dropped from 19,949,828 to 18,155,619. That's a 9% decline. What's the decrease equate to in student headcount? About 1.8 million fewer students during a period that stretched across the two years before the Covid-19 pandemic through the three years when it was at its worst. Even with a small bounce back in new freshmen enrollments in fall, 2022, total higher education enrollment fell every year during that five-year span.[6]

According to a 2023 *Chronicle of Higher Education* analysis of enrollment by first-time students at more than 2,600 colleges, almost three-quarters (74%) of those institutions sustained enrollment losses in the first year of the pandemic. And nearly half of them saw enrollment drops of 10% or more. What's more, among those institutions that had losses of 10% or more, very few recovered those enrollments the next year. Only 7% of public institutions, and 20% of private, nonprofit schools were able to recoup the students they lost in the prior year. Among two-year colleges, only 5% were able to recover their enrollment losses. Although doctoral universities tended to fare a bit better, a mere 25% saw their enrollments return to pre-pandemic levels.[7]

Hopes for a substantial, longer-term enrollment recovery must be tempered by demographic realities. In his book, *The Agile College*,[8] Nathan Grawe summarizes projections about college-going rates through the mid-2030s, based on expectations of the available population of high school seniors, the group that traditionally accounts for the vast majority of college enrollees. While the current decade might see a modest increase in college enrollment through at least the mid-2020s, declines of 10–15% are likely after that into the mid-2030s, and Grawe predicts that more than half of the states will see as many as 15% fewer students headed for college by 2029.

These rates vary depending on the region of the country. Colleges in the Northeast and Midwest can expect the sharpest declines, those in the South and the West the smallest. The type of institution will matter as well. Elite schools and national universities are expected to fare the best during this period, just as they did throughout the pandemic; two-year colleges and regional public institutions will suffer the worst. But the larger point is that, regardless of location or sector, hundreds—if not thousands—of colleges will have to confront the future problem of a declining population of traditional college-going age students, owing in large part to the nation's declining fertility rate after the 2008 recession. The premise is brutally simple: in the words of Bill Conley, Bucknell University's VP for enrollment management, "If they weren't born, they're not going to college."[9]

The pandemic may have supersized the loss of students, but the slide in enrollment significantly predates the outbreak of the virus. It goes all the way back to 2010, after the Great Recession, when the number of students attending college in the fall semester peaked at just over 21.5 million.[10] As of 2022, that number had fallen by more than three million students. In addition to these losses, a decrease in the number of international students coming to U.S. colleges and the migration of nearly two million students to virtual instruction further eroded key sources of college revenue for two years as students either chose to not live on campus—or were unable to—during much of the pandemic.

INFLATION, STRIKES, AND DOUBTS ABOUT THE VALUE OF COLLEGE

Now add to the nosedive in enrolled students the increased operating costs that colleges and universities are having to pay. According to the annual Commonfund Higher Education Price Index® (HEPI), inflation for U.S. colleges and universities rose 5.2% in fiscal year 2022, almost twice the increase of 2.7% in the previous fiscal year and the highest since 6.0% in FY 2001.[11] Costs rose in all eight HEPI categories—faculty salaries; administrative salaries; clerical salaries; service employee salaries; fringe benefits; miscellaneous services; supplies and materials; and utilities. These increased costs, coming at the same time as the decreased tuition revenue associated with relentlessly decreasing enrollments, compounded the budget deficits that many institutions are continuing to experience.

Related to inflationary pressures, campus strikes and union activism among academic workers have surged. The historic strike at the University of California (UC), which saw 48,000 academic employees at ten UC campuses walk off their jobs in the nation's largest higher education strike ever,[12] set the stage for faculty and graduate student workers to ramp up their unionization efforts and demands for better compensation at colleges across the country. Indiana University graduate students declared a strike in 2022; that was followed by grad student strikes at the University of Michigan and Temple University. Graduate students at Yale University, Johns Hopkins University, Northwestern University, the University of Chicago, and Boston University have voted to unionize, and several prominent universities proactively awarded graduate students substantial raises and better benefits in hopes to preempt unionization efforts. Rutgers University faculty went on strike in 2023, for the first time in that university's history. And in April of that year, workers at three universities in Illinois—Chicago State University, Eastern Illinois University and Governors State University—were all on strike at the same time. Most observers believe this new era of labor activism on campus will continue for some time, driving up college costs even further.

Well, so far, so bad. What about the public's perceptions of colleges and universities? If the past few years have been tough, perhaps higher education's future prospects will look brighter, with people once again understanding the importance of college, seeing it as the golden ticket to a good job, and embracing it as the key to a prosperous and fulfilling life. In fact, just the opposite has happened. Americans' confidence in higher education has eroded considerably in the past few years. According to a 2018 national poll by Gallup, only 48% of the public had "a great deal" or "quite a lot" of confidence in higher education. That's 9% lower than in 2015, and it was the largest drop among all the 16 institutions—including Congress, the presidency, banks, and newspapers—that were surveyed over that period.[13] But this sentiment has grown worse. By 2023, when Gallup asked the same question, it found that only 36% of Americans had either a "great deal" (19%) or "quite a lot" (17%) of confidence in higher education.

Only half of Americans believed that a college education was "very important" in 2018, a dramatic decrease from the 70% who said that it was very important in 2013. In addition, 13% of adults believed that higher education was "not too important," more than twice the percentage (6%) who held that negative view in 2013.[14] In short, most of the general public—of all political persuasions—has come to believe that college costs too much, takes too long, and does not adequately prepare students for the jobs they want to take and that the economy needs them to fill. A large percentage of American adults simply are no longer willing to buy the value proposition that colleges have been selling.

What's worse, an increasing number of young adults—higher education's main customers—also question the value of college. In 2021, during the peak of the pandemic, when presented with this survey statement—"higher education is not worth the cost to students anymore"—nearly two-thirds of both current college students (65%) and those students still in high school (64%) agreed.[15] Our frequent personal conversations with students confirm that skepticism. More of them are questioning whether an investment in a college degree will pay off. Instead, they feel that it might be better to pursue an alternative form of preparation for their future life and work.

The loss of confidence in higher education has continued—or even accelerated—after the pandemic, an ominous sign for college leaders in the years ahead. According to a 2023 poll conducted by the *Wall Street Journal* in collaboration with NORC at the University of Chicago, skepticism about college has grown. In 2023, 56% of Americans thought that earning a four-year degree was "not worth the cost because people often graduate without specific job skills and with a large amount of debt to pay off." That compares to 47% in 2017 and only 40% in 2013 who thought that earning a college degree was not worth it.[16]

Doubts about the value of a college degree were strongest among people ages 18–34, and even 42% of people with college degrees doubted that those degrees were worth it, an increase of more than 10 percentage points from two polls conducted in the prior decade. Belief in the value of a college degree dropped sharply among older people and women. People over the age of 65 with faith in college declined to 44% from 56% in 2017. Confidence among women fell to 44% from 54%, according to the poll.

Perceptions like these send shivers down the spines of higher education leaders as they struggle to contend with negative stories about the inequities, irrelevance, runaway costs, and overall state of higher education. Then there's the problem of college student loan debt, which, at the beginning of 2023 as we were writing this book, stood at an astounding $1.7 trillion in unpaid federal and private loans. Perhaps nothing has been as damaging to the image of higher education as the daily diet of stories about how much debt students have incurred to finance their college education and how many of them now fear they will never be able to escape that debt.

The staggering amount of student debt has exerted several negative effects on higher education, beyond the obvious fact that it's left so many Americans burdened with a financial obligation they may never be able to pay off. It has encouraged students to think about college in strictly monetary terms—such as what major they should choose or what career path they need to follow—even if those choices don't reflect what students personally value the most. And it has shifted the public attitude about higher education from one that historically emphasized the common good advanced by adequate public support for education to one that increasingly conceives of a college education as primarily a private investment purchased by individual consumers.

CAMPUS SCANDALS AND UNREST

Americans' view of college has also been clouded by a succession of embarrassing revelations and high-profile campus imbroglios.

- The Varsity Blues scandal involving bribery and corrupt admissions practices at dozens of prestigious universities resulted in more than 50 people being criminally charged for their complicity with the various scams. Many of the accused eventually pleaded guilty or were convicted by a jury, described in detail by Nicole Laporte in her book

Guilty Admissions.[17] College ambitions and anxieties turned dozens of parents into eager co-conspirators or gullible followers of Rick Singer, the hypomanic hustler behind the cheating, bribing, and lying that many rich families used to gain their children's admission to elite colleges. But the corruption didn't stop with Singer and cutthroat parents. Officials at several colleges were willing to go along with obviously immoral, or clearly criminal, schemes as they lined their pockets with little regard for the individuals or institutions they exploited.

- Allegations of price-fixing by 17 of the nation's most elite universities in 2022 led to them being sued for alleged violations of antitrust laws by colluding to unfairly limit student financial aid. The plaintiffs, which included students attending some of those universities, claimed the universities had illegally shared a methodology for how much financial aid they would award to prospective students. Specifically, the suit alleged that the defendant universities had "participated in a price-fixing cartel that is designed to reduce or eliminate financial aid as a locus of competition, and that in fact has artificially inflated the net price of attendance for students receiving financial aid.[18]" In 2023, the University of Chicago became the first defendant university to settle the price-fixing claims against it.
- Numerous embarrassing episodes of misconduct have led to the expensive, highly publicized ousters of presidents at well-known institutions like the University of Michigan, Michigan State University, and Liberty University. Other institutions, including Columbia University, Ohio State University, the University of Michigan, Michigan State University, and UCLA have been rocked by lawsuits over sexual abuse allegations against physicians formerly in their employ.

On top of it, colleges have become a favorite target of many conservative politicians who criticize them for a host of reasons, both real and imagined. That rhetoric has taken a cumulative toll, with views of college now revealing a sharp partisan divide. In that same Gallup poll cited above, fewer than half of Republicans (41%) said a college education was very important, much lower than the percentages of Democrats (62%) and independents (50%) who held that opinion.

To some extent, some of these opinions have been confirmed in the marketplace—at least in the short term—as major employers have begun to reduce the number of entry-level positions for which they once considered a college degree to be a hiring requirement. Plagued by a chronic talent shortage and hundreds of thousands of unfilled positions following the pandemic, a growing number of tech companies, manufacturers, and financial service employers have shed sheepskin requirements in favor of other proof of job qualifications.

For example, General Motors joined Google, Bank of America, IBM, and Tesla and dropped the requirement of a college degree for some jobs that had previously required it.[19] And as one of his first acts of official business, Pennsylvania Governor Josh Shapiro issued an executive order[20] stating that 92% of all Commonwealth of Pennsylvania employee positions—or about 65,000 jobs—did not require a four-year degree. Shapiro directed his administration to begin to post job listings that identified equivalent experience that would be considered in lieu of a college degree whenever possible. Shapiro's order followed similar directives from Utah Governor Spencer Cox and Maryland Governor Larry Hogan that rolled back college degree requirements for many government jobs in their states.

Financial woes have hit every kind of institution from community colleges to major universities, private and public, rural and urban. Even several elite colleges, which have enjoyed economic good times for decades and have been able to rely on multi-billion-dollar endowments to fund much of their operations, have found it necessary to tighten their belts and cut back on expenses, particularly following the financial hit that many of their endowments suffered in 2022.[21] After the value of Williams College's endowment fell by $635 million (more than 11%) in 2022, it said budget reductions would probably be required.[22] Citing costs that were rising faster than revenue, Bates College, a highly selective liberal arts college in Lewiston, Maine, indicated in January 2023, that it would need to reduce programmatic (nonpersonnel) budgets by 5%.[23] A number of other brand-name colleges have taken similar actions in the past two years.

THE IMPACT OF THE PANDEMIC

Although they had been building for some time, the financial challenges facing higher education intensified in 2020. That's when the first consequences of the Covid-19 pandemic began to be felt on almost every college campus in the nation. As the coronavirus pandemic swiftly spread around the world, colleges across the country closed their residence and dining halls, ended intercollegiate athletic competitions, shuttered their administrative offices, sent faculty and staff home, and began shifting their classes to online instruction. Campuses that had been bustling with activity became ghost towns in the space of just a few days. The pandemic's consequences were unprecedented in the history of American higher education, causing financial setbacks and enrollment losses that are still being felt.

Higher education will remember April, 2020 as the month the furloughs began. That's when college leaders began to shift their focus to the massive revenue losses and cost increases they knew were coming, both in that year and for years to come.[24] But even with that recognition, many administrators elected to delay permanent reductions in staffing as long as possible, preferring instead less severe measures, such as hiring freezes; cuts to travel and routine operating expenses; postponement of renovations, repairs and building projects; reductions in administrators' and highly paid coaches' salaries; and mandatory employee furloughs.

A furlough is an unpaid leave of absence that's imposed for a consecutive number of days or served intermittently across a semester or year. Furloughed employees remain employees of the institution and often retain key benefits like employer-provided health insurance. When institutions furlough rather than terminate employees, it's usually because they hope to bring them back to work after the college recovers from its financial difficulties.

Even when furloughs are temporary, the decision to force employees into unpaid leaves is still difficult because it immediately reduces their income. Furloughs may be intended to save jobs while at the same time yielding immediate savings, but their human costs are significant, nonetheless. The large number of colleges that were forced to resort to furloughs during the initial stages of the pandemic is a stark indicator of just how seriously and quickly their financial condition deteriorated.

Depending on the time of year, institutions may be able to furlough staff only, rather than also including faculty in the plan. As a result, that approach almost always causes the economic impact to fall most heavily on an institution's lowest paid employees. It's exactly those workers who can least afford to be furloughed who typically feel the brunt of the action.

In addition, institutions must be prepared for the staff attrition that furloughs leave in their wake. Employees who might have been considering retirement or a job change are often motivated by a furlough to leave the institution for good, feeling that they have been unfairly singled out for bad treatment. That may be an intended or an unintended consequence, but regardless, in most large-scale furloughs, institutions must consider that the loss of institutional effectiveness and productivity that frequently occurs throughout a furlough period will continue long after it has been ended.

In those first months of the pandemic, the list of universities forced to furlough workers spread almost as fast as the virus. The University of Arizona sent shock waves across higher education when its president Robert C. Robbins announced a massive furlough of employees to cope with a projected $250 million budget shortfall.[25] Even though those furloughs were delayed and shortened in the months to come, the scope of the initial decisions at a public institution with the stature of the University of Arizona, a member of the venerated Association of American Universities, was stunning.

But it was only the beginning. Whether at small colleges or large universities, decisions to impose furloughs, salary cuts, hiring freezes, slashes to supplies and travel budgets, and even some layoffs became common. While it's hard to calculate the full human impact of these actions, there's no doubt that the initial flurry of furloughs contributed to significant personnel attrition across the higher education landscape and led to a perception that higher education had become a less desirable sector in which to work.[26]

Like the University of Arizona, other flagship public universities, highly esteemed private research universities, and major university systems were not spared from actions that just months earlier would have been viewed as unthinkable. As examples:

- The University of Wisconsin Board of Regents approved a furlough policy for all its campuses.[27]
- The University of Oregon gave 30-day notice to 282 employees that they were being put on leave-without-pay status.[28]
- The University of Montana furloughed 63 staff.[29]
- The University of Tulsa announced that in order to cope with unanticipated budget losses of more than $10 million, it was furloughing most of its nonfaculty staff for at least two weeks.[30]
- Marquette University furloughed approximately 250 faculty and staff.[31]
- Small private colleges, including Valparaiso, Guilford, and Bob Jones University announced unpaid furloughs for hundreds of staff. Union College in New York put 30% of its staff on temporary furloughs.[32] The list went on and on.

Furloughs are a kind of fiscal purgatory where temporary reductions are tried first to avoid the permanent pain inflicted on personnel who are fired. They are used as an almost-last resort, after belt-tightening measures like freezing open positions, curtailing travel, trimming operating expenses, offering bonuses for early retirements, and postponing building and renovation projects have all been tried but proven insufficient. They're usually intended to stave off shutting down academic programs and laying off faculty and staff, which, short of an institution's outright closure, are the most severe cost-saving steps that colleges can take. At many schools, pandemic-era furloughs were accompanied by negotiated separation agreements and voluntary salary cuts for senior college administrators and intercollegiate athletics coaches. Salary reductions in the range of 10%-20% were common, although some reached as high as 30%.

Higher education's economic losses continued to mount as the pandemic dragged on.

- The University of Delaware announced it was facing a budget hole of $250 million and would be forced to take severe measures, including furloughs, layoffs and reductions in retirement benefits.[33]
- Yale University said the pandemic had cost it over $200 million in lost revenues and increased expenses in FY 2021 and over $350 million since the pandemic's onset in March 2020.[34]
- The University of Colorado revealed it would have to cut an additional $17 million from its budget after seeing its enrollment dip during the pandemic.[35]
- The University of Maryland estimated it would need to slash $292 million from its budget as a result of the coronavirus pandemic, a situation university leaders described as "by far the largest financial crisis in the history of the university."[36]
- And the University of Alaska reported losses of nearly $15 million in 2020 due to the pandemic, a loss its leaders predicted at the time would likely double by the end of the fiscal year.[37]

The financial devastation from the pandemic is still being calculated and, at many institutions, its repercussions continue to affect operations, albeit in less visible ways than during its peak in 2020 and 2021. As an illustration, the initial estimate of the economic impact from the coronavirus pandemic on the 14 institutions in the Big Ten Conference in 2020 was $1.7 billion. Those losses included millions in less tuition revenue due to decreased enrollments, refunds of room and board fees, unbudgeted costs for changes in large-scale operations such as transitioning instruction from in-class to online delivery, lower state appropriations, reduced athletic and other event income, and decreased business at their academic health centers.[38]

As one illustration of the overall economic impact of the pandemic, an analysis conducted by the *Chronicle of Higher Education* in 2023 found that during the initial part of the Covid-19 outbreak, 61% of the higher education institutions in the U.S. saw their net tuition revenue decline.[39] Net tuition revenue is the amount of tuition dollars a college collects after subtracting the financial aid and other allowances it gives to students. It constitutes the largest source of revenue for private four-year colleges, and it makes up about $1 of every $5 in revenue received at public four-year institutions, according to the *Chronicle* analysis.

Very few higher education institutions—regardless of their wealth or status—were spared from the hemorrhaging of tuition. For example, among the eight Ivy League institutions, five reported lower tuition receipts. Princeton

University sustained the largest loss of net tuition revenue (-21%), followed by Harvard (-18%), Yale and Brown (-11% each) and Columbia (- 6%). Three Ivies reported small increases—Cornell University saw a 3% bump, and Dartmouth College and the University of Pennsylvania each had a 1% net tuition revenue increase.

While most colleges saw their net tuition revenue drop during this period, the declines were felt most sharply at two-year institutions, where more than 70% experienced tuition revenue decreases. But they were far from being exceptions; 60% of public colleges and 58% of private colleges suffered drop-offs in their net tuition revenue. From 2020 to 2021, two-year colleges saw a 6.3% decline in net tuition revenue; four-year private nonprofits had a 2.2% decrease, and public four-year schools sustained a 1.6% loss. The only institutions to see an increase across those two years were the comparatively small number of schools in the four-year, for-profit sector, which realized an 8% gain. Selectivity in admissions did not make a big difference either. Among colleges identified as more selective in their admissions by their Carnegie classification, 55% had a decrease in revenue from tuition, compared to 62% of schools classified as selective, and 59% classified as inclusive institutions.

By September of 2020, estimates of the pandemic's financial impact on American colleges and universities had grown to more than $120 billion, according to a letter sent to the U.S. House of Representatives by the American Council of Education (ACE) and dozens of other higher education organizations.[40] The letter appealed to Congress to send more financial relief to the institutions, comparable to the stimulus checks, unemployment benefits for individual Americans, and loans and bailouts for small businesses and states that the federal government had already authorized, as the economy continued its struggle to recover from the effects of the pandemic.

In their letter, the education leaders stated, "Previously, our associations calculated that the financial impact of the pandemic on students and institutions would total at least $120 billion. Now, roughly one month into the fall semester, our members are reporting that their revenue losses and new costs have already greatly exceeded this amount, especially in areas such as testing, contact tracing, quarantine, treatment, and learning technology. For their part, many of our students and their families are struggling with reduced incomes and job losses, resulting in the need for billions of dollars in increased student aid."

As bad as higher ed's financial condition became, it could have been much worse had it not been for the extra money that the federal government—under both President Trump and President Biden—handed out to colleges and their students to mitigate the economic fallout. That aid came in the form of three rounds of Higher Education Emergency Relief Fund (HEERF) grants, totaling about $77 billion—$14 billion in the Coronavirus Aid, Relief and Economic Security Act (CARES), $23 billion in the Coronavirus Response and Relief Supplemental Appropriations Act (CRRSA), and $40 billion in the American Rescue Plan (ARP).[41]

Most institutions receiving these funds were required to spend at least 50% of their total HEERF allocation on direct financial grants to students (for-profit institutions had to spend 100% of their allotment for student support). The remainder could be used by institutions to cover expenses they had to pay because of the pandemic, including lost revenue, reimbursement for expenses they'd already incurred, increased technology costs involving the transition to distance education, faculty and staff training to accomplish that transition, and millions in costs to mitigate or treat the virus.

Just how essential those relief funds were was confirmed in a 2023 report from the Department of Education, which revealed that more than 18 million college students—80% of whom were recipients of federal Pell Grants—received federal relief funds during the worst years of the pandemic.[42] That money helped students pay their bills, and it kept many of them enrolled in college. It also enabled colleges to avoid even larger enrollment declines and greater reductions in their tuition, housing, and dining revenue during the pandemic.

Of the HEERF funds which colleges could spend at their discretion, about $13 billion went to replace revenue that institutions claimed they had lost from various sources,[43] with public doctoral institutions reporting $4.8 billion in lost revenue, representing 37% of the claimed losses. Losses from academic sources, including tuition and fees, enrollment declines, and supported research totaled $6.1 billion, while room and board revenue losses were about $3.7 billion, and lost revenue from auxiliaries like bookstores and campus events were reported at roughly $3 billion.[44]

Although the HEERF relief funds helped most colleges and universities weather the worst of the pandemic's financial storm, they also gave many college leaders a false sense of security. They masked the loss of students and decreases in institutional revenue and allowed most colleges to continue too much of their business as usual—at least temporarily. The result? Many colleges paused or avoided altogether a substantial resetting of their budgets and a meaningful curbing of their ongoing expenses that eventually would need to occur. They were about to experience the consequences captured in the famous words of Warren Buffett, "Only when the tide goes out, do you learn who has been swimming naked." HEERF may have been a lifeline, but it's proved to be a short one that would not save every sinking ship.[45]

COLLEGE CLOSURES AND CONSOLIDATIONS

Estimates about the number of colleges that have closed in recent years vary depending on what definition of a "college" is applied. If all institutions, including special-focus schools like art institutes and music academies, are counted, the number is considerably greater than if just four-year public and nonprofit private institutions are the sample of interest. The number also depends on whether satellite campuses are counted as separate institutions or as part of a larger university.

According to the National Center for Education Statistics, there were 4,583 degree-granting colleges and universities in the U.S. in academic year 2015–2016. In 2020–2021, that number stood at 3,931, representing a decline of more than 650 institutions.[46] The vast majority of that decrease—more than 90%—was accounted for by a decrease in the number of private institutions, either nonprofits, or for-profit colleges, with the for-profit group constituting more of the decline than all other sectors combined. There were about 1,300 fewer higher education institutions in 2020 than in 1970, according to the National Center for Education Statistics. In the five years between 2015 and 2020, there were 533 fewer institutions, compared with a decrease of 744 taking place across the 45 years prior.[47]

During the initial pandemic years, considering all types of degree-granting institutions, the rate of closures appears surprisingly to have stayed fairly steady. In academic year 2020–2021, there were 51 fewer institutions than in the prior year; in 2019–2020, there were 60 fewer than the previous year.[48] The pace of college closures and mergers did not pick up, as the major rating agencies had predicted it would several years earlier.[49] The average number of annual closures by just four-year, nonprofit colleges has hovered between five to 12 since 2000. An analysis by the *Chronicle of Higher Education* found that since 2000, as few as five stand-alone private nonprofit colleges had closed in a single year and as many as 21, occurring in 2018.[50]

How many colleges might be at risk of closure is another matter altogether. EY-Parthenon, a management-consulting company, has developed an index of financial health intended to single out institutions at risk. In a 2022 analysis that used federal data about a school's market demand, retention and graduation rates, the index identified about 20% of institutions to be "at risk" with another 20% in "monitor" status, meaning they could drop into the "at-risk" category.[51] That estimate is roughly the same as the post-pandemic, at-risk group identified by Robert Zemsky and his colleagues that we described in the Preface. Likewise, when Forbes assigned financial grades to more than 900 private institutions, based on nine operational and financial measures for fiscal year 2021, it handed out "Cs" or lower to about 20% of the institutions.[52]

Small, tuition-dependent institutions have been particularly susceptible to closure or mergers forced by pandemic-related financial woes. Mills College in California, Becker College in Massachusetts, Concordia College in New York, Marymount University in California, and MacMurray College and Lincoln College in Illinois are prominent examples.

One of the largest and most closely watched consolidations occurred in Pennsylvania where the Pennsylvania State System of Higher Education voted to consolidate six public universities into two regional campuses.[53] After a long process of debate about how best to address years of sagging enrollment and growing debt, the system board voted unanimously to turn its universities in Bloomsburg, Lock Haven, and Mansfield into a reconfigured Commonwealth University in the northeast part of Pennsylvania and the campuses at California, Clarion, and Edinboro into Pennsylvania Western University in the west. The mergers represented a necessary, but still controversial, attempt to salvage a system that was experiencing increasing financial instability. "We're bleeding cash," acknowledged Daniel Greenstein, the system's chancellor, at the time, adding that delaying the consolidation as some had urged would only have made the system's financial problems worse. That's a theme we will emphasize in the chapters to come.

In 2022 and 2023, several more colleges either reached or neared the end of their financial road. It seemed that every week brought news of another closure or near collapse. Cazenovia College, a small liberal arts college in New York announced it would close its doors after 200 years of operation.[54] Cazenovia's fate was sealed when it defaulted on a $25 million bond payment.[55] Contributing to the problem was a five-year enrollment drop of about 40% from a peak of more than 1,000 students, resulting in operating losses of $3.3 million in the fiscal year ending June 30, 2020. Cazenovia sustained another $2 million operational loss in the next fiscal year.[56]

"We're deeply disappointed that it has come to this," said Ken Gardiner, chair of Cazenovia's Board of Trustees. "Considerable time and effort have been spent on improving the College's financial position over the past several years. Unfortunately, the headwinds and market conditions were insurmountable, leading to a projected deficit of several million dollars for next year. As a result, the College won't have the funds necessary to be open and continue operations for Fall 2023 and beyond."

That same week, Holy Names University (HNU) in Oakland, California announced that it would close, after 154 years of operation, a decision necessitated by rising operational costs, declining enrollment, and an increased need for institutional operating support. "We have been doing our best to find a partner to keep the university functioning and continue HNU's mission," said HNU Board Chairperson Steven Borg. "While we've had interest in long-term collaboration from potential partners, we do not have the type of interest that would sustain HNU in continuing to offer its own programs and services, so we are forced to make the difficult decision to close and designate a transfer institution in the best interest of our students."[57]

Presentation College, a small private college in Aberdeen, South Dakota, announced in January, 2023 that it would close its doors at the end of the academic year.[58] Its enrollment had slipped from 821 students in fall 2016, to only 577 five years later, and its net tuition revenue decreased from $10.3 million a year to $7.5 million across the same period.

In March of 2023, Finlandia University, a small private institution in Hancock, Michigan, revealed it would cease operations "due to a combination of demographic changes, with fewer high school graduates available, a steep decrease in interest in going to college among those graduates, and an unbearable debt level."[59] The school had been established in 1896 (under the original name of Suomi College) and was affiliated with the Evangelical Lutheran Church of America. Despite that legacy and its best efforts to survive the crisis, Finlandia was unable to mend its finances or maintain its enrollment.

Iowa Wesleyan University also announced in March, 2023 that it would close at the end of that academic year. In its official statement, the university said, "The decision is based on a combination of financial challenges—increased operating costs due to inflationary pressures, changing enrollment trends, a significant drop in philanthropic giving, and the rejection of a proposal for federal Covid funding by Governor Reynolds."[60] We'll have more to say about this case and the role of governors as it pertains to college funding and financial exigency in Chapter 5.

In Alabama, Birmingham-Southern College (BSC), a small, liberal arts college, founded in 1856 and affiliated with the United Methodist Church, said it needed $37.5 million in public funds to keep its doors open. In a letter to members of the Jefferson County Delegation of the Alabama Legislature, Sen. Jabo Waggoner and Rep. Jim Carns wrote: "Birmingham-Southern has been operating in financial distress for over a decade. Without support, it will not be able to continue to operate after May 2023."[61] The college said its financial challenges began with "a building program in the mid-2000s that drew heavily upon the endowment and caused the College to take on significant debt. The financial crisis of 2008–2009 and an error in accounting of federal financial aid further depleted the College's resources." The college claimed that if it could not build back its endowment, which it was striving to do, "the economic model under which BSC operates is simply not sustainable for the long term."[62]

While the bailout plan drew initial support from lawmakers, it didn't fly with the governor. In March, 2023, Governor Kay Ivey's office announced that she would not use state dollars to prop up Birmingham-Southern's finances.

"The state has no plan to use the taxpayers' public funds to bail out a private college," said Gina Maiola, a spokeswoman for the governor.[63] Nonetheless, the college's trustees voted to keep the school open, hoping they could negotiate a loan from a newly created state fund that would keep it afloat.

Birmingham-Southern's situation illustrates the common reactions at many schools facing grim financial prospects. "If only we had more money," "if only we could increase private donations," "if only the state would give us more support," "if only we could enroll more students," "if only we had a little more time, this will turn around," are common sentiments one often hears from leaders of institutions on the brink. While those claims may serve short-term interests and give temporary assurances to a college's supporters, they also tempt campus leaders to postpone—sometimes until it's too late—the budget reductions and reallocation of resources that a candid appraisal would reveal are necessary.

While many of the colleges announcing their demise blamed the cascade of effects from the coronavirus as the precipitating cause, the fact is that their closure may actually have been delayed somewhat because of the HEERF funding and one-time increases in state appropriations that kept them afloat throughout much of the Covid-19 pandemic. Those bursts of funding proved to be only temporary buoys that couldn't prevent their ultimate sinking.

Now those federal relief funds have been spent. They're all gone. And it's very unlikely that funding by private foundations or more bailouts from the states will be offered as new lifelines. Most higher education observers—ourselves included—believe that many more institutions will be forced to close in the next decade or so. They waited too long. They avoided too many hard decisions. They kicked too many cans down the road. They came to the brink, and now they're at risk of falling.

In addition, it's important to understand that the recent run of college closures has taken place during a time when state financial support for higher education has rebounded in many (but not all) states. In some states, it's increased by a considerable amount. Like the federal HEERF allocations, increases in state funding may have temporarily kept the wolves from the doors of many public institutions, particularly those smaller regional universities that derive almost all of their revenue from a combination of state appropriations and tuition.

According to a recent Grapevine report from the State Higher Education Executive Officers Association (SHEEO), state support for higher education reached $112.3 billion in fiscal year 2023, a 6.6% increase over 2022. With that increase, overall state funding for higher ed had increased 27.5% between 2018 and 2023. The FY 2022 and FY 2023 funding levels marked the only two times in history that this support has topped $100 billion.[64] As a result of this increase, public higher education appropriation surpassed the pre-recession per-student funding level for the first time since 2008; inflation-adjusted education appropriations were 3.1% or $304 greater per FTE than in 2008. More than two-thirds of that state money has gone to fund the operations of public two-year and four-year colleges (most of the rest goes to student financial aid, research and support for public medical schools), providing them a cushion against inflation and reductions in tuition revenues associated with the protracted drop in enrollments.

Of course, the vast majority of private institutions don't have this kind of public financial backstop to call upon, which explains why small, private colleges that are not highly selective in the students they admit, are highly dependent on tuition dollars and don't have big endowments to fall back on, have suffered so much from sagging enrollment and have been the most likely to be forced into closure.

IS THIS DIFFERENT THAN BEFORE?

This is not the first time, of course, that higher education has faced tough economic times and been warned that it could be in trouble. As Karin Fisher has documented in a much-cited *Chronicle of Higher Education* article, "The Shrinking of Higher Ed," we've seen doomsday scenarios before.[65] In the past, however, American higher education has always been able to grow its way out of crises. It's been much more resilient than it's often given credit for, a fact confirmed by an important study by Melissa Tarrant, Nathaniel Bray, and Stephen Katsinas of the fate of 491 nonselective institutions that were labeled "invisible colleges" back in the 1970's because they were relatively unknown and viewed as susceptible to financial threats. Of those 491 original institutions, 80 had closed, but 84% were still open as of 2012–13, either as stand-alone or merged colleges.[66]

Colleges may get knocked down, but they tend to bounce back, having repeatedly devised and turned to a set of tried-and-true strategies to attract more students and bring in more revenue. They've increased their access to underrepresented groups; they've added new academic programs; and many have broadened their missions from undergraduate teaching to graduate training in an often-successful attempt to woo more students.

For example, after American colleges experienced low enrollments before and during World War II, higher ed went through decades of expansion, fueled both by thousands of returning GIs heading to college along with the children of the baby boom coming of college age. New institutions were opened, existing colleges expanded their capacity, and the federal government began pumping huge sums of money into university research and graduate education. It was what higher education historian John Thelin termed higher education's "Golden Age."[67]

However, by the 1980s, things began to slow down, once again. Birth rates had fallen, and colleges braced for a period where a serious enrollment contraction was predicted. Except for one thing: it didn't happen. Although the number of high school graduates decreased, college enrollment did not. Instead, it increased, owing largely to two factors. First, the number of women enrolling in college increased dramatically, such that by the 1990s—for the first time in history—women outnumbered men, an enrollment pattern that's been maintained ever since.

Second, the economy changed from one based largely on manufacturing that didn't require a college degree to land a good job and achieve economic success to one based on service and knowledge, where individuals with a college degree were much more likely to get ahead than those without one. So while the number of high school graduates might have decreased, the percentage of them who enrolled in college increased substantially for a straightforward reason. They had a strong financial incentive to do so.

Other factors have contributed in the past to colleges being able to maintain or even increase enrollments in the face of demographic trends and social changes. For example, the Vietnam War saw many men enroll in college in order to avoid being drafted. But when the threat of conscription ended in 1973 after President Nixon did away with the draft, it reduced the lure of attending college as a way to defer mandatory military service.

The 1970s was a period when, like now, higher education faced declining enrollments along with soaring inflation rates. It also had to contend with very negative public attitudes about college in the wake of widespread campus protests over the Vietnam War, civil rights, university investment strategies, free speech, and the "establishment." Like today, public opinion about higher education had soured. As Fisher noted, "The Carnegie Council, in a retrospective report with resonance for today's college leaders, said the unrest had "shattered confidence on campus and support in the community." Some prominent officials, like Gov. Ronald Reagan of California, successfully ran for elected public office by vowing to "clean up the mess" on college campuses. A significant percentage of the American public viewed college students and college faculty with impatience, disdain, or both.

By the 1970s, what Thelin had called higher education's "Golden Age" had turned into what he described as the time of the "troubled giant." Legislators, campus leaders, and the general public had become "fed up and worn out" with what they perceived to be the constantly troubled, always in turmoil college campus. But Congress came to a rescue of sorts, this time in the form of a new financial aid program—the federal Pell Grant, which it introduced in 1972 as a means of helping students with meager financial resources still be able to afford a college education. Pell Grants made it possible for millions of students from modest and low-income backgrounds to attend college, opening up new admissions opportunities for colleges and universities to pursue. They helped colleges regain their enrollments. Pell Grants offered not only a ladder of upward mobility for individual students, they served as a lifeline for colleges struggling to maintain their fiscal fitness.

Another higher education crisis occurred during the recession of 2008. While enrollments were strong during this period, as they typically have been during economic downturns, other sources of revenue were not. State appropriations to public institutions were cut, endowment returns hit the skids, and university budgets were slashed in response. But as before, colleges created ways to climb out of the hole. Two strategies were particularly useful. Institutions expanded their online course and degree offerings, and they intensified their efforts to recruit international undergraduate students, a large percentage of whom pay the full tuition pricetag, making them a very attractive target for revenue-depleted institutions.

Colleges are historically accustomed to boom and bust cycles, but since 2020 a unique combination of factors appears to have changed the equation. This time, it's less boom, more bust. While economic doldrums often result in more students enrolling in college, the pandemic resulted in just the opposite trend. Enrollments continued to fall at the same time there was a growing perception among the public that a college degree was no longer necessary to land a good job. Add to that mix an increasing number of new content and instructional providers entering the education marketplace and offering hundreds of short-term training and credentialing programs they've promoted as cheaper and quicker alternatives to traditional degrees, particularly those offered at community colleges. Those competitors have eaten into the potential college-going audience even further.

With enrollment of international students in American colleges stalling under the Trump administration's nationalistic rhetoric, the pandemic further weakened the U.S. domination of the international student market. It put a temporary, but protracted, stop to most international travel, and other counties are now competing more successfully with U.S. colleges for students who want to leave their home countries to pursue their education. The U.S. is no longer their only good choice. And not every school can plow the resources into online programming that large institutions can afford, leaving many colleges on the outside looking in on that recruitment strategy as well.

Where can colleges now turn for their enrollment boosts? Basically, they have two choices. Lure more of the students who've left college before they earned a degree to resume their education, or try to out-recruit other schools for the dwindling supply of traditional-age students and for whatever new markets of less traditional students can be developed.

The former strategy sounds good, but it's not yet yielded very large returns. The number of "some-college-no-degree" students who've returned to college remains relatively small; in fact, the percentage of them returning to college has decreased compared to earlier years. Nor is it probable that it will grow that much in the future, given the costs, scheduling obstacles and family obligations faced by many adults who might otherwise be tempted to return to college.

And the second option is likely to result in a zero sum game, where the rich get richer, and less well-resourced schools lose more ground. Most prestigious private institutions have been able to maintain their enrollments throughout and after the pandemic, and many public flagship universities have also attracted more students at the expense of other schools.

The biggest losers have been regional public universities, less selective, private liberal arts colleges and community colleges. These, of course, are the very institutions most likely to serve large numbers of traditionally underrepresented minority students, students from low- income families, and students who are the first in their families to attend college. No surprise then, these are the very same groups of students whose enrollment in college has eroded the most in recent years.

The steep enrollment drop off and the financial consequences associated with it are continuing, and many institutions are beginning to run out of all their relatively easy cost-containment options. In just the first few months of 2023, as we were writing this book, several institutions including Southern Oregon University; Indiana State University; Bemidji State University; St. Cloud State University; Marymount University in Virginia; the University of Holy Cross in New Orleans; the College of Saint Benedict and Saint John's University, two linked institutions in Minnesota; Milliken College and Bradley University in Illinois; Cardinal Stritch University and Marian University in Wisconsin plus the University of Wisconsin-Oshkosh; Antioch College in Ohio; Upper Iowa University; and North Dakota State University announced they were reducing their staff and faculty workforce, closing or combining many of their academic programs, or considering declarations of financial exigency in attempts to correct large budget deficits.

At other institutions, such as The King's College in New York, a complete closure of the school had not yet been finalized but appeared likely. In August 2023, Alderson Broaddus University in West Virginia relinquished its accreditation ahead of a planned closure. In Connecticut, leaders of the 17-campus Connecticut State Colleges and Universities system warned that it was bracing for layoffs, tuition increases, and possible campus closures as a result of what they said was a $335 million shortfall in the budget.[68] All these institutions had come to a similar realization—they weren't going to be able to grow out of their problems this time, or as Southern Oregon University

President Rick Bailey put it, just "pull the tuition lever" every year their budgets became more unbalanced.

A particularly poignant example of the extent to which university budgets have been stretched to the breaking point involves Valparaiso University, a private institution in northwest Indiana. Facing years of declining enrollment, Valparaiso revealed plans in 2022 to sell off several works of rare art from its Brauer Museum of Art in order to raise enough money to renovate two of its dormitories. Valparaiso had already closed its law school and terminated some of its academic programs, but its president, Jose Padilla, wanted to raise funds for the dorm renovations because he thought that spiffier residence halls would help boost enrollment. Padilla proposed the deaccession of three paintings from the college's museum collection: Frederic E. Church's *Mountain Landscape*, Childe Hassam's *The Silver Vale and the Golden Gate*, and Georgia O'Keeffe's *Rust Red Hills*. Combined, the paintings were estimated to be worth $20.5 million.

The proposal prompted an outcry from arts advocates, the university's faculty, and Richard Brauer, the museum's namesake, who sued the university and said he wanted his name removed from the museum if the deaccessioning took place. "For Valparaiso University's Museum of Art to have my name has conferred a high honor on me, but with this sale it will wrongly reflect my approval of its utterly disgraceful, irreparably existentially diminishing, unethical, and seemingly unnecessary, museum art collection sale actions!" Brauer wrote in an email to Padilla. Leaving aside the ethical considerations, the proposal illustrates the extent to which some college administrators will cling to fantasies about expansion or expensive capital improvements as a solution to their financial plight.[69]

Valparaiso is not the first university to sell off its art to raise money. Back in 2010, Fisk University, a private HBCU in Nashville, tried to sell two of its paintings from its Alfred Stieglitz art collection in order to raise money to keep the school open in the face of several ongoing financial problems. But a protracted legal challenge stopped the sale and eventually led to the university sharing the collection with an Arkansas museum founded by Walmart heiress Alice Walton in exchange for a $30 million payment. Several years later it was learned that Hazel O'Leary, Fisk's president at the time of the halted art sale, had also quietly managed to sell two other paintings to raise additional funds for the university.[70]

More and more often, colleges and universities are finding that their numbers simply are no longer adding up and that the prospects for them turning in a positive direction are dwindling. Their markets are collapsing. Their margins are sinking. Their missions are imperiled. They have been pushed to the brink.

COLLEGES ON THE BRINK

This book is about the steps that colleges on the brink can take to avoid financial crisis, collapse, and closure. We describe a set of tools, which when properly used, can help colleges step back from the brink, reassess their finances, restructure their academic programs, rebalance their budgets, and forge a more sustainable future. We concentrate specifically on financial exigency scenarios, when colleges are forced to employ every tool of transformation at their disposal. We discuss the proper steps as well as the common mistakes that colleges take either when they declare financial exigency or when they attempt a large-scale restructuring without formally declaring an exigency.

Even for those institutions that have cash reserves, large endowments, or other streams of revenue that make financial exigency only the most remote possibility, the tools described in the following chapters can be used to restructure budgets, enhance performance, improve outcomes, and forestall the spiral that other institutions are experiencing at speeds that are difficult to reverse.

Recent history suggests that the number of institutions in this category is growing. As examples, in 2023, DePaul University, the largest Catholic university in the nation, and West Virginia University, the flagship institution in that state, revealed they were both facing tens of millions in budget deficits. West Virginia University subsequently recommended terminating 32 academic programs and 169 faculty lines to help address its financial crisis. That same year, four universities in the Big Ten—Rutgers University, Pennsylvania State University, the University of Minnesota and the University of Nebraska—all announced that they were facing significant budget shortfalls (exceeding $100 million at both Rutgers and Penn State and $17 million and $13 million at Minnesota and Nebraska, respectively) that would require substantial cost reduction measures.[71] The Big Ten universities are among the best-resourced public institutions in the nation. For inflation and enrollment losses to hit their bottom lines this hard is an ominous sign of the economic setbacks many more less well-funded universities might soon be facing.

We also examine several of what we call "near exigency" procedures and related management maneuvers that have been used as substitutes for exigency. Some institutions avoid formal invocations of financial exigency because they want to circumvent the policies and procedures that their own regulations require for such declarations. They want to achieve the cost reductions that a financial exigency declaration can yield without having to go through all the time, steps, and public scrutiny that the process entails. These short-circuits are understandable, and in some emergency situations they may be necessary, but they come with at least one major drawback—they typically fail to educate the entire campus community the faculty, staff, and students—about the financial realities an institution is facing. The results from that approach include resentment over the lack of a transparent process, an inadequate understanding of the school's true financial condition, and a continuing, misplaced complacency about its economic security. They represent a missed opportunity for an institution to come to grips fully with the changes to its business model that will probably become necessary eventually.

We also discuss other ways that campuses seek to avoid restructuring—usually by nibbling around the edges of their budgets rather than taking the bigger bite that might be needed. The unfortunate result is that they often prolong their pain and decline and only deepen the financial reckoning when it finally does occur. When a college waits too long to tackle a budget that is structurally out of balance, it will typically add to the total cost of eventually bringing it under control.

We cover the timelines and processes that are often employed in a financial exigency. What are the mechanics of exigency? How long does it take for financial problems to accumulate to a serious crisis? How dire do financial conditions need to become for exigency to be justified? How is the situation best communicated to the campus community and external constituents?

Taking a college or university through financial exigency is not easy. It's not for the faint of heart. In most cases, a number of powerful forces will align to make it difficult for an institution to embark on and follow through with the fundamental changes involved in an exigency. The cultural playbook that's been written to delay or resist change in higher education is well-established, drafted by strong campus constituents, all guarding their own sacred cows. That playbook will be on full display during most financial exigency situations.

Alongside these protected interests are several false narratives and institutional myths about change-making that are prevalent in higher education—e.g., that you can never cut your way to improvement, that a college that doesn't grow is destined to wither, that small class size is the key to better learning, that the liberal arts are always unfairly targeted, and that better fundraising is the key to sustaining an institution's operations.

Confronting these resistances and myths is arduous, particularly given the ability of social media to amplify them. Overcoming them is even harder, as many presidents will attest. Few college presidents or chancellors sign up to be the target of a no-confidence vote, face angry alumni, be charged with wanting to destroy an institution, or be fingered as "the only college president who volunteered to shrink higher education." Nonetheless, we believe that such opposition can ultimately be overcome with the right combination of savvy, data, determination, and empathy.

Done properly, declaring financial exigency can revitalize an institution. It may actually increase its value, reengage major stakeholders who've been insisting on changes and calling for solutions, and introduce the type of discipline required to improve its financial integrity and survival. The institutional analyses that lead an institution to declare financial exigency are useful for—perhaps especially for—colleges that are not on the edge of going under, but that need a significant financial reset—a budget Mulligan—that realigns ongoing expenditures with actual revenue. A detailed understanding of a college's revenues and expenses—shared transparently with faculty, staff, students, trustees, alumni, and external constituents—can be used to avoid, rather than undertake, exigency.

Even when it is invoked, financial exigency need not be the death knell of a college, as it is sometimes characterized. Contrary to the prevailing myth, institutions can cut their spending and achieve sustainable success and fiscal integrity if they rebuild smartly at the same time. The long-term goal should be, whether through a regular, robust budget process, a major budget reset, or through the extraordinary conditions of exigency, to make a new financial model sustainable for an institution and to build a better college, dedicated to educating students well in the process.

NOTES

1. https://nces.ed.gov/programs/coe/indicator/csc/postsecondary-faculty

2. https://www.univstats.com/staffs/

3. Staley, D. J. and Endicott, D.D.J. (2023). *Knowledge Towns: Colleges and Universities As Talent Magnets*. Baltimore: Johns Hopkins University Press.

4. https://www.topuniversities.com/subject-rankings/2023

5. https://www.thecrimson.com/article/2023/3/28/harvard-cfo-hollister-caution/

6. https://nscresearchcenter.org/current-term-enrollment-estimates/

7. https://www.chronicle.com/article/big-drops-in-enrollment-hit-colleges-in-the-first-fall-of-the-pandemic-who-was-able-to-bounce-back

8. https://www.press.jhu.edu/books/title/12234/agile-college

9. https://www.chronicle.com/article/demographic-data-let-colleges-peer-into-the-future/

10. https://nces.ed.gov/pubs2012/2012280.pdf

11 https://www.commonfund.org/research-center/press-releases/2022-higher-education-price-index-hepi-report-released

12. https://www.theguardian.com/commentisfree/2022/dec/05/california-academic-strike-most-important-us-higher-education-history

13. https://news.gallup.com/opinion/gallup/242441/confidence-higher-education-down-2015.aspx

14. https://www.forbes.com/sites/michaeltnietzel/2019/12/12/americans-view-of-higher-education-takes-a-major-drop/?sh=446779615ba5

15. https://www.insidehighered.com/news/2021/07/07/students-see-less-value-college-despite-positive-experiences

16. https://www.wsj.com/articles/americans-are-losing-faith-in-college-education-wsj-norc-poll-finds-3a836ce1

17. https://www.twelvebooks.com/titles/nicole-laporte/guilty-admissions/9781538717097/

18. https://kval.com/news/local/uo-to-put-282-workers-on-leave-without-pay-status-to-help-with-budget-impact-of-covid-19

19. https://www.computerworld.com/article/3669412/companies-move-to-drop-college-degree-requirements-for-new-hires-focus-on-skills.html

20. https://www.governor.pa.gov/wp-content/uploads/2023/01/20230117_EO%202023-03_Final_EXECUTED.pdf

21. https://www.forbes.com/sites/michaeltnietzel/2022/10/13/elite-universities-saw-endowments-slide-in-fiscal-year-2022/?sh=385451ee5995

22. https://williamsrecord.com/461985/news/endowment-declines-11-2-percent-college-anticipates-budget-cuts-for-next-fiscal-year-as-inflation-persists/

23. https://www.bates.edu/finance-administration/2023/01/05/bates-in-2023-fi

24. https://www.forbes.com/sites/michaeltnietzel/2020/04/19/college-furloughs-have-begun/?sh=4d26473c23cd

25. https://tucson.com/news/local/university-of-arizona-sets-furloughs-pay-cuts-lasting-months-amid-pandemic/article_bbe1e7ff-9ae5-56e2-accd-9516e5421ffa.html

26. https://www.insidehighered.com/news/2022/05/04/turnover-burnout-and-demoralization-higher-ed

27. https://www.wisconsin.edu/uw-policies/uw-system-administrative-policies/interim-furlough/

28. https://kval.com/news/local/uo-to-put-282-workers-on-leave-without-pay-status-to-help-with-budget-impact-of-covid-19

29. https://missoulian.com/news/local/university-of-montana-63-staff-furloughed/article_952b24a9-c062-5e1a-b1c9-a97e5d8d9b54.html

30. https://tulsaworld.com/news/local/education/university-of-tulsa-announces-furloughs-as-financial-losses-grow-due-to-covid-19/article_9db8d7fe-d622-5f32-b47b-e3c83aaeb6f2.html

31. https://marquettewire.org/4031224/news/breaking-mu-announces-unpaid-furloughs-to-curb-covid-19-financial-impact/

32. https://www.forbes.com/sites/michaeltnietzel/2020/04/19/college-furloughs-have-begun/?sh=1cbb505223cd

33. https://www.wdel.com/news/facing-250m-deficit-university-of-delaware-turns-to-layoffs-furloughs/article_78076b68-fe7b-11ea-ae60-63f7dd5f786a.html

34. https://provost.yale.edu/news/university-budget-update-2021-22

35. https://www.denverpost.com/2020/09/03/cu-boulder-budget-cuts-coronavirus-enrollment/

36. https://dbknews.com/2020/09/11/umd-budget-cut-coronavirus-salary/

37. https://www.adn.com/alaska-news/education/2020/09/16/on-top-of-budget-cuts-covid-19-has-cost-the-university-of-alaska-15-million-so-far/
38. https://www.forbes.com/sites/michaeltnietzel/2020/05/03/big-ten-universities-estimate-they-have-already-lost-more-than--17-billion-from-the-coronavirus/?sh=73f84d433716
39. https://www.chronicle.com/article/tuition-revenue-has-fallen-at-two-thirds-of-colleges-during-the-pandemic?sra=true&cid=gen_sign_in
40. https://www.acenet.edu/Documents/Letter-House-Fall-COVID-Supplemental-092520.pdf
41. https://www2.ed.gov/about/offices/list/ope/arp.html
42. https://www2.ed.gov/about/offices/list/ope/heerf-2021-annual-performance-report.pdf
43. https://www.chronicle.com/article/higher-ed-received-billions-in-covid-relief-money-where-did-it- go?cid=gen_sign_in
44. https://www.chronicle.com/article/these-were-higher-eds-biggest-financial-losses-from-the- pandemic?sra=true&cid=gen_sign_in
45. https://www.newamerica.org/education-policy/reports/from-crisis-to-recovery/introduction
46. https://nces.ed.gov/programs/digest/d21/tables/dt21_317.10.asp
47. https://www.forbes.com/sites/emmawhitford/2022/11/15/after-colleges-close-most-displaced-students-never-earn-a-degree/?sh=79b4c66e1b9a
48. https://www.insidehighered.com/news/2021/08/02/number-colleges-shrinks-again-including-publics-and-private-nonprofits
49. https://www.insidehighered.com/quicktakes/2018/07/25/moodys-private-college-closures-11-year
50. https://www.chronicle.com/article/when-it-comes-to-college-closures-the-sky-is-never-going-to-fall
51. https://www.ey.com/en_us/education/strategy-consulting/six-key-financial-and-operational-metrics-pinpoint-higher-ed-risk
52. https://www.forbes.com/sites/emmawhitford/2023/04/26/forbes-2023-college-financial-grades-the-strongest-and-weakest-colleges/?sh=207a4d121097
53. https://www.insidehighered.com/news/2021/07/15/pennsylvania-system-approves-plan-merge-six-universities
54. https://www.cazenovia.edu/closing
55. https://www.insidehighered.com/quicktakes/2022/10/17/cazenovia-defaulted-bond-payments
56. https://www.syracuse.com/news/2022/12/cazenovia-college-to-close-after-nearly-200-years.html
57. https://hnu.edu/news/holy-names-university-in-oakland-to-close-after-spring-semester-in-may-2023/
58. https://www.highereddive.com/news/presentation-college-south-dakota-closing/640665/
59. https://www.freep.com/story/news/education/2023/03/02/up-north-private-university-to-close/69964941007/
60. https://www.iw.edu/iowa-wesleyan-university-announces-closure/

61. https://www.al.com/news/birmingham/2022/12/birmingham-southern-college
-in-financial-distress-in-danger-of-closing-in-2023-lawmakers-say.html

62. https://www.forbes.com/sites/michaeltnietzel/2022/12/20/at-years-end-several
-colleges-face-a-financial-reckoning/?sh=62566264505c

63. https://www.al.com/educationlab/2023/03/gov-kay-ivey-says-she-wont
-support-state-bailout-of-birmingham-southern-college.html

64. https://shef.sheeo.org/grapevine/

65. https://www.chronicle.com/article/the-shrinking-of-higher-ed?cid2=gen_login
_refresh&cid=gen_sign_in

66. https://www.tandfonline.com/doi/full/10.1080/00221546.2017.1390971

67. Thelin, J. R. (2004). *A History of American Higher Education*. Baltimore: John
Hopkins University Press.

68. https://www.insidehighered.com/news/government/state-policy/2023/05/01/
connecticut-state-system-warns-devastating-cuts

69. https://news.artnet.com/art-world/valparaiso-university-faculty-vote-halt
-brauer-museum-deaccessioning-2266904

70. https://www.nytimes.com/2016/07/27/arts/design/florine-stettheimer-painting
-fisk-university-sold.html?emc=edit_tnt_20160726&nlid=28239917&tntemail0
=y&_r=0&referer

71. https://www.forbes.com/sites/michaeltnietzel/2023/03/18/budget-woes-hit
-several-big-ten-universities/?sh=7f6cee845f72

Chapter 2

Financial Exigency

Financial exigency is not a familiar term to most individuals outside of higher education, or even for many within it. Those who do know about financial exigency often have only a cursory understanding of what it means or involves. They simply know it's not good, and that it should be avoided whenever possible, just like "going out of business" sales and bankruptcy in the business world.

In fact, financial exigency is often compared to a business bankruptcy, and while there are some similarities, exigency differs from a formal bankruptcy in fundamental ways. For example, it does not extend the various legal protections provided by a formal bankruptcy against collections, lawsuits, foreclosures, and other legal proceedings—so while the analogy is clear, it's not a perfect one.

Although there are different definitions of financial exigency, most colleges and universities recognize some version of the one first promulgated, and later revised several times, by the American Association of University Professors (AAUP), which was founded in 1915 by Arthur Lovejoy and John Dewey and continues to be the nation's leading advocacy organization for higher education faculty and a frequent thorn in the side of some college administrators.[1]

The term *financial exigencies* first appeared in a policy statement issued by a group of higher education organizations, including the AAUP, in 1925. In the *Conference Statement on Academic Freedom and Tenure,* one provision on academic tenure stated: "Termination of permanent or long-term appointments because of financial exigencies should be sought only as a last resort, after every effort has been made to meet the need in other ways and to find for the teacher other employment in the institution. Situations which make drastic retrenchment of this sort necessary should preclude expansions of the staff at other points at the same time, except in extraordinary circumstances."[2] Concerns about the adequacy of that statement soon surfaced and intensified as an increasing number of colleges were forced to close because of growing financial problems in the wake of the Great Depression. Before the Great Depression, the best estimate was that an average of 5–10 colleges wer. shuttering their doors annually. In 1935, 29 colleges closed.

In its 1940 *Statement of Principles on Academic Freedom and Tenure*, AAUP said simply that "[t]ermination of a continuous appointment because of financial exigency should be demonstrably bona fide."[3] That's brief and to the point, but not all that informative. In addition to that statement, AAUP's *Statement on Government of Colleges and Universities* called for faculty to have primary responsibility for decisions affecting academic programs and faculty status, but clearly a more comprehensive definition of financial exigency was needed.

AAUP's Regulation 4(c), initially drafted in 1957 and contained in subsequent versions of AAUP's guidance, has undergone several revisions over the years. Its definition of financial exigency was updated in the 1970s during another period of economic recession in the country. The 1976 version of Regulation 4(c) in *Statement of Principles on Academic Freedom and Tenure* provided AAUP's most complete description of financial exigency up to that point in time. It defined financial exigency as an "imminent financial crisis which threatens the survival of the institution as a whole and which cannot be alleviated by less drastic means."[4]

The intent of the regulation was to require that exigency involve more than just a single budget shortfall or a temporary operating loss. To meet that AAUP definition, the financial crisis should be of a magnitude to threaten the survival of the institution and be one that cannot be resolved by anything less drastic than terminating faculty appointments.

That definition was revised once more in 2013, during a period when most colleges and universities were again struggling through the aftermath of another major financial crisis—the Great Recession of 2008—as well as the economic woes that befell several institutions in Louisiana in the wake of Hurricane Katrina in 2005. This time, the AAUP definition of financial exigency was modified to "a severe financial crisis that fundamentally compromises the academic integrity of the institution as a whole and that cannot be alleviated by less drastic means."

That change reflected a recognition that while the earlier definitions of exigency might have been appropriate for small, private institutions, they did not translate as well to public universities, which, because of annual state funding, seldom faced complete institutional extinction but still might experience severe financial difficulties that could compromise their academic integrity. One concern AAUP was trying to address was that without a definition better attuned to such fiscal realities, institutions would proceed with widespread program closures including faculty layoffs but skirt the procedural and policy standards that should follow from a formal exigency declaration.

The 2013 definition of financial exigency is broader than previous versions primarily because it was intended to be more widely applicable to institutions that were not about to go into total collapse, but whose budget problems had become severe enough that they threatened a school's academic mission. While the definition appears to be less dramatic than its predecessor; at least in theory, its overall reach had been extended. Whether the new definition has encouraged or discouraged colleges in financial peril to formally declare financial exigency is a matter of continuing debate, and we anticipate the definition will likely be refined again as more institutions cope with an ever-evolving range of financial challenges.

Paragraph 4.c of the AAUP's *Policy Documents and Report* provides several pieces of additional guidance concerning a declaration of financial exigency. They're summarized in Textbox 2.1.

Terminating the contracts of tenured faculty is the unique feature of a financial exigency.[5] It's what sets it apart from all the other cost-cutting measures that colleges might employ. (In our subsequent discussions of faculty dismissals for financial reasons, we use the terms *layoff, termination of appointment, retrenchment*, and *reduction in force* interchangeably.) Because tenured faculty are any college's most valuable resource and most costly expense, forcing the end of their employment is the most extreme step an institution can take, and it's the reason that most university leaders prefer to avoid it if at all possible.

However, for all the reasons that faculty tenure is an important principle and condition of employment for higher education institutions to protect, it also introduces substantial fixed costs that are difficult to reduce or manage in ways that an emerging financial crisis can demand. Speed and nimbleness are recognized as strategic advantages when responding to a changing market or managing a business, but tenure is an obligation in higher education that typically makes a prompt reallocation of a large pool of resources difficult. This is not an argument against tenure. It's a recognition that colleges have unique limits on how they can respond to rapidly deteriorating budget conditions. These limits also differentiate higher education in terms of its relationships with employees from those that exist at most businesses in the private sector.

The importance of faculty tenure is a primary reason that AAUP developed an elaborate—some might call it "cumbersome"—set of recommendations for how declarations of financial exigency should be done.[6] And it's also why most colleges and universities have written policies and procedures detailing how a financial exigency is to be conducted should it ever be invoked. Whether institutions follow, amend, or ignore those procedures when "the chips are down" in a financial emergency is another matter we discuss shortly and in subsequent chapters.

TEXTBOX 2.1 OTHER INSTITUTIONAL REGULATIONS ON ACADEMIC FREEDOM AND TENURE RECOMMENDED BY THE AAUP

As a first step, an elected faculty governance body, or a body designated by a collective bargaining agreement, should participate in decisions that a condition of financial exigency exists or is imminent and that all feasible alternatives to termination of appointments have been pursued.

According to AAUP guidance, before any proposals for program discontinuance on financial grounds are made or entertained, the faculty should have the opportunity to render an assessment in writing on the institution's financial condition. Included in that assessment should be:

1. Faculty access to at least five years of audited financial statements, current and following-year budgets, and detailed cash-flow estimates for future years.
2. Faculty access to detailed program, department, and administrative-unit budgets.
3. Prompt written notification of faculty being considered for discontinuance including at least thirty days in which to respond to it.

Faculty members facing termination of their appointment should have the right to a full hearing before a faculty committee that considers the extent of financial exigency, the validity of the educational judgments and the criteria for identifying a termination, and whether the criteria are being properly applied in the individual case.

If an institution terminates appointments because of financial exigency, it should not at the same time make new appointments, except in extraordinary circumstances where a serious distortion in the academic program would otherwise result. In addition, the appointment of a faculty member with tenure will not be terminated in favor of retaining a faculty member without tenure, except in extraordinary circumstances where a serious distortion of the academic program would otherwise result.

Before terminating an appointment because of financial exigency, the institution, with faculty participation, should make every effort to find the faculty member another suitable position at the institution. It should give faculty whose positions are slated to be terminated notice or severance salary in various amounts depending on when in the academic year the termination occurs and how long the faculty member has been employed.

Finally, the lines of faculty members terminated under financial exigency should not be filled by other individuals within a period of three years unless the faculty members concerned have been offered an opportunity for reinstatement.

Many universities adopt the AAUP standards almost verbatim. Others make changes to them that retain basic concepts, but weaken other provisions. For example, Lincoln University, a Historically Black College and University (HBCU) in Jefferson City, Missouri, revised its exigency definition in 2017 to allow it to declare exigency not only at the university level, but also "for specific colleges, schools, departments or programs." Lincoln also made another change at the time, stating that faculty members with the shortest term of service now "will generally," but not definitively, be terminated before those with longer periods of service. Both of those changes were substantial and gave the university greater flexibility in how to conduct a faculty retrenchment. Three years later in 2020, Lincoln University declared a state of exigency.

If a university's official faculty policies or its collective bargaining agreement with faculty differ from the AAUP's standards, and a faculty retrenchment is legally contested, a court is likely to defer to the university policies or the contractual language. However, if an institution does not have an official policy or collective bargaining agreement in place, a court might rely on AAUP policies to interpret what are the usual academic customs that should be followed. Table 2.1 gives a few examples of official exigency policies at different kinds of colleges, but it's important to understand this is just a sample; there are dozens of variations in these definitions used by institutions across the country.[7]

Table 2.1. Examples of Financial Exigency Policies

Institution	Educational Sector	Exigency Policy
Missouri State University	Public Doctoral/ Professional University	A financial crisis of such magnitude that all other reasonable measures have been taken and there is no reasonable alternative to termination of university employees.
Southern Methodist University	Private R1 Research University	An imminent financial crisis which threatens the survival of the institution as a whole and which cannot be alleviated by less drastic means than to terminate appointments of tenured faculty or those with an unexpired term.
Oklahoma State University	Public R1 Research University	A state of financial crisis which affects the University as a whole, to the extent that it may become necessary to terminate tenured appointments or other appointments prior to their normal expiration, and a state in which the survival of programs deemed essential to the mission of the University is in doubt.
University System of Georgia	Public University System	When circumstances cause a shortfall in projected revenues for general operations as compared with projected expenditures over the same period, and such shortfall would have a material adverse effect on the operation of either an institution, an academic or other unit of an institution, or the USG generally.
Dillard University	Private HBCU	A serious financial condition that threatens the academic integrity of the university or of one of its academic programs or school of instruction. Financial exigency permitting termination of a tenured faculty member need not threaten the viability of the University as a whole, but may apply only to a specific academic program, division, or department.
Community College of Baltimore County	Public Two-Year College	A serious condition wherein the operating funds of the college are inadequate to successfully maintain the established level of programs and services. The college's response to the financial deficiency will include a reduction in force.

WHEN BAD BECOMES REALLY BAD

In the typical case of financial exigency, all the elements that can jeopardize a college's financial or academic viability have come together at the same time and at the same place. It's the nearest thing that the academy has to a bankruptcy in the business world, a time when "bad" has become "really bad."

1. Across the institution, financial deficits coupled with increases in debt and reductions in net revenue have accumulated to an unprecedented size;
2. At state institutions, drops in tax receipts have led to large decreases in state appropriations, sometimes for two or more years in a row;
3. As institutions struggle to maintain student enrollment, they often discount tuition—via institutional scholarships paid from operating funds—in an effort to attract more students. While increasing institutional financial aid is intended to improve a college's "yield"—the percentage of accepted students who ultimately attend—the discount sometimes doesn't increase yield enough to offset the lower tuition collected per student. The result is a losing proposition. The college realizes less net revenue, exactly the outcome the discount was meant to avoid. This vicious cycle has been evident for decades at private institutions, but as public institutions have accelerated their discount rates, they too run the risk of losing net revenue.
4. Student success as measured by rates of retention and completion are in decline, often disproportionately affecting the most academically at-risk students at the highest rates; and
5. Budgets have become broken, with instructional and other ongoing institutional expenditures no longer financially responsible.

The path to financial exigency is usually paved by an ongoing combination of these structural deficits and systemic disparities that push a college to the brink of what in the corporate world would be insolvency, a time for a "fire sale," or a liquidation. The margins between viability and failure have narrowed to the point that extreme measures are necessary to save the institution. It's sink or swim, do or die.

EARLY EXAMPLES OF FINANCIAL EXIGENCY

Declaring financial exigency is not new. While it's difficult to pinpoint the first time it was invoked, one of the earliest instances was at Adelphi College (now Adelphi University), which successfully sought federal bankruptcy protection in 1937, followed by the dismissal of five faculty members in 1939 for financial reasons, a move that eventually earned the institution censure from the AAUP.

Over the next decade, exigency was declared at a rate of about one school per year. The AAUP began to examine the termination of faculty appointments for financial reasons in earnest in 1974, a year after Bloomfield College in New Jersey had declared financial exigency, a decision AAUP later characterized as "outlandish."[8] The 1970s saw exigency declared at a number of institutions, a not surprising consequence of the troubled economic times and social protests that, as we alluded to in the previous chapter, had ensnared higher education during that decade.

Beginning with the Bloomfield College report, the AAUP published twenty-eight investigative reports over the next several years involving terminations of faculty appointments for financial reasons.[9] They covered a range of institutions in every region of the country and focused on three basic questions:

1. whether the institution's financial problems were so severe that they necessitated the termination of faculty appointments;
2. whether the faculty had a meaningful opportunity to participate in the decisions to terminate appointments; and
3. whether the individual faculty members facing termination of their appointments were given opportunities for hearings before faculty peers on the disputed issues.

AAUP committees concluded that, in their opinion, a bona fide financial exigency existed at only four of the 28 schools investigated—the City University of New York, Westminster College of Salt Lake City, Saint Bonaventure University, and the University of the District of Columbia. In all the other instances, the investigating committees doubted that the institutions "were confronting such severe financial problems as to necessitate the termination of faculty appointments." In nearly all of the 28 cases, AAUP investigating committees found that faculty involvement in the decisions leading to terminations was either inadequate or nonexistent. Examples included the University of Idaho, Goucher College, Essex Community College, and Alaska Pacific University.

Finally, at most of the institutions AAUP investigated during this period, the committees concluded that the individual faculty facing termination of appointment did not receive a hearing before faculty peers on disputed issues as 4.c guidance calls for. The purpose of such hearings is to give the affected faculty members an opportunity to raise issues about why they might have been unfairly singled out for release or whether exigency was being used as a smoke screen for getting rid of faculty who administrators disliked or viewed as too controversial. This issue was examined and found problematic in exigency cases at the University of Texas of the Permian Basin, Sonoma State University, Southern Nazarene University, and St. Bonaventure University.

In 1996, the trustees of City University of New York (CUNY) proceeded with one of the nation's largest layoffs of faculty pursuant to declaring financial exigency. Citing budget cuts of about $160 million for CUNY made by then-Governor George Pataki, the university initially terminated appointments of more than 100 professors, closed or merged a number of academic departments, and cut some of its remedial education programs.

Those actions were subsequently challenged by CUNY's Faculty Senate and faculty union, which claimed the university was using exigency as a pretext for a consolidation plan that it wanted to make independent of any financial emergency. As part of their challenge, they pointed to the fact that the state of New York had later restored $58 million of CUNY's proposed cuts, and that CUNY had been able to cover the remaining $102 million gap by increasing tuition by $750 a year and offering early retirement incentives to several faculty members. A judge initially found for the faculty union,[10] but CUNY appealed that decision and ultimately prevailed. A compromise was subsequently worked out by the parties.

Another exigency circumstance resulting from severe cutbacks in public funding occurred in 1997 at the University of the District of Columbia, a public HBCU. In that case, a combination of reduced financial support from the District of Columbia and steep drops in enrollment led to the university's accrediting agency placing it on a warning status, which was followed by the university notifying more than 100 faculty along with several staff that their appointments were being terminated.[11]

MORE RECENT EXAMPLES

Table 2.2 gives a representative, but not exhaustive, list of institutions that have been forced into exigency since 2000. It's important to understand that not every college that initially declares exigency ultimately proceeds all the way to the stage of terminating faculty appointments or ending academic programs. In some cases, as we discuss in Chapter 4, the state comes to the rescue with an increased recurring or one-time appropriation that pulls an institution back from the brink. In other cases, the institution itself finds an alternative to exigency, either after receiving a pulse of private donations, turning to other budget-cutting alternatives, or reevaluating its financial condition.

38

Chapter 2

Table 2.2 reveals one notable pattern about recent exigency declarations—they tend to be more common at public institutions than private ones. Although the list of institutions is not exhaustive, we believe it's representative of the field.

Why is exigency more frequent at public colleges? First, it may be because private institutions are more concerned that the acknowledgment of a severe financial crisis might worry donors so much that their support for the institution will dry up. Because public universities are accustomed to frequently publicizing their financial needs to governors and legislators, they are not as worried about the implications of disclosing a financial emergency.[12] Another likely reason is that private colleges don't have an annual state appropriation that can serve as a financial backstop, giving them more time to work themselves out of the red. The path from a financial problem to a financial collapse is shorter for private schools who don't have any state funding to help compensate for declining enrollments or a sagging endowment. They are more likely to be forced past any last-ditch attempt to restructure through exigency into an outright closure.[13]

However, in other instances, it's been the failure of the state to provide its regular, annual appropriation that precipitated a financial exigency. One of the more highly publicized examples of this problem took place at Chicago State University, a public institution whose enrollment is largely composed of minority students from the Chicago area. Following years of declining enrollments and other problems including whistleblower lawsuits and questions about its accreditation status, Chicago State was dealt a nearly fatal blow in 2016 when a months-long budget impasse between Republican Governor Bruce Rauner and the Democrat-controlled Illinois legislature resulted in the state's universities receiving no appropriations for months.

While the withholding of state funds resulted in cutbacks at all of Illinois' public institutions, Chicago State University was the hardest hit primarily because of how much it depended on state funding to keep the doors open. About 30% of its total budget at the time came from the $36 million annual state appropriation. Chicago State declared financial exigency on February 4, 2016, and later that same month, all 900 of its employees, including its faculty, received notices of potential layoffs. Those actions led the Higher Learning Commission, the university's accrediting agency, to place it on notice over its deteriorating financial condition.[14] Months later the state's budget stalemate was resolved, and a stopgap budget was passed, but Chicago State and the other state institutions still received only a portion of their annual appropriation, which was not enough to spare them from some very deep cuts. At Chicago State, the result was that approximately 300 employees, including several faculty, were terminated.

Southeast Missouri State University was another institution where steadily declining state appropriations resulted in financial exigency being declared. On June 12, 2002, the university's Board of Regents invoked exigency, a decision that received the support of the Faculty Senate and university budget committee, following a three-year reduction of more than 16% in state funding contemporaneous with attempts to offset those losses with one-time budget cuts of 16%. A mandated institution-wide program review, which evaluated multiple dimensions of program productivity, resulted in the eventual closing or merger of several academic majors along with the termination of ten faculty positions, which included individuals with tenure.

Table 2.2. A Sample of Institutions Declaring Financial Exigency Since 2000

Institution	Sector	Date	Institution	Sector	Date
Southeast Missouri State Univ.	Public Four Year	2002	Missouri Western State University	Public Four Year	2020
Tulane University	Private Nonprofit	2005	Lincoln University	Public HBCU	2020
University of New Orleans	Public Four Year	2006	Central Washington University	Public Four Year	2020
Antioch College	Private, Nonprofit	2007	Cornish College of the Arts	Private Nonprofit	2020
Southern University	Public HBCU	2011	Pacific Lutheran University	Private, Nonprofit	2020
South Carolina State Univ.	Public HBCU	2015	Hannibal-LaGrange University	Private Nonprofit	2022
Chicago State University	Public Four Year	2016	Kentucky State University	Public HBCU	2022
Wheeling Jesuit University	Private Nonprofit	2019	Henderson State University	Public Four Year	2022
University of Alaska	Public Four Year	2019	New Jersey City University	Public Four Year	2022
			Upper Iowa University	Private Four Year	2023

There's also a frequent flip side to the exigency coin—acting like an exigency is in effect without actually declaring it, a practice that AAUP has condemned numerous times over the years. This short-circuiting approach was taken by several colleges during the pandemic, as they attempted to manage their financial woes by not formally declaring financial exigency but proceeding with the termination of faculty and academic programs anyway.

Institutions using such exigency workarounds typically refer to a "financial crisis," "dire financial straits," "financial emergency," "financial stringency," or "budgetary hardship" as the justification for cutting personnel and programs, claiming that the severity and the immediacy of their financial problems necessitated a suspension of the normal process that a formal exigency declaration would have required.[15] In other scenarios, even though the financial situations were extremely grave, institutions did not find it technically necessary, even by their own policies, to invoke exigency because their personnel actions did not involve terminating any tenured faculty appointments.

How institutions reacted to the economic threats posed by the pandemic depended in large measure on their preexisting condition. For some, like those we describe below, their financial health was so precarious before the pandemic that they quickly fell into critical condition as the consequences of the pandemic mounted. They had to call a "code blue" and immediately take extreme actions to preserve the institution.

Others might not have faced quite so severe a diagnosis, but the warning signs were serious enough that they knew they needed to make substantial "lifestyle changes"—in the form of major budget readjustments to prevent more serious problems down the road. And many colleges fell into a middle ground; they were part of the "worried well." While they weren't in bad fiscal health at the time, they understood nonetheless that the pandemic had dramatized how they could be at risk for further deterioration and that much greater attention to the expenditure side of the institution was warranted.

As we've already shown, when an institution acts quickly and declares exigency or takes other extreme budget steps under a different name, it often elicits formal complaints from the faculty, resulting in the possibility that the AAUP will form a special committee to investigate and report on the matter. For example, a May, 2021 AAUP report details investigations of eight institutions—Canisius College, Illinois Wesleyan University, Keuka College, Marian University, Medaille College, National University, University of Akron, and Wittenberg University—that took emergency austerity measures during the pandemic, resulting in the termination of faculty contracts and academic programs.[16] Not surprisingly, AAUP found—similar to what it's concluded in most of its previous investigations—that the institutions failed to respect "the norms of academic governance" and proceeded largely "by administrative fiat, with little or no consultation with the faculty even where austerity and emergency measures had dramatic effects on the curriculum . . . "[17]

The report characterized the institutions' actions as being "prompted largely by opportunistic exploitations of catastrophic events . . . (a) phenomenon, generally known as 'disaster capitalism.'" That's a term coined by Canadian author Naomi Klein to refer to the tactic of using the fear and confusion following some kind of shocking event—political coups, market crashes, natural catastrophes, or budget disasters—to push through extreme measures where typical norms of operation are suspended in favor of more business-friendly policies.

This type of accusation might not always be wrong. Neither might it always be accurate. But when such judgments are always made in hindsight as the case with AAUP committee investigations, university leadership is likely to reject them and put up strong defenses against the charges. Or, as in many of these cases, a college administration will try to find a way to finesse any criticisms from the beginning. Faced with the need to declare financial exigency, a university president might decide to not invoke it but proceed with a full set of austerity measures—including faculty retrenchment—regardless, believing that no matter how much faculty consultation and input are sought during an exigency process, it will never be good enough to satisfy the AAUP. We will revisit this issue in later chapters.

The AAUP has also investigated and condemned numerous exigency work-arounds that occurred before the pandemic. One took place at the Vermont Law School, which proceeded with a 2018 restructuring that lowered faculty salaries, reduced the number of full-time positions, and eliminated the tenured status of fourteen of nineteen tenured faculty members. According to the AAUP, those actions were taken without meaningful faculty participation in the process.[18]

Another well-publicized example of major cuts in personnel and academic programs without a formal exigency declaration occurred at Cabrini University, a private Catholic school in Pennsylvania. Facing years of mounting deficits and sliding enrollment, Cabrini had made at least two rounds of faculty, administration, and staff reductions, many done through voluntary separation agreements. Faced with a deficit estimated at between $5–6 million, it also began a major reorganization in 2022, downsized the number of academic departments, and made public overtures for other institutions to consider merging with it. But none of that was enough to save the school. Through a deal brokered with Villanova University in 2023, Cabrini will continue its operations only through the 2023–24 academic year, and then Villanova will assume ownership of the Cabrini campus and whatever it decides to retain in terms of academic programming.

In 2013, AAUP put National Louis University (Illinois) on its censure list following an investigation of numerous financially related faculty and program terminations that were seen as particularly egregious departures from proper procedures.[19]

What is the AAUP censure list, and what does it mean to be on it? Basically, it's a public identification of college administrations that AAUP believes have seriously violated recognized principles of academic freedom and tenure. AAUP censure is intended to serve at least a couple of purposes. First, it's an industry-wide shaming of institutions aimed at pressuring them into cleaning up their act. Second, the threat of censure is also meant to serve as a deterrent to institutions straying from accepted norms of shared governance.

AAUP has no governing power over any college or university. It does not establish any laws. It can't compel institutions to do anything or to refrain from taking the steps the institution deems to be necessary. It can't hire or fire anyone at a wayward college. It can't accredit or disaccredit schools. Nonetheless, an AAUP censure carries weight in many higher education circles, and colleges don't like to have their reputations tarnished by being censured. While most institutions will work hard to have their names removed from the list, a handful regard censure as a badge of honor, a sign of their proud independence. Witness the fact that one school—Frank Phillips College, a public two-year college in Texas—has been on the censure list since 1969. Ten other institutions placed on censure prior to 1990 have remained on the censure list ever since.[20] We discuss censure as a reaction to financial exigency more in Chapter 6.

An extreme version of an exigency workaround occurred in the state of Kansas, where in 2021 the Kansas Board of Regents unanimously voted in a policy that allowed the six public universities it oversees (the University of Kansas, Kansas State University, Wichita State University, Fort Hays State University, Emporia State University, and Pittsburg State University) to terminate or suspend employees—including tenured faculty—without having to follow established processes such as the declaration of financial exigency.

According to that policy, "In light of the extreme financial pressures placed on the state universities due to the COVID-19 pandemic, decreased program and university enrollment, and state fiscal issues," any employee—including one with tenure—"may be suspended, dismissed, or terminated from employment by their respective university. Declaration of financial exigency and the processes associated with declaration of financial exigency shall not be a prerequisite to any suspension, dismissal, or termination authorized by this provision, and no existing university policy hearing procedures shall apply to such decisions."[21]

It was not initially clear how many of the schools would shelve their existing procedures and use the new policy instead, but it didn't take long to discover that one of them would. In September 2022, Emporia State University notified 33 faculty and staff that they were being dismissed under the controversial new provision.[22] Those actions were subsequently condemned in a strongly worded AAUP investigative report,[23] which found them to constitute "a direct assault on tenure and, by extension, academic freedom," and to indicate that "conditions for shared governance at Emporia State University are deficient."

THE FINANCIAL EXIGENCY BALANCING ACT

Whether and when to declare financial exigency involves a delicate balance. Do it too soon or without first having taken other steps to cut costs, and it can inflict serious damage on the institution—affecting student and faculty morale and sending the signal that the college is failing, a message likely to speed up the downward spiral.

Delay for too long or avoid altogether a recognition of exigent circumstances, and the budget cuts that will eventually be required may be even deeper, leaving the institution in a tailspin from which it may never recover. The deficits, the debts, and the doubts about its leadership will become too great for the college to survive. It will not be able to pay its bills, meet its payroll, or make required payments on its debt.

Most institutions that are in serious enough financial trouble to justify declaring exigency have had to confront one of two kinds of circumstances. Either they've been struck with a sudden, catastrophic event like the pandemic, or Hurricane Katrina in 2005, which forced several universities in Louisiana to shutter operations temporarily at the same time they invoked financial exigency.[24] Or they've been spinning downward for some time and are already suffering a set of bad consequences—low faculty morale, enrollment declines, increases in student attrition, reductions in state appropriations in the case of public colleges, too much deferred maintenance, stingy operating budgets, downgrades by rating agencies, and recent staff departures.

In this latter situation, most students and the existing faculty and staff know that tough times and hard decisions are ahead, and they want campus leaders to level with them, collect and share the necessary data, and tell the truth about their school's financial realities. However, they also want any retrenchment of faculty and staff positions and closures of academic programs to be done fairly, as deliberatively as possible, and with due process for all affected. Declaring exigency without adequate participation of faculty, staff, and students will almost always lead to unnecessary conflicts and unsatisfactory results. Done without a fair and transparent process, it can lead to lawsuits alleging discrimination, breach of contract, or wrongful termination.

A noteworthy example is the previously cited case at Bloomfield College in Bloomfield, New Jersey. Founded in the mid 1800s as a theological seminary, Bloomfield gradually evolved into a college that enrolled a large percentage of minority students. Over that time, however, it also faced sagging enrollments and unmanageable debt, leading it to declare financial exigency in 1973. As part of its exigency plan, Bloomfield ended the employment of 13 faculty and notified its remaining faculty members that they would be placed on one-year contracts for the 1973–74 academic year.

The faculty sued the university, and they prevailed, with the judge ordering their reinstatement. The university appealed that decision and lost again. To avoid a total shutdown, Bloomfield sought protection through federal bankruptcy, buying it time to reorganize, sell off some assets and cut a new deal with the tenured faculty. Bloomfield came out of the bankruptcy in 1974 with enough funds to continue operations and its focus on becoming an institution that primarily served students of color and first-generation college students, which it has done ever since.

But that's not the end of the Bloomfield saga. In 2022, after years of running in the red, its financial crisis deepened, and Bloomfield came close to having to shut down again. It was spared when the state of New Jersey and Montclair State University, a public college located about 10 miles away, offered enough financial support for Bloomfield to remain open temporarily during the 2022–23 academic year, after which it would merge with Montclair State and continue to operate as "Bloomfield College of Montclair State University."[25]

Another early legal case involved the University of Dubuque, which in 1974 dismissed a tenured faculty member, citing a $100,000 operating deficit and the following contractual provision: "After the expiration of the probationary period, continuous appointment shall be established and services are to be terminated only for adequate cause. It is understood that continuous appointment is based upon the need for the services of the appointee and the financial ability of the institution to continue the appointment." The faculty member sued and although the jury found in the plaintiff's favor, the judge sustained the university's motion for judgment notwithstanding the verdict, noting that the university's accounting records offered sufficient evidence of exigency and that its financial trends had convinced the university's creditors that failure to cut back faculty would be negligent.[26]

A similar finding was reached in the case of *Krotkoff v. Goucher College*, where a court ruled that the termination of a tenured professor of German at Goucher College due to a bona fide financial exigency was permissible and not precluded by the status of tenure.[27]

As we discuss more fully in Chapter 4, neglecting to be in constant communications with an institution's governing board during a period of exigency is another potential pitfall, bad enough to qualify as presidential negligence. Silence in such circumstances is never golden; it will almost certainly cause the problem to become worse. Likewise, conspiring with the board to try to keep secret or to delay acknowledging an administration's plan for drastic budget cuts will also usually backfire. Universities are notoriously bad at keeping secrets.

The failure to include the input of key constituents like alumni, students, and policy makers including—particularly in the case of a public institution—a state's governor and legislature—will only serve to aggravate already serious problems, as illustrated by the case of Kentucky State University (KSU), an HBCU in Frankfort, Kentucky. After years of fiscal problems and numerous instances of apparent mismanagement, KSU had financial exigency declared for it by the Kentucky General Assembly, when it passed—and the governor signed into law—HB 250 in 2022. That legislation also authorized a $23 million non-interest-bearing loan to KSU in fiscal year 2021–2022 and created the KSU loan repayment trust fund. It further required that the Kentucky Council on Postsecondary Education create and oversee a management improvement plan for KSU, which, if the university met the benchmarks in the plan, would result in additional appropriation of $5 million in 2022–2023 and $10 million in 2023–2024.[28]

But KSU's budget issues were far from being resolved by those interventions. In 2023, Mike Harmon, the auditor for the state of Kentucky referred the findings of his investigation into the "chaotic" finances at KSU to state and federal prosecutors.

DECLARING FINANCIAL EXIGENCY

Financial exigency need not be the means of institutional self-destruction. Indeed, almost all of the colleges that have invoked it in the past have survived. Whether that proves that the exigency process was necessary for the institution's survival, or it means that the financial crisis was not as dire as it first appeared cannot be known for certain. But in most cases, the downward trajectory had been spiraling for years, and it's not obvious what else could have turned it around except for an extreme remedy.

Bond rating agencies—a very important observer of any college's finances—are inclined to view a carefully executed, properly timed exigency plan in a positive light, particularly if it is also aimed at realigning expenses with revenues going forward. For universities that have gone through protracted periods of financial stress before declaring a financial exigency, rating agencies are more likely to take such a declaration as a negative sign, viewing it as an indication that all other options had been exhausted. But for those institutions that use exigency more promptly to balance expenses with revenue and invest in high-demand academic programs, bond rating agencies are inclined to see it as a positive management strategy. As an example, one of Moody's periodic assessments of the financial outlook for the higher education sector ran under this headline in 2015: "Financial Exigency Is A Credit Positive Tool For Struggling Universities."

Done properly, financial exigency can be an instrument for institutional survival and even renewal. It can restore confidence, sharpen the mission, boost bond ratings, build back a school's financial reserves, and put a college back on the road to financial stability and educational success. It can become not merely a reactive tool, but a proactive step that colleges on the brink can use to help solve the existential challenges they face.

That's what we hope to show in the remainder of the book as we explore the why, what, how, and when of financial exigency. We start with a personal, up-close, detailed look at a university that has recently gone through the process, and we discuss the tools it used to move from crisis to solutions. These same tools can also be used by other institutions that find themselves at the brink of a financial emergency.

VOICES FROM THE FIELD

It's highly unusual for new presidents or chancellors to begin their duties on November 15, near the end of a fall semester at most colleges, but Henderson State University was facing unusual circumstances. As the university's new chancellor, I (Chuck Ambrose) understood not only that my appointment was a bit out of sync with the normal rhythm of the fall semester, but I also was about to understand that I had little more than half of a fiscal year remaining to right a fast-sinking fiscal ship.

After 20 years as a campus head, Ambrose had plenty of experience managing financial crises of one sort or the other. Like many campus heads, he recognized the inevitable ups and downs of college budgets, and like most of his colleagues, he hoped to avoid using the extreme budgetary tools—like program terminations and employee layoffs—that were sometimes necessary for an institution to survive. Over those 20 years, Ambrose had kicked his share of cans down the road, hoping that institutions with which he was affiliated would grow themselves out of many of the challenges we discuss here.

After 12 years at a small, private, church-related university and eight at a public comprehensive institution, he had also learned how colleges needed to face up to their fiscal challenges or risk their long-term viability. Somehow, most of the financial challenges facing both public and private institutions had found a home at Henderson—all at the same time and at the same place. In Ambrose's own words, "I was hopeful to join a community at Henderson that was willing to prove that we could actually do college differently, that we could transform our service to students and focus our institutional outcomes on college completion and purposeful learning outcomes. In other words, I was looking to lead a place that was required to change. But I also have to admit—in the spirit of waiting too long—I was hoping for a transformational opportunity, not an existential crisis."

People often asked me—"How long did it take you to figure out Henderson's plight?" And I told them, "about two meetings, maybe four hours. When an institution is slow to pay its bills, when students owe millions in unpaid tuition and fees, when you are running out of funds to meet your debt obligations, and when you're worried about making payroll in the spring, you know it's time."

"I realized that we basically had no cash. And at the same time our student outcomes like retention and graduation rates were the lowest in Arkansas, a state that ranks near the bottom for student success. A quick glance at the National Center for Educational Statistics' College Navigator website* revealed that all these deficits were disproportionately affecting our most at-risk students, who were experiencing the most negative outcomes. Clearly, there was no time to delay. We had a matter of weeks, not months, to act."

---

* https://nces.ed.gov/collegenavigator/

FINANCIAL EXIGENCY AT HENDERSON STATE UNIVERSITY

One of us—Chuck Ambrose—has direct personal experience taking an institution through financial exigency. Here is that story.

Ambrose became Chancellor of Henderson State University (HSU), a public university in the small community of Arkadelphia, Arkansas, on November 15, 2022. Founded in 1890 as Arkadelphia Methodist College, Henderson State is the home to the Reddies, as its intercollegiate athletic teams are called.

HSU has an interesting, even inspiring history. On February 3, 1914, a fire destroyed what was then the main campus building and nearly caused the school to close up shop completely. But instead of causing Henderson to close, the fire brought the students and faculty together the very next day, determined to build the school back—literally from the ground up. The first person to offer financial support to rebuild the school was Malachi Smith, a Black citizen of Arkadelphia and the college's cook, who gave a $25 donation for the cause. A new, shared purpose took form that day. Known as the

"Reddie Spirit," it's been summoned ever since. And every year, during the opening of school, HSU students gather to hear what's become known on campus as the "pine-tree speech," a retelling of the saga of the fire and the college spirit it first kindled. On Founders' Day in 2023, HSU named its on-campus dining facility after Smith.

When Ambrose took the Henderson job, he was familiar with the university's well-known history of financial problems stretching back at least a decade. But he did not know the depth of those problems until he asked his leadership team for a more detailed accounting of the books showing where the institution stood. What he learned was that HSU's dire financial condition had been ongoing for years despite multiple attempts to chip away at the problem. A combination of factors—the construction of several new campus facilities, the addition of academic programs and faculty it could not afford, and the accumulation of unpaid tuition bills—had put the institution deep in the hole. Add to that list the failure of a succession of administrators—some of them serving on an interim basis—to keep institutional spending of all kinds in check, and the recipe for financial failure was complete.

In 2017, an official sign of trouble surfaced when HSU received a non-compliance letter from the Higher Learning Commission, its regional accrediting agency, questioning its financial health and Title IV compliance.

In 2018, HSU discovered that it had the unenviable combination of the highest enrollment but at the same time the lowest net tuition per student of any public university in Arkansas. In other words, even as Henderson enrolled more students, it earned less net tuition revenue. This problem is not all that uncommon—many institutions brag about their increasing enroll-ment, at the same time they bury the fact they're discounting tuition so much to lure students that they are collecting less net tuition. In addition, a case history of HSU's restructuring, written by Scott Carlson for the *Chronicle of Higher Education,* noted another tuition problem—even though HSU had a policy of not permitting students who had large unpaid bills to register for courses, it was ignoring that restriction and allowing students who owed as much as $20,000 to re-enroll.[29]

On July 29, 2019, realizing that its financial problems had become too large for it to manage alone, Henderson signed an agreement with the Arkansas State University System that the system would provide operational support to HSU and assist it with restoring financial integrity. After working together through the contractual agreement for about four months, the ASU System Board of Trustees approved a merger agreement and transition plan with Henderson State on November 21, 2019, establishing a more formal interim management process.

With the approval of the Higher Learning Commission and the Arkansas General Assembly, Henderson officially joined the Arkansas State University System on February 1, 2021. The support of the ASU System brought immediate help in the form of support for governance, policy, financial, legal, institutional research, and governmental relations functions. Additionally, through shared services with ASU, Henderson was able to achieve substantial savings in health care costs, payroll and benefits, procurement, purchasing, travel, and human resources. These arrangements helped HSU save money and increase the efficiency in several of its administrative offices and other areas. Nonetheless, it was not enough. Henderson was still deep in the hole.

In 2015, HSU had about 105 days of cash on hand. By 2019, its position had eroded so badly that it had only seven days of cash on hand with $64,037,276 in ongoing annual operating expenses. In addition, it required a $6 million loan from the state of Arkansas just to make payroll and pay its bills. In 2020, Henderson and ASU System leadership reduced operating expenses to $61,978,279, increasing its cash on hand to 38 days. Additional cuts in 2021 further reduced expenses to $56,560,209 and a further improvement to 42 days of cash on hand. Those reductions included staff furloughs as well as cutbacks in nonfaculty positions, retirement benefits, travel, and supplies.

According to the Arkansas Higher Education Coordinating Board, HSU was the only public institution in Arkansas with negative operating margins in the 2016–17 and 2020–21 evaluation periods. It ran up negative fund balances in fiscal years 2019 and 2020. If Henderson was ever going to restore financial integrity and stabilize its finances, it would require finding ways to eliminate its large annual operating deficits, improve its overall cash position, and adjust its instructional spending to the revenue it generated.

In 2022, Henderson State University began a new, and in many ways more difficult, history when it embarked on one of the largest institutional cost reductions in the shortest timeframe in the history of U.S. public higher education. At the time, the university was facing a $12.5 million projected budget shortfall for the fiscal year ending June 30, 2022. It was carrying long-term debt of $78 million, an amount that had increased about 500% since 2001 largely due to the construction of new residence halls and other campus facilities, including a student recreation center, a dining hall, and athletic facilities. The result of that construction was $6.9 million in required annual debt service payments. In addition, its financial reserves were almost gone, even after it received the $6 million dollar advance from the State of Arkansas in July 2019 and another $12 million in federal Higher Education Emergency Relief Funding after that. In addition, its enrollment was plummeting, falling from a peak of 4,037 students in 2019 to 2,919 in 2021.

Beginning in January 2022, Henderson introduced a modified cash budget—where expenditures had to be balanced against cash on hand—to achieve immediate cost savings. The cost reductions that were realized in the remaining months of that fiscal year included:

- furloughs and administrative salary rollbacks ($1.2 million),
- position management, including hiring freezes and the consolidation of positions ($335,160),
- reductions in the administrative stipends paid to academic deans ($130,403),
- a reduction from 25 department chairs and four deans to four academic program directors and one dean of the faculty,
- an elimination of more than $7.2 million in payroll, with the majority of that in the last five months of the fiscal year.

These initiatives created enough temporary liquidity for the university to make payroll and debt service payments, but the structural deficits that had accumulated over more than a decade meant that significant systemic changes would still be required to ensure sustainable operations. Furloughing staff, rolling-back administrative salaries and stipends, cutting travel, and introducing other spending controls improved Henderson's cash position, but they were not enough to put it on a sound financial footing going forward.

On February 3, 2022, 108 years to the day after the campus fire, Ambrose sent a letter[30] to the HSU community informing it that he was beginning the process of declaring the university to be in a state of financial exigency. The letter indicated the immediate steps that were being taken to curtail costs, and it warned that the process ahead would be painful, likely resulting in the termination of faculty and staff, a large reduction in academic programs, and a significant restructuring of the university's administration.

Consistent with the HSU Faculty Handbook,[31] the Faculty Senate and the university's academic administrators, including the deans and department heads, were given 14 days to indicate whether they concurred with the chancellor's recommendation and to submit their own recommendation, along with the chancellor's, to the Board of Trustees. HSU's Faculty Handbook provides that "[a] financial exigency will be certified when a unit (college or school) of the University or the University itself is threatened by a financial crisis that cannot be ameliorated by means less drastic than the reduction or elimination of programs which results in the termination of personnel." Also, as outlined in the Faculty Handbook, a Financial Exigency Committee was formed to provide its own recommendations for budget reductions and academic program restructuring.

While the Faculty Senate concurred with the need for exigency, the Financial Exigency Committee forwarded recommendations to the Board for cuts that were not as deep as those proposed by Ambrose. Instead of the 25 programs that the chancellor eventually recommended be eliminated, the Committee recommended 12, and instead of terminating any current full-time faculty, it recommended cutting only part-time/adjunct positions along with eliminating only those faculty lines that were unfilled at the time.

Unlike past exigency situations at other institutions, the HSU faculty were generally supportive of the Chancellor's decision, albeit with qualms about the magnitude of the cuts and the time frame he was projecting. Some found the financial analysis "flawed," and others believed it was "rushed." But on February, 11, 2022, the HSU Faculty Senate agreed that a condition of financial exigency existed, a finding that also was supported by the provost and other academic administrators within the week.

Certainly there were HSU faculty and staff who strongly objected to the plan, mounting an aggressive legal, personal, and social media campaign against exigency, which, as we discuss in Chapter 6, is a common and expected reaction to most academic program cuts and faculty retrenchment, whether they're executed through financial exigency or not. Nonetheless, only two EEOC complaints were filed that evolved into subsequent legal claims.

Ambrose's exigency recommendations were also informed by input from the Huron Consulting Group, which he and the university system had hired to analyze HSU's financial data and make recommendations for a future academic portfolio that would be aligned with both its financial resources as well as its primary job markets. As an illustration of a point we emphasize in Chapters 4 and 5—the importance of involving key policy makers and other stakeholders in an exigency process—Arkansas Governor Asa Hutchinson also became involved, paying most of Huron's $480,000 consultancy fees from his discretionary funds.

On March 18, 2022, Ambrose submitted his formal request that the Arkansas State University System Board of Trustees approve the declaration of exigency at HSU. On March 28, the ASU Board of Trustees voted to do so, requiring HSU to conduct a top-to-bottom review of its organizational size and shape, align its academic portfolio with available resources, and set priorities that would enable the university to emerge as a financially healthy institution, better prepared to serve the educational needs of students and answer the workforce needs of the region and the state.

Decisions about personnel and academic programs were based on four primary metrics:

- The net costs of delivering courses compared to the net revenue they produced,
- The unit-based cost of instruction defined at the student seat level,
- Student success rates, with a weighted priority given to degree completion, and
- Alignment of academic programs with community workforce needs.

Here are some key findings from those analyses.

- In 2020–2021, Henderson's academic portfolio lost $13.7 million on an operating basis. In other words, that was the loss when overall instructional expenditures for all of Henderson's course offerings were subtracted from the tuition and fees generated from those courses. Every one of the university's academic units operated at a loss. That stands in contrast to what is the reality or goal at most institutions—where up to 50% of academic programs may be net positive.
- In fall 2021, Henderson enrolled 2,919 students, a 7.7% decrease from the previous year and a 28% drop—equal to more than 1,000 fewer students—since 2019. And across the five years prior to 2022, of the 10,809 new students who had enrolled, 47% had left HSU without graduating. Their unpaid tuition and fees represented 60% of all of Henderson's receivables.
- At the same time, total credit hours produced across the university had fallen roughly 9% every year since 2019. Its average annual credit hour production per instructional line had dropped to 298 hours, compared to the 600 credit hours per teaching position that were estimated to be necessary for HSU to bring its instructional budget into balance.
- Retention of full-time students had also declined sharply, adding to the headcount losses. In 2016, HSU retained 64.6% of its full-time students who were enrolled the year before; in 2021, the retention rate sagged to 55.8%. What did those losses mean for the bottom line? In terms of net tuition revenue, HSU suffered a 26% decrease, from $12,204,810 collected in 2016–2017 to $8,988,093 in 2020–2021. That amount of revenue loss caused by the steep enrollment decline was unsustainable, revealing to the campus why it had to take prompt and extreme steps.
- Not surprisingly, given that attrition, Henderson's graduation rate was less than half the national average for four-year colleges, and it was even worse for students with demonstrated financial need. The overall six-year graduation rate for HSU students receiving Pell Grant support was a dismal 26%.
- For additional context, in 2020–2021, Henderson's instructional salaries and benefits comprised 70% of its operating budget, a level not

too different from what would be found at institutions of similar size and mission. Tenured and tenure-line faculty represented 75% of that amount.

Here was the bottom line. Henderson State was teaching fewer students with an instructional cost basis that had not been adjusted to its student headcount, and that ratio was worsening year by year. Given the size and structural nature of the operating losses, Henderson State had to bring instructional costs in line with its actual revenues. It needed to offer an array of academic programs that it could afford, that fit student interests, and that answered community workforce needs. In other words, it required a realignment of its academic portfolio with its mission and its resources.

By May 2022, in a mere five months, February's warning had become Henderson State's new reality, with extensive cuts to personnel and programs made under a declaration of financial exigency officially approved at a meeting of the Arkansas State University System Board of Trustees. During that meeting, Ambrose informed the Board that if it did not approve the exigency recommendation, it would need to answer the question of how the state of Arkansas would address the $78 million in debt that was owed by HSU. The Board voted to approve the recommendation, with ASU System President Chuck Welch explaining, "Our only two options were to make the hard recommendations necessary to keep the university open, or to do nothing and see the university cease to be a stand-alone institution. The latter was not an option."

HSU then developed an Academic Performance and Program Viability Tool to support a 30-day process for the Faculty Senate-appointed Financial Exigency Committee to meet three primary objectives:

1. Restructure the academic program to meet the goal of reducing instructional costs by $5 million dollars,
2. Determine the number of programs for elimination or reduction,
3. Determine the number of faculty lines for elimination or reduction.

Under the plan[32] recommended by Ambrose and ultimately followed, Henderson State University would eliminate 37.5% of its undergraduate degree programs, including geography, history, political science, public administration, social science, criminal justice, early childhood development, family and consumer sciences, human services, biology, radiography, chemistry, mathematics, nuclear medicine technology, medical lab science, studio art, art education, communication, mass media communication, theater arts, English, and Spanish.

As part of those cutbacks, 88 faculty jobs would be eliminated, 67 of which were filled, at the time, while 21 were vacant. The 88 targeted positions represented 37% of the 237 total instructional lines at HSU in spring 2022. Of those 67 filled positions, 44 were held by tenured professors. Of the 21 unfilled lines, 12 were on the tenure track.

The faculty cuts would ultimately save about $5.3 million—$2.55 million in FY 2023 and another $2.78 million in FY 2024. In addition, by reducing its non-instructional staff positions, Henderson anticipated saving an additional $1.5 million. All told, HSU cut its total workforce from 330 to 230 employees, a reduction of about 30%. Finally, by restructuring dozens of administrative positions, it was able to find another $600,000 in cost savings.

At the same time, Henderson introduced the program and faculty rollbacks under the exigency plan, it made several commitments to students and faculty. For example, Ambrose promised that the university would maintain undergraduate instruction in its liberal arts core. While the majors in disciplines such as English, history, mathematics and history would be ended, instruction in those subjects would still be continued as part of the general education requirements expected of all Henderson students.

Students were also reassured that they would be allowed to complete the degree programs in which they were currently enrolled, a "teach-out" guarantee that should always be extended to students attending any college that ends academic programs or closes entirely. In some cases, that guarantee might require arranging for students to transfer to another school or negotiating a cooperative agreement with a neighboring college, but currently enrolled students should never be left without the option of finishing the degree they came to a college to pursue.

In place of the discontinued degree programs and the reduced number of departments and colleges, HSU formed four meta-majors (or learning communities) that were configured to align with regional workforce needs:

- Health, Education, and Social Sustainability (including majors such as psychology, education, sociology and social work);
- Applied Professional Science and Technology (programs such as aviation, computer science, and physics);
- Business Innovation and Entrepreneurship (accounting, business administration and management information systems)
- Arts and Humanities (innovative media, music, and music education).

In addition, going forward, it planned to offer more than 30 certificate programs at the undergraduate level in subjects such as social media, creative writing, gerontology, and criminal justice and more than a dozen graduate certificates in areas like supply chain management, dyslexia therapy, and project management.

A year after first introducing the need for financial exigency, Henderson State began to find out where it stood financially. The initial results confirmed that as a result of the steps taken in 2022, the university had made significant progress in restoring fiscal integrity and was on a path to sustainable operations.

Based on a FY 22 audited financial statement:

- The combined efforts of Henderson State's modified cash budget and financial exigency helped decrease accounts payable from $6,926,687 to $1,383,746, an improvement of $5,542,941.
- Personal services expenses decreased from $30,768,950 to $23,498,322, a reduction of $7,270,628, or 23.4%.
- Henderson State's overall net position increased from $21,013,662 in FY21 to $31,946,526 in FY22.
- Henderson State improved from seven days of cash on hand in 2019 to 50 days of cash on hand in 2022.

What about enrollment, an area that critics of many financial exigency plans—including Henderson State's—had predicted would decline dramatically? The fall 2022 student headcount stood at 2,519, down 400 students from 2,919 the prior fall. That was a 14% decrease, clearly a cause for continuing concern and an important target for future efforts at rebuilding, which we discuss in Chapters 7 and 8.

On the other hand, there were encouraging signs, pointing to a possible recovery on the horizon. First-time freshmen increased to 437 compared to 416 in fall 2021, and graduate student enrollment increased as well—from 689 in fall 2021 to 708 in fall 2022. A notable increase was seen in Henderson's MBA program, which grew from 76 students in 2021 to 130 students in 2022. And by the end of FY 2023, Henderson State's net cash position had increased by nearly $3 million.

Another indication of progress came from the Higher Learning Commission (HLC), Henderson State's accrediting agency. In February 2022, after learning of HSU's exigency, HLC informed the institution that in light of the serious questions raised about its financial capacity, it was planning to assign a Financial Distress designation to the university. HLC had visited Henderson State in November 2021 and based on that site visit and other materials had recommended a reaffirmation of Henderson State's accreditation. It had apparently not detected the seriousness of the university's financial problems. In fact, it took a phone call the day before exigency was declared from Chancellor Ambrose informing HLC of the exigency declaration before the commission understood how precarious Henderson State's finances had become. However, within three months of the exigency being declared, HLC subsequently decided to not proceed with such a designation after considering the steps Henderson State had taken to right its fiscal ship since financial exigency was invoked.

One other outcome from the financial exigency at Henderson State University also needs to be recognized. On July 31, 2023, Chuck Ambrose announced that he was resigning as chancellor, effective September 15 and would be joining the Husch Blackwell law firm as a senior consultant for higher education strategy. The work of leading an institution through the painful process of financial exigency is different from the job of rebuilding it, a challenge that we explore in depth in Chapters 7 and 8. Ambrose believed he had accomplished the task he had been presented: to establish the financial foundation that would allow HSU to continue to operate. But in the course of achieving that goal, he also understood that too many battles had been fought, too much political capital had been spent, and too great a personal toll had been taken for him to be the right person to lead the institution into its new future.

This is one of the many difficult lessons—on both a professional and personal level—to be learned from institutions that go through financial exigency. The individual who oversees an institution's exigency process may not be the individual who is in the best position to lead that institution to its full recovery. We will have more to say about these kinds of considerations in future chapters, but for now, as we turn our attention to the fundamental questions that financially distressed colleges must address, we wanted to acknowledge this portion of the HSU story.

In the chapters that follow, we use the Henderson State case and lessons learned from it and other colleges that have gone through financial exigency to explore more fully the processes involved, including the institutional data that are required, the roles and responsibilities of college leadership and board governance, the most common pitfalls, the campus reactions and other fallout to an exigency declaration, and the ultimate purposes to which an exigency transformation should be directed. Next, in Chapter 3, we turn our attention to the first crucial ingredient—the institutional data that colleges must collect and analyze so they can understand exactly what it costs to operate the academic programs and services they provide to students.

NOTES

1. The American Association of University Professors (AAUP) mission "is to advance academic freedom and shared governance; to define fundamental

professional values and standards for higher education; to promote the economic security of faculty, academic professionals, graduate students, postdoctoral fellows, and all those engaged in teaching and research in higher education; to help the higher education community organize to make our goals a reality; and to ensure higher education's contribution to the common good."

2. https://www.aaup.org/file/FinancialExigency.pdf

3. Ibid

4. Ibid

5. Regulation 4.d, by contrast, provides procedures for tenure terminations as a result of program closings that are not mandated by financial exigency, but are based on educational factors: "Termination of an appointment with continuous tenure, or of a probationary or special appointment before the end of the specified term, may occur as a result of bona fide formal discontinuance of a program or department of instruction." Unlike financial exigency, decisions to discontinue a program or department of instruction under 4.d should be based "essentially upon educational considerations, as determined primarily by the faculty as a whole or an appropriate committee thereof." In practice, institutions often blend or conflate 4.c and 4.d in ways that AAUP finds objectionable. Such commingling was one of the reasons leading to its revised definition of exigency in 2013.

6. AAUP also provides guidelines for how faculty should be involved in an institution's regular budgeting process.

7. https://www.lawinsider.com/dictionary/financial-exigency

8. https://www.jstor.org/stable/40224955?read-now=1&seq=2#page_scan_tab_contents

9. https://www.aaup.org/report/financial-exigency-academic-governance-and-related-matters

10. https://www.nytimes.com/1996/05/03/nyregion/cuny-misused-fiscal-emergency-to-cut-staff-and-costs-judge-rules.html

11. https://www.acenet.edu/Documents/Faculty-in-Times-of-Financial-Distress-Examining-Governance,-Exigency,-Layoffs-and-Alternatives.pdf

12. J. R. Jordan. (2018) Sign of the times: Financial exigency in higher education. In S. Green (Ed.) *Declaring Financial Exigency in Higher Education: How Do You recover?* New York: Nova Science Publishers.

13. It's yet to be seen whether this pattern might change if small, private institutions continue to suffer enrollments losses as is generally expected, raising the possibility that financial exigency might become more common at private schools.

14. https://www.diverseeducation.com/students/article/15098817/shaky-finances-putting-chicago-state-accreditation-at-risk

15. Another vehicle is to terminate faculty contracts through *force majeure*, a clause in some collective bargaining contracts that frees the parties from liability or obligations when an extraordinary circumstance beyond the control of the parties—such as an epidemic—prevents one or both parties from fulfilling their obligations under the contract.

16. https://www.aaup.org/file/Special-Report_COVID-19-and-Academic-Governance.pdf

17. https://www.aaup.org/file/Special Report_COVID 19 and Academic Go

18. https://www.aaup.org/report/college-and-university-governance-vermont-law -school

19. https://www.aaup.org/file/National_Louis.pdf

20. https://www.aaup.org/our-programs/academic-freedom/censure-list

21. https://www.kansasregents.org/resources/PDF/About/Board_Meetings/FY _2022/E_May_18-19_2022_Board_Minutes.pdf

22. https://www.insidehighered.com/news/2022/09/21/why-emporia-state-axed-33 -employees

23. https://www.aaup.org/file/Emporia_State_University_embargoed.pdf

24. https://www.aaup.org/NR/rdonlyres/6BBEDF23-3FA6-4BBB-85BA -73424C41B5B3/0/KatrinaReportt.pdf

25. https://bloomfield.edu/about-us/news/montclair-state-university-and -bloomfield-college-announce-efforts-forge-permanent. See also: https://www .diverseeducation.com/leadership-policy/article/15090133/einvented-new-jersey -college-embraces-minority-identity

26. https://www.repository.law.indiana.edu/cgi/viewcontent.cgi?article=3160 &context=ilj

27. https://openjurist.org/585/f2d/675/krotkoff-v-goucher-college

28. https://cpe.ky.gov/news/stories/cpe-approves-17M-ksu.html

29. https://store.chronicle.com/collections/reports-guides/products/restructuring-a -university

30. http://www.magnoliareporter.com/education/colleges_universities/article _2c116d3a-85a7-11ec-9a3d-238557d3cf0f.html

31. https://www.hsu.edu/uploads/pages/2016_faculty_handbookwith_fully_ approved_recommendations_for_2018.pdf

32. https://hsu.edu/pages/creating-the-future-of-college-reimagining-henderson/

Chapter 3

The Numbers Every College Should Know

Financial exigency is a very data-demanding process. Any college leader who's considering declaring exigency is likely to be unsuccessful unless the restructuring strategy begins with the collection and analysis of at least three years of institution-wide and department-specific data about finances and academic performance. Unless those data are available and accurate, a financial exigency probably should not be pursued.

A financial exigency may still be necessary, but absent reliable data, the institution will not be able to recognize that it's required or pursue it responsibly. The standard for declaring exigency is high, as it should be—students will be adversely affected, jobs are at stake, and the long-term survival of the institution is at risk. Reliable institutional data have a special power: They reveal the truth. Nothing tells the story of the threats to a college's viability or its claims of prosperity like objective data. Ultimately, the only real leverage a college leader has for bringing about lasting institutional change is to call upon the truth.

Hard, cold numbers can compel a campus to face the reality of an institution's red ink and pinpoint the source of the bleeding. How much money is in the bank? What debts must be serviced? How much revenue is coming in? What expenses must be paid? How big is the endowment, and how much of it is being spent? Are we adding or losing students? How many students are graduating? Are they passing licensure exams, and what kinds of jobs are they getting after graduation? Is too much institutional aid being awarded or not enough? Are there too many administrators? Too many staff? Too many faculty? Can we afford our intercollegiate athletics program? Which academic programs net positive revenue annually, and which lose money each year? How much did we rely on federal relief funding to operate during the pandemic, masking the full financial impact of Covid-19?

Many colleges never ask these questions or face their answers head on. Some may not want to know the answers. They avoid the hard truths even as they accumulate. Presidents may not share financial data sufficiently with their boards. Boards may not fully understand what the numbers mean. Boards and presidents may not share the data or educate their campus community about the significance of the numbers.

In other situations, while the president and maybe the institution's chief financial officer have examined the numbers, the majority of faculty and staff have not. They move on year after year, assuming the budget will somehow take care of itself. That a down year will be followed by a good one. That declining student enrollment can eventually be turned around. That the state will recognize how important they are and come to their financial rescue whenever it's necessary. Or that a big donor will make a major gift that saves the day.

The alternative scenarios—where enrollments keep sliding and revenue continues to plunge, where expenses continue to mount, where the state makes further cuts to appropriations, and where donors find other good causes to support with their gifts—are less often entertained or are not taken seriously until it's too late.

A good case in point is Saint Leo University, a Catholic four-year college, located outside of Tampa, Florida. In 2012, enrollment at Saint Leo stood at about 13,000 students, and it was operating dozens of satellite learning centers across several states. It was in full growth mode. In fact, St. Leo even made a bid in 2021 to acquire or merge with Marymount California University as part of its expansion plans.

Saint Leo's vision to acquire Marymount California took place even as it was sustaining serious enrollment losses of its own. By 2022, following the pandemic, its enrollment had dropped to about 7,500 students, and Saint Leo found itself scrambling. Its debt—a whopping $66 million—was downgraded to speculative status, and it began to pull back its operations. It closed several of its satellite education centers, began to phase out a number of its intercollegiate athletic programs, terminated three of its degree programs, and eliminated 111 faculty and staff positions, 27% of which were vacant at the time.[1]

Remember, all these cuts came less than a year after it had tried to grow out of its financial problems by taking over California Marymount, a strategy it was finally forced to abandon after its accreditor, the Southern Association of Colleges and Schools, refused to sign off on the deal, citing concerns about Saint Leo's financial condition. The merger fiasco ultimately resulted in Jeffrey Senese, the Saint Leo president who had tried to broker the Marymount takeover, resigning from office.

Faculty often argue that you can't run a college like a business. That's almost always an overly simplified or frankly false narrative. If by that

VOICES FROM THE FIELD

The all-too-frequent cycle of scrambling to hide from—or make up for scarcity—is particularly common at small, enrollment-driven, private colleges that don't have large endowments to draw upon. When these cycles become more frequent or they take on new burdens that threaten the bottom line, declaring financial exigency may ultimately become necessary to bring about the restructuring necessary to contain costs and reverse downward trends.

This cycle often begins early in the spring semester when preliminary application and acceptance reports from the enrollment management team are tracked to estimate what enrollment is expected for the fast-approaching fall semester. Along with those estimates, a college will also project how much financial aid will need to be awarded in the form of institutional scholarships to hit the enrollment target. And public colleges will also learn in the spring how much the state will be increasing or decreasing their appropriations for the next year.

When the fall semester finally arrives, and new students are officially registered and begin their classes, even small gains and losses in the final enrollment numbers can mean the difference between ecstasy and despair as college leaders ponder these basic questions: Did we hit our first-year enrollment and transfer targets? How many students signed contracts to live in the dorms? How much financial aid did we disburse, and what is our discount rate? What is our retention rate for current students? Are we going to produce enough revenue to support our budget, or are we coming up short? Is it going to be a great year or a tough one for the campus?

If the answer is that tuition revenue is not going to be able to cover the expenses expected for the year—the greater costs for utilities, the employee raises and benefits, and the inflationary expenses in everything from food services and supplies to maintenance and repairs—administrators will begin to plan for the funds they'll need to find or the expenses they'll need to pare back in order to make it through the end of the academic year or have enough money to pay people in the summer.

In a tough year, college leaders will begin to focus their attention on annual private giving and what estate gifts may or may not mature. Or they may consider how a push for enrollment of transfer students in the fall could yield new revenue for the spring semester. They may explore the potential of increasing enrollment in the summer or adding an inter-session over the winter break, with the hope that those classes could generate more net revenue. They will look for any dollars that might be available in institutional reserves or the unrestricted endowment to patch the hole. The overwhelming preference of all college leaders is to look for more money before they're forced to cut everyday expenses, freeze hiring, or defer maintenance and repairs.

When this cycle repeats itself year over year, operating margins will continue to contract. The need to make permanent operating cuts through structural changes in the institution will grow at the same time a president's willingness to do so may weaken in the face of faculty and staff resistance to any meaningful belt-tightening. But the consequence of waiting can pile up and ultimately increase the severity of the fiscal crisis an institution must face. In that respect, Shakespeare was right, when in the Twelfth Night, he wrote "In delay there lies no plenty."

In the post-Covid 19 environment, colleges are learning that bad budget news has become more of an annual, rather than a cyclical, problem. Both private and public institutions are finding their revenues dropping, their costs rising, and students increasingly questioning whether they can afford what a college education costs. The seasonal cycles are becoming the annual norm, and the options available—other than substantial reduction in expenses—are running out.

claim, faculty simply mean that the point of most colleges is not to turn a profit, they're clearly correct. Except for the relatively small, for-profit sector of higher education, colleges are not operated to turn profits for owners or stockholders. Or, if with that claim, they mean that the success of a college should not be judged solely on its endowment wealth, property holdings, or the annual earnings of its graduates, we concur.

But if they mean that colleges and universities are—or should be—immune from financial realities, or that they don't have to respect a bottom line where revenues are sufficient to pay expenses, not only are they wrong, but they're also staking out a position that could eventually endanger their institution's long-term viability. Colleges and universities must maintain the same level of fiscal integrity and economic stability that are expected from government, non-profit organizations, hospitals, small businesses, and big corporations.

In this chapter we show why it's imperative that every college and its various constituents be presented with accurate, up-to-date financial data about how it generates its revenues and spends its resources. That requires more than just knowing what the budget is. It means understanding the actual revenue and expenses the institution is realizing and how the many complex parts come together for it to operate with the best financial stewardship possible.

The reason is simple. A college whose leaders, faculty, and staff are financially literate about its costs and who develop basic financial competencies is a college more likely to survive in the increasingly turbulent economic environment in which higher education finds itself.

A college that is well-informed about its finances is much more likely to develop the shared sense of responsibility that will be required to cope with whatever structural deficits have been identified. Shared knowledge provides shared power to affect outcomes and drive change. Next, we discuss what kinds of data are important and what fiscal steps may need to be taken following a thorough financial reckoning.

WHAT EVERY PRESIDENT KNOWS OR SHOULD KNOW

Hardly a day goes by—especially since 2020 and the onset of the pandemic—that college presidents don't wake up and read a new story about higher education's dire budget problems in the *Chronicle of Higher Education* or *Inside Higher Education,* two leading publications covering the higher education sector. Those articles focus on one of the following two themes.

First, how it's becoming harder for colleges to generate revenue. There are many reasons for this problem, as we alluded to in Chapter 1, but, as a reminder, here are the chief culprits.

- Fewer students are going to college, and the forecasts suggest that demographic trends will only worsen that problem in the upcoming decade.
- Tuition revenues are shrinking through a combination of lower enrollment of new students, stagnant or declining retention of current students, and too steep of a discounting of tuition through institutionally funded scholarships.
- Endowment returns have decreased or remained stagnant, reducing the ability to spend more from those investments.
- Compounding the enrollment slide is the emergence of apprenticeships, employer-provided training, industry certifications, and alternative-credentialing programs, each marketed as offering faster and more convenient delivery of information and lower prices than that offered through traditional college degrees.
- A greater percentage of students are attending large public flagship universities or brand-name private colleges, leaving regional universities,

small private institutions, and community colleges competing for a progressively smaller slice of the enrollment pie.
- Increases in online or virtual enrollment are eating away at sources of
  auxiliary revenues, such as room and board fees, that have traditionally
  been lucrative revenue sources at many colleges.
- Inconsistent state funding, where appropriations to public institutions
  rise and fall annually depending on the economy and state tax receipts,
  leaves colleges uncertain about their funding base.
- The federal faucet out of which billions of dollars flowed to keep institutions afloat during the pandemic is not likely to be turned on again.
  Colleges balancing their budgets with any of those remaining funds are
  learning that this tide has turned.

The second theme is how colleges have bigger bills to pay, owing to several
factors that have become all too familiar to college administrators as illustrated by Figure 3.1.

- Many institutions have followed a strategy of trying to grow their way
  out of a financial hole. They've added new majors, expanded graduate
  degree programs, increased the number of their intercollegiate athletic
  teams, created multidisciplinary research centers, hired more personnel,
  and/or made new, large investments in capital renovations and building projects.
- This expansion strategy is too often the default option for colleges facing
  money problems. That's because for decades higher education has had a
  perpetual growth-is-good mindset. Growth is good—when it really happens, is accurately measured, and pays for itself. At too many colleges,
  however, none of those results occurs. Many colleges have "built it,"
  but unlike in the cornfields of Iowa, they didn't come. The anticipated
  growth, if it occurs at all, is usually not as large as had been projected.
  Consequently, it's insufficient to cover the additional expenses that were
  incurred. Rather than helping the institution increase net revenue, expansion often fails to pay for itself and forces the institution to increase its
  internal subsidies.
- Another frequent by-product of growth strategies is increased debt as
  institutions borrow money to fund major capital projects, including the
  construction of new facilities and renovation and repair of existing ones.
  The build-it-and-they-will-come mentality was dealt a severe blow by
  the pandemic, which left many schools that had banked on the drawing
  power of a spruced-up campus in the lurch of shrinking enrollments and
  mounting debts.

- Hidden debt can also be contained within vendor contracts and other financial relationships where cash or capital has been leveraged and amortized, binding the institutions to years of increased spending.
- As we discussed in Chapter 1, inflationary increases have driven up costs in every category of college spending—salaries, materials and supplies, utilities, transportation, health care, insurance, and capital repairs and renovations.
- Accompanying this inflation has been a renewed union activism on campus. Beginning with the historic six-week strike by tens of thousands of academic workers at the University of California in 2022, strikes have been authorized at scores of institutions ever since. Faculty, staff, graduate assistants, and postdoctoral researchers have united to demand higher wages, increased benefits and better working conditions. Labor activism on college campuses is reaching unprecedented levels. With colleges still grappling to rejuvenate their Covid-depleted workforce, workers have been very successful in negotiating increased compensation and benefit packages.
- Institutions also face the rising costs of greater compliance and regulatory pressures from both federal and state governments. New mandates and regulations require more staff to monitor and enforce them, further driving up labor costs. For most of these staff, there is no revenue stream to support them, as there is—at least theoretically—when a college adds a new academic program or builds a new residence hall.
- Institutions continue to invest more in educational and student service technology, which drives up expenses associated with acquiring the necessary hardware and software, in addition to hiring additional personnel trained to use it.
- Additional investments have been driven by colleges attempting to respond to important student needs in areas such as behavioral health, food and housing security, and other support services. These efforts are important, but they almost always require more staff, swelling the annual payroll and placing more strain on operating margins.

College presidents and their chief financial officers acknowledge most of these problems—at least they do so for higher education in general. Whether they fully appreciate their significance at their home institutions is another matter, however. In 2023, *Inside Higher Education* commissioned Hanover Research to conduct a survey of what college presidents believed about their institution's future.[2] A total of 442 campus heads responded, representing two-year and four-year institutions, in both the public and private higher ed sectors.

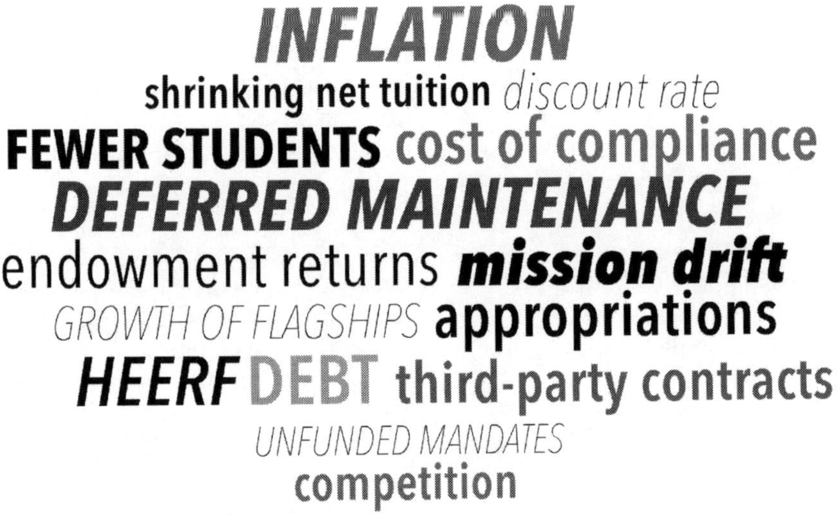

INFLATION
shrinking net tuition *discount rate*
FEWER STUDENTS cost of compliance
DEFERRED MAINTENANCE
endowment returns *mission drift*
GROWTH OF FLAGSHIPS appropriations
HEERF DEBT third-party contracts
UNFUNDED MANDATES
competition

Figure 3.1. Chief Culprits

The survey found the college chief executives to be mostly upbeat about their institutions' futures. More than three-quarters of them (85%) thought that their college would be financially stable over the next decade. Most also thought their institution was in stronger shape now than it had been compared to 2019 before the onset of the pandemic. Presidents were twice as likely to say their institution would be better off "next year" than it is now (58%) than believe that "next year" would be worse (22%).

Presidents and chancellors acknowledged that the pandemic had changed higher education in important ways: 76% agreed (27% strongly) that "the pandemic and subsequent necessary changes (e.g., adopting more remote learning) has created an opportunity for my institution to make other institutional changes we have been needing to make anyway." Almost three-quarters (72%) said their institution needed to fundamentally change its business model or other operations, and 87% agreed (37% strongly) that their institution would maintain some of Covid-19–related changes it had been forced to make even after the pandemic ends, particularly an expanded use of online learning.

Nonetheless, the campus leaders were reluctant to endorse the need for major transformations at their home institutions. Most appeared to think their institution has settled into a "new normal" despite all the disruptions from the pandemic. Fewer than one in five presidents (18%) said that senior administrators at their institution had had "serious internal discussions" in the last year about merging with another college, and only 28% said they'd had serious internal discussions about consolidating some of their institution's programs or operations with another college. About eight in 10 campus leaders indicated that their institution was unlikely to shrink its physical campus over the next five years. An earlier survey had found that community college presidents were more open to the possibility of downsizing their schools' footprint, but even among them, only about 25% acknowledged some physical consolidation might need to occur.

What should we make of these results? On the one hand, college leaders overwhelmingly acknowledged that institutions must change their basic business model in the upcoming years. On the other hand, they didn't express much enthusiasm or urgency for doing so at their own institution. There were some sector differences for sure. A greater percentage of public doctoral university presidents and leaders of private colleges expressed great confidence in their schools' financial future, compared to the heads of community colleges or public master's/baccalaureate institutions. But overall, most of the leaders were sanguine about their institution's financial security and did not express an urgent need for structural changes. "Not in my back yard" was their unspoken mantra.

Perhaps the presidents are right. Maybe the worst of higher education's tough fiscal times is over, and the nation's colleges can look forward to a rosier future. After all, America higher ed has survived boom and doom cycles repeatedly before. It's proven to be a very sturdy enterprise, able to adapt and recover. History is on their side. Why should now be any different?

Much more likely, we believe, is that if the future looks rosy to presidents, it's because too many of them are looking at it and their institutions through rose-tinted glasses. The result is an optimistic distortion that may be reassuring in the short run, but risky over the longer haul. Although we don't believe higher education is facing the financial Armageddon that some pundits have predicted, we do think it is in store for a prolonged period of economic challenges.

The presidents' prevailing optimism invites an all-too-well known temptation—when in doubt about what to do, punt the ball. Don't upset the status quo even when you know you probably need to. Somehow, things will work out. Our universities are sturdy, built to last; they've always bounced back, and they'll do so again. We think that perspective is unrealistic. We believe many campus leaders and their communities have run out the clock. Surveys aside, whether a college should be optimistic or pessimistic about its financial future ought to be based primarily not on its president's grand aspirations or sanguine attitude, but on data that accurately depict the college's financial realities and operations and a projection of its future based on an analysis of those data. Those are the numbers we turn to next.

THE BASIC QUESTIONS EVERY
COLLEGE SHOULD ANSWER

Every college collects and maintains annual institutional data on its total enrollment; on the number of new and transfer students who apply, are accepted, and eventually enroll; on its student retention and graduation rates; and on graduates' performance on various licensure and certification exams. For the most part, these numbers are trustworthy and can be relied upon to give an accurate portrayal of a college's enrollment and completion numbers. Several websites, such as the National Center for Education Statistics' College Navigator puts these kinds of data in the hands of students and parents as they consider their own college options and make their decisions about where to attend.[3]

Colleges also collect generally reliable data on annual revenue by different sources—tuition, state appropriations, endowment spending, private gifts, investments, grants and contracts, money earned by auxiliary units (e.g., residence and dining halls, a campus bookstore or university press, ticket sales, and other services) and at some major universities, the income from an affiliated medical center. Likewise, colleges keep close track on their annual expenditures, usually divided into such categories as employee compensation (wages, salaries, and benefits); student financial aid; supplies and other expenses like communications, travel and equipment; debt service; capital improvements; and operations and maintenance of facilities.

Colleges spend months preparing annual operating budgets that show the funds they plan to receive and the ways they plan to spend money on both day-to-day operations and one-time expenses. Budgeting can be approached in several ways, and different institutions use different methods to build their budget each year.

- Most common is *incremental/decremental budgeting* where individual unit budgets are increased or decreased by a specific percentage annually. Because most aspects of these programs or activities don't change that much from year to year, it's assumed that a relatively small percentage increase/decrease will be adequate in most cases.
- Other institutions use what's called a *zero-based budgeting* approach, which unlike incremental/decremental budgeting, assumes—at least in theory—no budget base from prior years. Instead, each unit begins at a base of zero, and its budget is built and justified from there. In actual practice at most colleges, a large portion of the prior budget is treated as a base, with any annual adjustments to it applying to maybe only 20–25% of the total.

- A few institutions use *responsibility center budgeting*. In this method, academic units are assigned the revenues they generate through their programs. They then are "taxed" by the central administration to pay for the various units on campus that serve them such as the library, the counseling center, the admissions office, and other administrative units. These taxes, or "franchise fees," are combined with other revenues, such as state appropriations, to fund the institution, including subsidies for those academic programs that don't bring in enough tuition to cover their costs. Although responsibility center budgeting is commonly portrayed as a more transparent process intended to increase entrepreneurial activity at the unit level, its implementation is often uneven with some units enjoying allocations and subventions that are adjusted for a variety of historical reasons and opaque justifications.

What's important to remember for our purposes is that a budget is a statement of policy or strategic priorities translated into the dollars those priorities are expected to cost. A budget is not the same as cash, a mistake that faculty and staff—and sometimes presidents—forget. Focus only on the budget, and you may never know an institution's actual cash position or how money flows throughout a fiscal year. Just because an expense is listed in a budget does not mean that an institution has the necessary funds to pay for it, a fact that we will often repeat throughout this book. A good example of this disconnect was found at Henderson State University, where just prior to declaring financial exigency, it discovered that while it had budgeted $68.3 million in annual revenue, it was in fact going to bring in only $55.8 million.

College budgeting differs from budgeting in private businesses in several ways, one of the most important of which is that a college typically only sets its prices—its tuition and fees and room and board rates—one time a year, while business frequently adjust their prices to reflect supply and demand as each one changes. In college budgeting, the tuition price is established at the beginning of each year to enable the institution to bring in the revenue it intends to spend. In other words, anticipated spending helps determine the revenue a college needs to generate. When you think about it, that's a peculiar—and substantial—twist from the business world, where revenues typically influence the costs of whatever the business is selling. It's one of the reasons why most colleges, which are perpetually attempting to expand, continue to set their tuition higher year after year or seek more funding from the state when enrollment falls. How many businesses do you know that, when faced with a shrinking customer base, raise their prices or ask for bigger public subsidies?

Colleges follow a standard nomenclature for financial accounting and budgeting developed by the National Association of College and University Business Officers (NACUBO).[4] Those designations organize an institution's expenditures under several categories of activity such as instruction, research, public service, academic support, student support, institutional administration, and subsidies to auxiliaries such as athletics, performing arts centers, health clinics, and student recreation centers. Institutional budgets are further subdivided down to the academic department and administrative unit level.

Colleges also prepare annual financial statements that summarize their financial results and position at the end of a fiscal year, which at most institutions is the same as the academic year, running from July 1 through June 30 of the next year. A college's financial statement will include a statement of its assets and liabilities, its net position, statements of revenues, expenses, and changes in net position from the prior year, cash flows, and various notes explaining the report's findings. The financial report may also have a separate section on component units affiliated with the institution such as a foundation, intercollegiate athletics department, or an academic health center.

Financial statements are audited by certified accountants, who certify that they fairly represent, in all material respects, the financial position of the institution in accordance with auditing standards contained in *Government Auditing Standards*, issued by the Comptroller General of the United States.[5] A college's administration is responsible for preparing its financial statements. An auditor's responsibility is to use professional judgment and give a reasonable—but not absolute—assurance about whether the financial statement is free from material misstatements either because of fraud or error.

The budget and the financial statement are the starting points for gaining an overview of an institution's finances. Anyone who wants to understand a college's financial health must start with those documents. But with the growing complexity of higher education—both in the ways it generates revenues and spends its dollars—these standard financial metrics do not capture the full measure of how a college is faring, and more importantly, how its primary core business of instruction is performing and how its stewardship of increasingly scarce resources can be improved.

For a detailed understanding of an institution's financial well-being—particularly in those cases where financial problems point to the need for substantial cost reductions that might extend as far as declaring a financial exigency—budgets and financial statements are necessary, but they are not sufficient. They are the place to start a discussion, not end it. A more fine-grained analysis is called for.

A well-managed college should know the answer to this first, basic question: How much do our degrees cost? Then, it needs to understand what it costs to operate every unit on campus and how those costs have changed over the years. This understanding is particularly important for colleges that are in financial trouble. Such cost accounting should include the offices of the president, the provost and vice-presidents, and all the various units reporting to them. It also should include financial aid, athletics, and campus maintenance and repairs. It needs to address debt service and other contractual obligations. Every unit should be put under the microscope.

Because most of a college's costs occur from the delivery of academic programs, they must be given special scrutiny. Specifically, a college needs to know how much it costs to offer each of its academic programs and how much those programs generate in tuition revenue. Calculating the net costs or gains of academic programs involves the following metrics: the number of students in the program, the credit hours and net tuition they generate, student retention and completion rates, and the per-student or per-credit costs of instruction associated with the program, including both general education requirements, other service courses, and courses specific to the major.

The focus on academic program costs will need to be broadened at institutions where the mission is not focused solely on teaching. At many universities, significant internal funds are invested in research, both in terms of faculty's work effort but also in specialized equipment, laboratory facilities, graduate assistants, and research administration. Because science and engineering have become increasingly interdisciplinary, research-intensive universities have created centers to bring together investigators from different departments to tackle complex research topics in areas like data science, climate change, health promotion, urban studies, and artificial intelligence. These centers usually require additional skilled staff and capital expenditures, and while they may have been founded with external grant support or private gifts, their long-term operation can require substantial institutional underwriting that needs regular monitoring to determine if it can or should be continued.

Some academic program performance measures—e.g., student enrollment and completion in different majors—are also monitored by state higher education coordinating boards and agencies that periodically review the academic productivity at public institutions within the state to determine if their programs are meeting minimum thresholds of productivity or if there is unnecessary duplication of programs that could be reduced. Many of these coordinating agencies were established in the 1970s, during a prior period of economic straitening for higher education. (These agencies are sometimes referred to as "1202 commissions" because they were authorized under Section 1202 of the Higher Education Act of 1965.)

For example, Missouri's Coordinating Board for Higher Education (CBHE) has the statutory responsibility to review existing programs at the state's public colleges and universities and make recommendations to modify, consolidate or eliminate them if it determines such action is in the best interest of the institutions and the state. One component of the CBHE review is an analysis of program productivity, using this standard: "Unless there is sufficient justification for exceptions, particularly in the arts and sciences, programs shall maintain a critical mass of majors and graduate annually an average, calculated over the prior three years of at least 10 graduates at the associate or baccalaureate degree level, five graduates at the master's degree level, and three graduates at the doctoral degree level."

In a 2018 review, the Missouri Department of Higher Education and Workforce Development identified 775 programs statewide that fell below these productivity thresholds.[6] That number equaled about 46% of approved programs in the state. Once the list of each institution's programs and completions was compiled, the department sent the data to each public institution to review and verify their accuracy. After the accuracy of the data was affirmed, institutions were sent a list of the programs that fell below the productivity thresholds and asked to review them.

After that review, institutions then indicated what action they intended to take regarding those programs falling below a threshold—close them, modify them, or retain them. If it intended to retain a low-productivity program, the institution was required to justify that decision. For example, it could point to unique institutional circumstances that called for the program to be continued, or it could document how the program was going to be changed to increase its appeal and productivity in the future.

Just because a review flags a low productivity program, it doesn't mean that the program is necessarily destined for closure. In some cases, a program with low enrollments and graduates will be retained because an institution believes it's too central to its mission to jettison. Its faculty may be conducting highly influential research, or it may be responsible for important service to the state. In other cases, as we will discuss shortly, a program may have a special historical or community significance that results in it being maintained despite its recent disappointing performance.

Sometimes, rather than closing a program with low productivity, a college will redesign it so that it is better aligned with new trends in the discipline or an emerging job market. For example, in the case of the Missouri review, 41% of the programs targeted for low productivity were retained, and another 16% were provisionally retained, pending further review and possible modifications. Approximately 30% of the programs were slated to be terminated, and the remainder were still under review at the time of the final report.

It's not uncommon to hear college presidents complain publicly about these kinds of required external reviews. They may grumble that the coordinating board is trampling on their institution's autonomy and should defer to the judgment of the institution's faculty, administration, and governing board about what programs are offered or discontinued. Or they might object to the numerical thresholds, calling them "arbitrary" or "unfair" metrics to apply to small, but still important, majors. They might say the numbers are anomalous, that they singled out a particularly bad stretch that's not been characteristic of a program's overall history.

Here's a tip. No matter what public objections presidents make to such mandated external reviews, privately they usually welcome them because they force their institutions to undergo the scrutiny they know is necessary but are reluctant to impose, often because they fear pushback from the faculty. Presidents know these reviews might compel their institutions to take the difficult—but consistently resisted—step of closing a program that's no longer academically successful or fiscally viable. In some cases, campus CEOs might even ask the state to conduct an updated or expedited program review to provide them enough outside cover to make such hard decisions. We know because one of us was one of those CEOs.

Whether they are mandated by an outside agency or conducted periodically by a college itself, academic program reviews can also help institutions identify a set of what are often called "signature programs." These are the high performing, drawing-card programs that enjoy an excellent reputation among the higher education community. They are the programs that institutions would like to be known for. Typically, these signature programs are the ones that produce more credit hours, generate more net revenue, place more graduates, and help the institution attract more attention and resources than its other academic offerings. A select, well-funded portion of any college's academic portfolio needs to include such signature programs.

Beyond a consideration of enrollments and degree production, how would the basic metrics described above influence a possible financial exigency process? For starters, they enable an institution to ask fundamental questions such as: "How much does it cost to operate each academic department?" or "How much does each major cost?"

Let's return to Henderson State University for an illustration. Examining the books for academic year 2021 reveals that HSU's instructional programs—its majors and minors—were organized into 20 academic departments. Combined, those 20 departments generated just about $8.3 million in revenue, but it cost $22 million to operate them, with most of those operating costs—about 70%—occurring in personnel (salaries, wages, and benefits).

The result was a $13.7 million deficit in the academic portfolio. Every single department operated at a loss, considering only the salaries and benefits of faculty members. Those losses ranged from about $76,500 in Educational Leadership and $112,000 in Aviation at the low end, to $2.189 million in Music and $1.944 million in the School of Business at the high end of the distribution. This pattern is unusual. At most colleges, there are several academic units that generate a "profit," enabling them to help subsidize important, but smaller programs that operate at a loss. But at HSU, there were no subsidizing departments—all of them were operating at a loss.

The overall academic program deficit can be explained by two factors: (1) low levels of student enrollment and persistence, resulting in declining levels of net revenue; and (2) instructional spending that exceeded the net tuition generated from credit hour production. As examples of the costs and revenue associated with credit hour production, consider these three departments. In the Art department, each credit hour brought in $40 of revenue, at a cost of $338 per credit hour. In Communications and Theatre Arts, the ratio was $40 of revenue for $307 of costs per credit hour. In the School of Business, $82 in revenue per credit hour was offset by $290 in corresponding costs.

At HSU, instructors taught an average of 298 credit hours per year. For a teaching institution like Henderson, that number should have been closer to 600 credit hours per instructional line. And, to make it worse, those numbers were on the decline. Between 2019 and 2021, total credit hour production decreased an average of 9.1% a year, as overall university enrollment decreased by about 1,000 students during that same interval.

Credit hour production declines were widespread during that interval. In the Department of English, Foreign Languages, and Philosophy, credit hours decreased 22.9%. In Math, Computer Science, and Statistics, credit hours were down 19.4%. In the Social Sciences department, they were off 16.8%, and in Art the decrease was 15.9%. Only three of 20 departments showed an increase in credit hours across this period. Nursing was up 24.2%; Aviation gained 4.8%; and Sociology, Human Services, and Criminology increased 3.8%.

The costs of delivering HSU's academic programs were concentrated overwhelmingly in personnel salaries and benefits, just as they are at every college. Institution-wide, personnel compensation accounted for 70% of academic program costs, from a low of 23% in the Aviation department, where there were large annual costs for aircraft, fuel, equipment, and maintenance and lower-than-average instructional costs because most of the instructors were part-time, to highs of 80% in Chemistry and Biochemistry and 83% in the School of Business. Of those costs, 75% involved compensation to faculty who either were tenured or were on the tenure track. For one quarter of HSU's academic departments, tenure and tenure-track faculty accounted for 90% or more of the department's compensation. For another quarter, tenure and tenure-track faculty were responsible for 80% or more of departmental compensation.

Figure 3.2 summarizes these data for ten HSU departments—five with the largest financial losses and five with the smallest.

Program	Estimated Operating Margin	Total Operating Costs	Total Cost per Credit Hour	Compensation % of Total Costs	Net Tuition Revenue
Art	$ (603,096)	$ 684,725	$ 338	74%	$ 71,384
Biological Sciences	$ (835,890)	$ 1,025,106	$ 210	74%	$ 164,281
Chemistry	$ (576,275)	$ 666,338	$ 249	80%	$ 81,738
Communication & Theatre Arts	$ (1,111,361)	$ 1,275,440	$ 307	79%	$ 163,229
Curriculum & Instruction	$ (530,239)	$ 966,980	$ 1,492	94%	$ 417,612
English, Foreign Language & Philosophy	$ (1,681,317)	$ 1,781,816	$ 224	80%	$ 100,499
Math, Computer Science & Statistics	$ (1,178,336)	$ 1,277,534	$ 238	82%	$ 78,378
Music	$ (2,188,988)	$ 2,099,437	$ 646	53%	$ (148,802)
School of Business	$ (1,944,244)	$ 2,709,314	$ 290	83%	$ 682,880
Social Sciences	$ (810,085)	$ 993,951	$ 172	76%	$ 183,865

Figure 3.2. HSU Departments with Biggest Operating Losses

Reiterating a point we made earlier, just because an academic department is flagged for running a deficit doesn't mean that it should be put on the chopping block. The music department at HSU is an excellent example of this point. It was running an annual deficit of more than $2 million, the largest of any department at the university. Music is a small department at Henderson

State, with relatively few majors or graduates. Yet, it was spared from termination. Why? Because the leadership of the institution, along with the faculty, decided that for historical purposes and institutional culture, music was simply too important a program to abandon. It was downsized, but it was still preserved, despite its dismal financial numbers.

Other majors, however, were scheduled to be phased out because their enrollments were too small and their operating deficits too large. For example, in academic year 2021, the BA program in Spanish had three majors and one graduate; the BA in Business Administration had two majors and one graduate. The Early Childhood Development program had one undergraduate student declaring it as a major; it had no graduates in 2021.

Another point is worth emphasizing here. Just because an undergraduate major is eliminated from the curriculum, doesn't mean that students will no longer complete courses in that subject matter. This is a common misconception made—sometimes knowingly, sometimes unintentionally—by critics of academic downsizing. When a college eliminates its Spanish major, that doesn't necessarily result in its students suddenly being unable to take courses in Spanish. It means that the faculty may now concentrate on teaching lower-division Spanish courses, emphasizing oral and written communication in the language. Rather than an upper division seminar on Catalan Language and Culture or an advanced course on Films of the Hispanic World, faculty will teach first- and second-year Spanish.

Is an institution academically diminished by the fact that it will no longer offer a major in Spanish? Yes, assuming the program was of good quality, it probably will be to some extent. Nor can there be any denying the personal loss felt by scholars, who, having devoted their professional lives to becoming an expert in a field, will no longer be able to conduct the advanced classes they love the most. These are examples of the agonizing decisions that a financial exigency demands. But they're also the kinds of decisions that may be necessary to keep an institution open.

FROM SHARED GOVERNANCE TO
SHARED RESPONSIBILITY

Expecting college faculty and staff to understand the need for—and help in implementing—severe spending cuts, including the extreme ones involved in a financial exigency, requires that they are well-informed about the institution's financial condition. It necessitates that they understand program-level data like those we just discussed. In the best-case scenario, using these types of unit-based data will result in the reallocation of resources that keeps an institution out of an exigency situation altogether.

Waiting until an emergency arises to develop those financial competencies is a major, but avoidable, misstep. Faculty and staff need to be well-represented in budget preparations year in and year out, and those budget discussions need to drill down to the unit level. That process needs to be the routine, not the exception. When a wider number of faculty and staff are provided with those data, they are better positioned to engage in the process of allocating resources at their institution. And when they understand those data, the narrative about continuing or discontinuing academic programs changes dramatically.

Good management practice as well as the norms of shared governance dictate that faculty and staff should be meaningfully involved in developing and monitoring an institution's budget. These practices can move institutional culture from simply valuing shared governance to a more meaningful level of taking shared responsibility for institutional outcomes. According to AAUP's 1966 *Statement on Government of Colleges and Universities*:

> "The allocation of resources among competing demands is central in the formal responsibility of the governing board, in the administrative authority of the president, and in the educational function of the faculty. Each component should therefore have a voice in the determination of short—and long-range priorities, and each should receive appropriate analyses of past budgetary experiences, reports on current budgets and expenditures, and short—and long-range budgetary projections. The function of each component in budgetary matters should be understood by all; the allocation of authority will determine the flow of information and the scope of participation in decisions."[7]

Faculty and staff participation in budgeting can be achieved in a couple of ways. One is to include elected representatives from each group on departmental, college, and university-wide budget committees. Another is for faculty and staff to form budget committees that then provide recommendations to a central budgeting group made up of the president, provost, chief financial officer, and other administrators. Whichever is used, the intent is for these groups to be able to understand and influence decisions about the overall allocation of institutional resources and the proportion allocated to individual academic programs and other campus units. For those inputs to be well-informed, faculty and staff need access to the same financial information that the administration uses. It's an open-book approach to management that develops budgeting expertise while it also increases the likelihood of greater buy-in for the ultimate decisions made by the president and governing board.

A STRATEGIC FRAMEWORK FOR RESOURCE ALLOCATION AND INSTITUTIONAL PERFORMANCE

The combination of reduced revenues and increased expenses produce the structural deficits that have brought some institutions to the brink of a financial crisis and are leading others down a slippery slope they need to escape before they reach the edge.

Financial deficits are also often associated with—both as causes and consequences of—unacceptably low rates of student success, a problem experienced at many institutions. Lower enrollments and poor rates of student retention mean less revenue for a college to invest in the student support services and other resources that can help students persist until they reach the graduation finish line. It's a vicious cycle resulting in resources being spread too thin across too many programs, leaving few of them capable of doing their jobs well.

Colleges strive to accomplish three important outcomes for their students. First, they want to open doors of access and give as many students as possible the opportunity for a college education. Second, they want to help students be successful so that they graduate in a timely manner. And third, they want to provide the sort of education that prepares their graduates well for life and work. Institutions that are successful at these three goals have a sustainable model for the future. Those that are not successful must discover how to reallocate their resources going forward so they can become institutions that serve students better.

At HSU, problems of student success became more obvious as the financial exigency process began to unfold. In 2020, according to the National Center for Education Statistics, the average first-to-second year retention rate of first-time undergraduates at four-year public universities was 82%.[8] The corresponding rate at HSU was 56%. The average national six-year graduation rate, again considering first-time, full-time undergraduates attending public four-year institutions, was 64%. At HSU, it was 37%, and it was only 26% for those students receiving Pell Grants.

It would be one thing for a college to be running large financial deficits, if it was also achieving high rates of degree completion at the same time. That pattern would suggest that while the institution might be spending its money relatively wisely, it just didn't have enough of it. It's a completely different situation when a college is seeing below-average levels of student success and is also running deep in the red. That scenario calls for a top-to-bottom examination of how the institution's resources are being allocated, and more importantly, how they could be reallocated to achieve greater student success.

Figure 3.3 displays what we call a Strategic Resource Allocation Model (SRAM). It summarizes four interrelated areas of analysis and action that a campus should consider when evaluating how to become more fiscally responsible and academically successful. It requires answering the basic questions we've already identified in this chapter—how much does it cost at the individual program level for an institution to deliver its degrees.

The upper left quadrant summarizes an institutions' academic performance and net financial position. It represents what should become the next new normal for higher education, a focus not on how schools can grow themselves out of financial difficulties, but how they can reset their expenditures to maximize good student outcomes—greater retention, higher graduation rates, improved learning, and better preparation for the job market.

The upper right quadrant addresses the necessity of sound fiscal management and financial responsibility. These key elements help define what it means to be good stewards of an institution's resources. Governance and

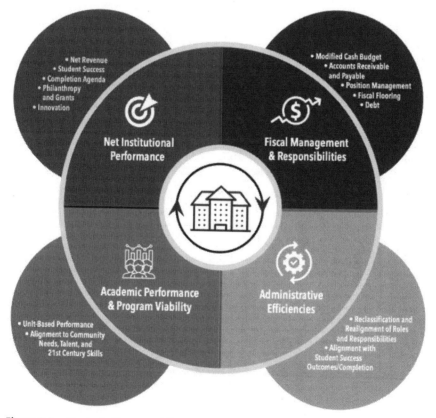

Figure 3.3.   Strategic Resource Allocation Model [SRAM]

leadership must provide the tools and training necessary to engage faculty and staff in understanding and ultimately managing the resources for which they are responsible. An effective resource allocation model should support an institution's mission, serve its student markets, and ultimately improve its bottom line. Doing so requires an institutional wide awareness of what degrees cost, what students can afford to pay, and how internal reallocations can improve performance. It also means defining an institution's financial floor—adjusting spending in real time to match the revenue a college receives.

The lower right quadrant addresses the need for administrative efficiencies. It includes the traditional means of saving money such as consolidating departments and colleges, sharing back-of-the-house services and benefits (e.g., legal staff, HR, procurement offices, employee insurance) with other colleges, and trimming other sources of overhead. But it also requires something much harder—saving money where so much of it is spent—on personnel. Today's reality is that, given their revenue problems, more colleges need to recognize the fact that they are overstaffed. A flattening of administrative structure and a reduction in support staff will likely be necessary for them to align realizable revenue with required expenses. Simply put, it's no longer possible for colleges to have a staffer for everything and an assistant for everything else.

The lower left quadrant involves what we've earlier illustrated, in part, with the HSU case study—the need to conduct a review of academic performance and program productivity. Such reviews should address two bottom-line questions: How much does it cost to offer our degree programs, and how well do they prepare our students to be effective citizens and have productive, satisfying careers.

College leaders ultimately have one important tool available to bring about change—the truth. Carefully vetted and widely shared, the data we've discussed in this chapter should increase faculty and staff's understanding of their institution's financial condition. While those of us who work in higher education have a general appreciation for its problems—that it costs too much, that too many students are shut out of it, that student learning and completion rates are far below where they should be, and that Americans are losing faith in its value—we are generally less well-informed—sometimes downright ignorant—about how our home campuses are affected by basic financial realities.

Whether this is from a willful desire not to know the score or from a false sense of security based on past experiences, the fact remains that it's becoming increasingly more important for every college to understand the viability and sustainability of its business model. Only with such understanding is it likely that a campus community will be able to reevaluate those policies and practices that must be changed for it to achieve the outcomes that are most needed.

In the next chapter, we turn to several steps that a college can take to move back from the brink. What are the tools that can help them make data-informed decisions? What actions might they take that would precede or avoid financial exigency? And what is the sequence of actions that is involved if financial exigency is ultimately declared?

NOTES

1. https://www.tampabay.com/news/education/2023/02/16/saint-leo-university-close-8-satellites-cut-staff-degree-programs/

2. https://www.insidehighered.com/news/governance/executive-leadership/2023/04/11/hopeful-despite-headwinds-survey-presidents

3. https://nces.ed.gov/collegenavigator/

4. https://www.nacubo.org/topics/planning-and-budgeting

5. https://www.gao.gov/assets/gao-18-568g.pdf

6. https://dhewd.mo.gov/cbhe/boardbook/documents/tabp0318.pdf

7. https://www.aaup.org/report/statement-government-colleges-and-universities

8. https://nces.ed.gov/programs/coe/indicator/ctr/undergrad-retention-graduation

Chapter 4

The Journey Through
Financial Exigency

When does a college know that a declaration of financial exigency has become necessary? How long does it take for financial problems to accumulate to that level of crisis? How dire do financial conditions need to be for exigency—rather than less severe measures—to be justified? When and how should the decision to proceed with exigency be communicated to the campus community and external constituents?

The answers to these questions depend largely on the unique current circumstances of a given college as well as its history. Some campuses are much better buffered against a money crisis than others. They may have economies of scale that allow them more options for saving money by combining offices or functions. Some have large unrestricted endowments from which they can draw to tide them over through a rough period. As we mentioned in Chapter 2, public institutions are more likely to declare an exigency when in deep financial trouble than private institutions, and they are also more likely to be able to rebound from it. That's because private institutions don't have any state funding to fall back on as a cushion against hard times, leaving them much more susceptible than public colleges to tumble directly from a crisis to a closure. For example, in the case of the University of Alaska, it rescinded its declaration of financial exigency after only about a month largely because of the legislature coming forward to increase its appropriation.[1] Public institutions may also be part of a university system affording them the chance to use central—rather than local campus—resources for many operations. Some colleges are not burdened with debt, while others owe so much they are left with little cash to pay for current operations.

A college's overall morale and psychological capacity to weather a crisis need to be considered as well. As one observer of exigency observed, "In raw terms, it is a money crisis. But it is more. A financial exigency is a crisis of purpose, a crisis of authority, a crisis of management, a crisis of spirit."[2] So

while it's not possible to say with precision when an institution's fiscal crisis
has become bad enough to warrant declaring exigency, several factors will
be encountered in almost every case. In this chapter we discuss those considerations and offer some guidelines about how a journey through exigency
might typically unfold.

THE MAJOR WARNING SIGNS

For starters, let's review the major warning signs that we've already discussed
in the previous chapters. These problems all involve more serious problems
than just one budget that's out of balance, a fall semester with disappointing enrollment, a downturn in private donations, or a single bad year for
state appropriations. Those kinds of ups and downs are to be expected at
any college. One or two difficult budget cycles does not constitute a case
for exigency unless they have been extraordinarily bad ones and augur the
probability that an institution will not be able to work itself out of the hole
in the future.

Some of the factors that can precipitate a financial exigency are external,
over which institutions have no control. Runaway inflation, a stock market
that's turned suddenly bearish, a natural disaster that threatens an entire
region's economy, a global pandemic, or a state with several consecutive
years of plunging tax receipts and reduced appropriations for higher education are examples. There are few shelters from those economic storms,
which can deal a devastating blow to all kinds of campuses. They are largely
unavoidable hazards.

In other instances, the culprits are mostly internal and reflect an institution's bad fiscal decisions, including loose spending habits, excessive expansion of programs, a too aggressive commitment to major capital projects, and
poor planning and flawed fiscal management. They are avoidable.

Without quantifying every hazardous factor that might be encountered,
here are some of the major problems, especially when they occur together,
that a college should consider as clear danger signals. When several are present at the same time, they point to an institution whose long-term financial
health is at risk.

- Years of static or declining state appropriations particularly during a
  period of sustained inflation.
- Increased reliance on debt financing for operations, capital renovations
  and maintenance/repair projects for an aging physical plant. Difficulties
  in a college's ability to service institutional debt is a fundamental sign
  of financial weakness. A common guideline is that a college should

not carry a long-term debt load that exceeds 50% of its annual revenue.[3] Credit ratings, accrediting bodies, state-wide coordinating agencies, and auditors all have a role in monitoring long-term debt, and they pay close attention to an institution's ability to pay it.

- A spend-down of an institution's unrestricted endowment or an abrupt increase in its annual spending policy, resulting in it spending more than the endowment is earning and depleting its overall net assets.

- A failing physical plant showing obvious signs of disrepair, neglect and/or safety issues and signaling a lack of resources available for maintenance and repairs. When institutions cut their budgets, neglecting the physical plant and avoiding the funding of depreciation are easy targets for initial reductions. But the consequences of those reductions soon become obvious, and they can be ominous. When a parent of a student states: "the residence halls are 25 years behind; I would not let my child live in these dorms," or "we've never seen the campus grounds look so bad," the financial plight of a college is being noticed. The same is true when the faculty comment, "they don't even empty the trash once a month in my office," or "this elevator has not worked for years; we are not even ADA compliant." When a college does not have adequate resources to provide a safe and healthy environment for students, faculty, and staff, its poor financial health becomes readily apparent.

- A progressively rising tuition discount rate, suggesting a desperate attempt to lure more students to enroll. The extent of this strategy is revealed by a 2023 National Association of College and University Business Officer survey[4] of 341 private, nonprofit colleges and universities, which found that the average tuition discount for first-year, full time students was 56.2% for academic year 2022–23, and it was 50.9% for all undergraduates—both record highs. In other words, after providing grants, fellowships, and scholarships from their own funds, these institutions were forgoing more than half the revenue they otherwise would have collected if they had charged all students the full tuition and fee sticker price. How well did this discount gambit work? According to the survey, after accounting for inflation, net tuition declined by more than 5% for these schools, and their undergraduate enrollment fell by an average of 1%.

- Enrollment shifts in a state or region where more students elect to attend the public flagship, the land-grant university, or brand-name private colleges than the less selective institutions in the region.

- Fewer students graduating from high schools in a college's traditional recruiting base, especially when coupled with higher numbers of students simply choosing not to attend college.

- A sustained period of poor financial management, resulting in uncontrolled spending, a lack of budget transparency, lax internal controls on hiring, and insufficient oversight of institutional staffing patterns.
- A sell-off of an institution's physical assets.
- A growing amount of accounts payable (the money an institution owes others), indicating its inability to pay its bills on time and a generally good indicator of a school's days of cash on hand. When a college's vendors suddenly become its lenders because the institution can't pay its bills, it sends a ripple effect across a local economy. For smaller colleges and regional institutions located in small communities, the institution will probably be one of the area's largest employers so the ripple can soon become a wave. No one element sounds a louder—or more frequently repeated—warning to external constituents that an institution is in financial trouble than its delay or failure to pay its bills.
- A rising tide of student accounts receivables (the money students owe the institution), indicating that students are not paying their bills. Not only can this element translate into a significant lack of cash, but it also represents a driving force of educational inequity. As an institution carries a growing balance on student accounts, it may resort to a series of unpleasant remedies that include payment plans (sometimes with interest), holding a student's transcript (to incentivize payment after a student has graduated), and as a last resort, sending a student's debt to collections. Some states garnish wages and withhold tax refunds to collect these lost tuition payments. (As an example, in the financial exigency at Henderson State University there were twice the number of students in receivables as students enrolled.)
- Inflationary increases in personnel and other fixed costs (wages and salaries, health care, utilities, supplies, third-party contracts for housing or food services, and technology).
- Mission drift and curricular spread, involving the expansion of academic programs, intercollegiate athletics, research activities, service commitments, and co-curricular offerings without a commensurate increase in revenue to support such expansion.
- A governing board that consistently fails to provide sufficient oversight of the administration's financial decision-making.

An institution should have a very high bar to clear before it declares financial exigency, but when it does it will usually be because several of the above elements have accumulated over time. The decision to invoke exigency should mean that a campus consensus has emerged that the mission and survival of the institution are at risk. The bar also must be high to justify the enormous academic and personal impacts that will be caused by program closures, termination of faculty and staff, and in most cases, a fundamental restructuring of the scope and offerings of the institution.

WHEN THE ALTERNATIVES HAVE BEEN EXHAUSTED

Another way to evaluate the necessity of an exigency declaration is to consider what other alternatives have been—or could be—attempted to turn the ship around. Managing scarcity is an art, and universities have several ways to lower or delay spending besides breaking tenure, firing staff, and cutting academic programs, the most extreme measures associated with financial exigency. In fact, it would be a rare institution that hasn't used one or more of the following measures to steer it though tough financial times. That doesn't mean such steps are easy or that they will be popular, but they are clearly less draconian than what will be demanded in financial exigency.

Here are some steps that would—and we would argue should—precede a decision to invoke exigency. These options are not offered as a check list or a formula. Some of them won't be available to every type of college or will have only a minimal effect at others. Institutions can "mix and match" the measures listed below and in Figure 4.1, relying on those most likely to achieve sufficient savings or additional revenue in a suitable period.

- Cutting spending for routine supplies, special events, communications, and travel
- Refinancing institutional debt
- Eliminating or consolidating administrative offices
- Reducing the number of schools, colleges, and departments
- Lowering the subsidies the institution pays to its auxiliary units, like intercollegiate athletics, a performing arts center, or residence life
- Freezing hiring for open staff and faculty positions
- Cancelling sabbaticals and other paid leaves of absence
- Eliminating open staff and faculty positions
- Using any "carry forward" money or year-end reserves to fund current operations
- Increasing annual spending from the endowment
- Implementing a mid-year tuition increase or surcharge, a move that for obvious reasons is sure to bring strong condemnation from students
- Reducing departmental spending across the board by a certain percentage (often in the 1%-5% range)
- Increasing faculty teaching loads
- Canceling low-enrollment courses

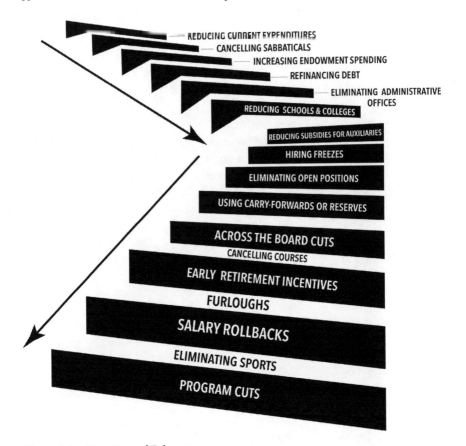

REDUCING CURRENT EXPENDITURES
CANCELLING SABBATICALS
INCREASING ENDOWMENT SPENDING
REFINANCING DEBT
ELIMINATING ADMINISTRATIVE OFFICES
REDUCING SCHOOLS & COLLEGES
REDUCING SUBSIDIES FOR AUXILIARIES
HIRING FREEZES
ELIMINATING OPEN POSITIONS
USING CARRY-FORWARDS OR RESERVES
ACROSS THE BOARD CUTS
CANCELLING COURSES
EARLY RETIREMENT INCENTIVES
FURLOUGHS
SALARY ROLLBACKS
ELIMINATING SPORTS
PROGRAM CUTS

Figure 4.1. Steps Toward Exigency

- Increasing class sizes in multiple-section courses to reduce the number of classes that need to be staffed
- Offering incentives for employees to take early retirement
- Furloughing employees
- Rolling back salaries, often structured so that more highly paid employees are assigned greater percentage reductions
- Ending participation in intercollegiate athletics for some of its varsity teams. Decreasing the number of intercollegiate sports can save money, especially for the "big time" sports schools that award "full-ride" athletic scholarships and pay hefty coaching salaries. However, for smaller schools that offer no or only limited athletic scholarships, cutting sports might hurt their bottom line given the relatively high percentage of tuition-paying students participating on athletic teams at these schools.

Cutting intercollegiate sports also deserves a bit more discussion because of two external constraints associated with it.

The extent to which an institution cuts back the number of intercollegiate sports it supports is governed by two sets of regulations. First, for the roughly 350 universities that are members of the National Collegiate Athletic Association (NCAA) Division I, they must offer a minimum of 14 sports (at least seven for men and seven for women, or six for men and eight for women). Dropping down one or two NCAA notches from Division I is an option of course, but it's rarely taken largely because of the outcry it will cause from alumni and boosters. However, one school that took that route was the University of Hartford, which dropped from Division I to Division III, a move that was projected to save the school $9.2 million per year, primarily in the costs of athletics scholarships, once the transition was complete.[5] On the other hand, some colleges with non-scholarship athletic programs formerly in Division III have migrated to Division II because they believe they can realize more net revenue from a partial scholarship model that will attract more students to enroll.

The second constraint is Title IX of the Education Amendments of 1972 (20 U.S.C. 1681 et seq.) which prohibits discrimination on the basis of sex in education programs receiving federal financial assistance.[6] Because intercollegiate athletics are considered an integral part of an institution's education program, they are covered by this law and are therefore required to show that their athletic programs are operated in a manner that is free from discrimination on the basis of sex. That requirement is interpreted to mean that an institution must offer equal opportunities to its men and women students and that eliminating costs in athletic program must be balanced in terms of its impact on gender equity.

SMALL NIBBLES VS. BIG BITES

Some combination of the above steps is usually sufficient to allow an institution to manage and survive a difficult financial situation. Administrators have been able to do it countless times over the years, even when they've hoped not to have to do so. But these actions don't always prove adequate to the task at hand. Sometimes, trimming expenses, banning travel, limiting purchases, and imposing hiring freezes add up to a mere nibbling around the edges that does not produce enough savings to sufficiently improve an institution's cash position.

In those instances, the problems are too large or have gone on too long. They have exhausted the strength of routine cost containments, even in

combination, to get the job done. Nibbles will no longer do; bigger bites are
required. And given the large emotional toll that usually results from even
small bites, it may be preferable to take as big a bite as you can all at once.
Establishing an institution's financial floor is never easy, so it may be better
to only have to do it once. That's one value—albeit a painful one—of declaring financial exigency.

While the temptations to resist exigency will be strong, waiting too long to
declare it can be a fatal decision for an institution. Exigency will inevitably
involve very difficult actions, including terminating the employment of staff,
retrenching both non-tenured and tenured faculty, and closing academic and
student support programs. As bad as those alternatives are, they are not as
devastating as the outcome they are intended to avoid—the complete and
final closing of an institution.

Waiting too long to recognize the need for exigency can be as damaging
to an economically fragile institution as proceeding too quickly. Waiting too
long increases the probability that a financial crisis will worsen, requiring
that even larger reductions in faculty, staff, and programs will ultimately
have to be made. Too long of a delay can also backfire because it drags out
the process of restructuring, adding to the public perception that a college is
failing to meet its obligations and may not have the leadership necessary to
take difficult actions that will be required to save it.

FOUR KEY TOOLS FOR MANAGING
A FINANCIAL EXIGENCY

Institutions that take the course of financial exigency will benefit from a set
of management instruments that can help inform the decisions they will need
to make throughout the process. The following four strategic tools should
be considered: A modified cash budget, an academic productivity portfolio,
student success measures, and a strategic resource allocation model (see
Figure 4.2). Each one can be modified to suit the unique circumstances of a
given college, but together they provide a useful way to organize and analyze the institutional data that are key to a well-conceived and successfully
executed exigency plan.

A Modified Cash Budget

One of the first changes required by financial exigency is to develop and use a
modified cash budget—both during the crisis and for the long-term financial
stability of the institution. Current institutional budget policies and practices,
along with the standard financial operating statements seldom give a timely,

VOICES FROM THE FIELD: CHUCK AMBROSE— WHEN ALL THE BAD NEWS FINALLY ADDS UP TO FINANCIAL EXIGENCY

After just two meetings and a few noteworthy conversations with Henderson State University's senior administrative staff, I knew that a financial exigency process would be unavoidable. A couple of those conversations still stand out in my mind. I remember my CFO telling me we were squirreling away cash just to make debt service payments. I also recall staff admitting to me that we were slow in paying our bills, a fact confirmed when I began receiving regular calls from vendors about their invoices not being paid. And, then there was this warning: "oh, by the way, it looks like we may be having a hard time making payroll in the summer."

The realization was all too obvious. HSU was out of cash. I had a sudden flashback to the summer of 1998 and my first few months at Pfeiffer University, where we were not paying our bills, facilities were literally falling down, and students owed us far more money than we were collecting. I'd always believed that "managing scarcity is an art," and now I was going to get to do it all over again.

I'd seen how bad things can become at a financially stressed college, but across 40 years in higher education, I'd never seen a public institution in such a depleted cash position as the situation at Henderson State. I admit I wondered at the time how a public institution could work itself through all the structural deficits we had identified, with essentially no alternative sources of revenue, to extend our work beyond the academic year.

I knew that the case for exigency at HSU was indisputable. It was now time to use data to change the narrative, roll up our sleeves, and begin the process of educating the campus about its dire condition and the actions we were going to have to take to pull it out of the hole and restore its viability.

Once I realized that Henderson's finances were so bad that the survival of the institution was at risk, I knew it was time to use every mechanism at our disposal to try to rectify the situation. At this point, financial exigency felt like a liberating tool that would refocus us on solutions instead of being consumed with our overwhelming problems. It provided the hope we could make the fundamental changes necessary to sustain the university.

On December 7, 2021, I wrote the following email to the key campus leaders that I would ultimately rely on, outlining the first steps I believed the university needed to take in the sequence leading to exigency.

Good morning team:

I wanted to outline next steps as we discussed in yesterday's first budget meeting. As we move forward, I'd like to schedule our ongoing weekly budget meetings alongside our Strategic Leadership Team (SLT) to elevate focus on measurable results. We will utilize the budget meeting to design and implement the immediate steps required to restore fiscal integrity, responsibility, and improve our cash position. As we begin the new semester, the following are the deliverables we discussed that will define the work ahead for the remainder of the fiscal year:

1. Development of a Modified Cash Budget—This will serve as the roadmap for operations (generating/collecting cash and spending/allocating cash for the remainder of the fiscal year). This monthly schedule will be utilized as our "budget" and reframe key processes including purchasing, requisitions, P Cards, travel and internal accountabilities.

2. Active Management Plan for Account Payables—This includes the centralization and required processes for managing all expenses, invoices, contracts, and other encumbrances. Current assessments of payables must include utilization or development of purchasing/procurement policies and practices that are designed to improve/manage cash position. A P Card process improvement plan must be developed and articulated for immediate implementation.

3. Active Management of Accounts Receivables—AR needs to be recalibrated to accurately reflect expected cash collections, known revenue, and bad debt (that will not improve our financial position).

4. Expenditure Controls—These expenditure controls need to be designed and implemented (and communicated) in the priority order of the impact they have on our cash position: payroll, travel, operating, contracts, etc. . . . Active interventions must include a 90-day hiring freeze, P Card charges, travel policies for spring, etc. . . . A set of actionable items that we are going to ask all budget managers to implement and be held accountable to needs to be clearly communicated—utilizing regular communications and FAQs.

5. Data Dashboards—A set of the elements that we are going to pay attention to, track, teach, and measure our performance needs to

be aligned and support the utilization of a Modified Cash Budget for the remainder of FY 2022.

6. Reconciliation—Utilize the modified cash budget to assess institutional performance to the FY 2022 budget and the utilization of the Modified Cash Budget to serve as a realistic starting point for the FY 2023 budget.

7. Transparency to Inform/Teach Internal Stakeholders—Briefing or Summary Documents/Reports/Dashboards that can inform internal constituencies including institutional debt, cash position (payables/receivables), monthly and annual spend required to operate, utilization of one time or non-recurring resources to build the FY 2022 budget that will not be available for FY 2023, and the fundamental differences between "our budget" and available cash.

8. A Retention/Completion/Student Success driven set of beginning interventions to improve our FY 2023 enrollment/revenue potential communicating the reasons why this is our foundation for improving our overall institutional performance. This can be linked to the larger campus engagement process of considering what's possible for creating a positive future at the same time we restore the financial integrity/stewardship. This key learning process needs to consider who students are and how we serve them. Communicating how our students will help transform Henderson, that something is different and happening, and built on what's best about the University will be the "Why?" of the semester. As we consider metrics, managing resources, and interventions to improve performance, we must consider the reality of today in terms of the disproportionate impact it is having on our most at-risk students. And why this level of student success cannot be our future.

9. We need to be ready to begin a new semester ready to manage our now and then quickly consider designing our future (realities and aspirations). And then, utilize this data and the help of ASUS, and other partners to begin the redesign of FY and academic year 2023 in light of a new paradigm for the University.

Please review and provide missing, added, or edited responses to build this memo out to be a clear set of deliverables that we will utilize to operate.

Thank you for all of your efforts,

Chuck

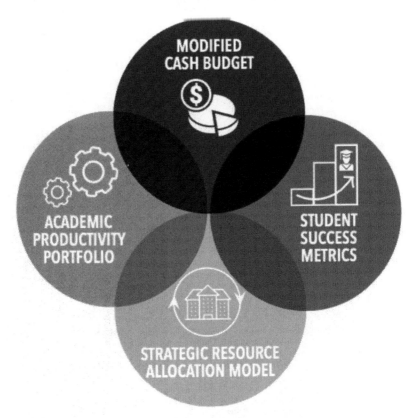

Figure 4.2. Four Key Tools

accurate picture of a college's cash position. Almost always when resources are strained, relying on these budgets has been a significant factor contributing to, rather than warding off, a financial meltdown. They encourage thoughts like: "If it's in my budget there must be cash," or "if I do not spend it before the end of the year, I will lose it." They neglect the more fundamental question that a financially troubled institution should be asking: "are we collecting cash at the same rate that we are spending it." Regular annual budgets no longer matter if a college can't pay its bills on time or meet its payroll throughout the fiscal year.

The best way to assess and then subsequently improve an institution's cash position is with a modified cash budget. In the simplest of terms, a modified cash budget is built on a cash flow model that tracks how much cash is being brought in and how much cash is going out monthly.

Many states and institutions track cash on hand as a fundamental measure of financial health. But a modified cash budget goes beyond simply counting cash on hand. It develops a monthly operating statement very much like you would in your own home, asking questions like: How much take-home income am I bringing in, how much money do I have in my checking account, what are my monthly expenses, and how much do I have to dig into my savings monthly to pay my bills. When your savings are depleted and your monthly expenses are outpacing your monthly income, you are moving precariously close to your own personal financial exigency.

A modified cash budget offers three primary benefits:

1. It is a clear and unquestionable metric that gives a real-time assessment of annual operating performance. If cash flow is regularly misaligned with ongoing operational costs, an institution is headed in the wrong direction where financial exigency may be required.
2. It is a powerful communications tool that translates a school's financial position into metrics that the entire campus community can understand.
3. It provides an operating tool that eliminates reliance on the standard budget-to-actual practices and moves to an effective cost containment strategy focused on your most valuable asset: cash.

An institution will seldom improve its cash position unless and until it pays close attention to what it spends and what revenue it generates. As a best practice, every institution could benefit from utilizing a modified cash budget alongside their normal operating procedures to track how cash informs overall institutional performance.

Once a financial crisis is identified, an institution can respond with a variety of cost-containment measures. In the case of Henderson State University furloughs and administrative salary rollbacks saved $1.2 million, position management reduced another $335,160, and academic dean salary and stipend rollbacks yielded $130,403 in current year savings. While these initiatives created temporary liquidity for the university to meet payroll and make debt service payments, existing structural deficits meant that greater systemic changes were required to ensure sustainable operations. The institution was too deep into a financial hole for these measures to solve its long-term problems.

A modified cash budget takes you back to the fundamentals. It focuses on needs and not wants, it cures the "if it's in my budget, I must have it" syndrome, and it provides a mechanism to track the progress of subsequent cost containment strategies. For institutions needing to define and manage the scope of a crisis, a modified cash budget defines how unsustainable the current model is. As we discuss further in Chapter 7, for institutions that are emerging out of a crisis, a modified cash budget keeps a focus on the essentials—improving their cash position, tracking progress, and most importantly, not sliding back into the historical policies and practices that caused the crisis.

In one form or another, a modified cash budget should be a part of every institution's operating toolbox.

An Academic Productivity Portfolio

An *Academic Productivity Portfolio* shows how much it costs to deliver a degree. Within the context of a financial exigency process, it:

- Summarizes the full array of an institution's instructional allocations and outcomes.
- Pinpoints courses that are chronically under-enrolled and might be dropped from the curriculum, offered less often, modified in some way, or combined with other courses.
- Identifies how much each academic program is contributing to operating surpluses or deficits and how much specific programs, if they were enhanced, could generate in potential revenue.
- Provides data that are required for smarter resource allocations in the future.

The portfolio is an essential tool. It defines academic productivity and program viability. The metrics within the portfolio can help inform the need for financial exigency and build a campus consensus that it's required. The portfolio can guide decisions about program and instructional reductions or eliminations and serve as a road map for restructuring the curriculum with a focus on programs that can contribute to the renewal and revitalization of the institution. There are several practical guides to conducting this kind of academic program assessment; one of the most frequently used is the now updated version of Robert Dickeson's *Prioritizing Academic Programs and Services.*[7]

Used as a regular and ongoing management resource, academic productivity portfolios can help avert the need that financial exigency would ever be required. They allow for instructional allocations to be made in a responsible manner based on:

- The number of instructor and faculty lines
- The employment relationships with those instructors (full-time, part-time, on the tenure track, tenured)
- The costs of instruction
- The number of credit hours produced by each instructional line
- Program enrollments and trends
- Student success outcomes, such as year-to-year persistence and degree completion

- Program alignment with community employment needs
- Student's career readiness as measured by licensure exam results, job placements, alumni surveys, and average salaries
- Net tuition and net costs at the unit or student seat level

While a modified cash budget identifies current financial deficits and the progress being made toward containing costs, the academic portfolio illuminates academic program or unit productivity and provides an empirical basis for subsequent decisions to maintain, invest, grow, or eliminate programs. The information contained within an academic portfolio changes the narrative with faculty about which academic programs should be pruned and which should be spared. It broadens the understanding of how a college generates and allocates its resources, and it serves as the foundation for enhancing institutional performance. It provides a data-driven management tool that, within a financial exigency, sets the parameters for program reductions and eliminations.

Every institution should use an academic portfolio and integrate it into its regular decision-making and accountability measures. It need not be limited only to times of gloom and doom. If academic leaders used it on an ongoing basis, overall institutional performance and financial outcomes would be enhanced. Put another way—it would be unlikely, if not impossible, for a college to find itself in exigency if it had been regularly evaluating its academic performance data. Just like weather radar can help motorists steer clear of a storm, the academic portfolio can alert provosts, deans, department chairs, and faculty of risky conditions on the curricular front, enabling them to make smarter decisions that lead to improved overall institutional performance.[8]

Student Success Measures

Student success measures include several important progress milestones— student persistence from year to year, graduation rates and post-graduation outcomes such as acceptance to graduate or professional school, pass rates on licensure and certification exams, and job placements and career progress. They also involve an analysis of how these outcomes differ by important student characteristics such as age, part-time/full-time enrollment, socioeconomic status, racial and ethnic background, and whether the student is the first in his or her family to attend college.

A successful college is one that achieves excellent outcomes for its students in a timely manner and does so equally for all of them, regardless of background. The business model for higher education should no longer be driven primarily by its enrollment numbers. It should be based on its ability to retain and support students throughout their college years, help them finish their degrees within six years or less, and produce graduates capable of performing well in their careers and living personally satisfying lives. Think of student success as the extent to which colleges perform three basic jobs that students hire—and society pays—them for:

1. Opening the doors of access to advanced education
2. Providing students with the support they need to complete their degree
3. Equipping students with the knowledge and skills needed to be effective citizens who are also economically successful

At the national level, this emphasis on student outcomes has been referred to as the *completion agenda*. Initially, that agenda emphasized a set of policies aimed at increasing graduation rates and the earning of college degrees and other postsecondary credentials. More recently, the completion agenda has emphasized the role of higher education in increasing social and economic mobility for students.

That agenda has been supported by several national intermediaries that have advocated for institutional strategies to improve college completion rates and give a boost to graduates' upward economic mobility. The Gates Foundation; Achieving the Dream; the Lumina Foundation; Complete College America; the Hope Center for College, Community and Justice; and the National Center for Student Success are some of the most prominent examples of organizations supporting the completion agenda.

In addition, several policy institutes and private companies are providing students and their families with data about the economic return on investment (ROI) they can expect from attending a given college or graduating with a major in a specific field. These calculations, inspired by the U.S. Department of Education's College Scorecard,[9] are not without their limitations, but they

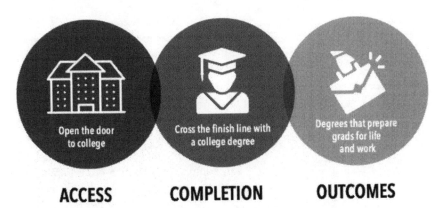

ACCESS   **COMPLETION**   **OUTCOMES**

Figure 4.3. Three Jobs Students Hire Us to Do

do offer reasonable answers to fundamental questions that many students have about the value of a college education — "will college be worth it to me financially," "how long will it take me to recoup the costs of attending this college," "how much can I expect to make if I major in this subject," and "how do my top choices for where to attend college compare on these measures?"

As one example, Third Way, the independent think tank, calculates what it calls a Price-to-Earnings Premium (PEP) for thousands of colleges in the United States.[10] The PEP measures how long it takes on average for low-income students attending a given college to recoup the costs of paying for their education. It's like the Obama-era "gainful employment" regulation that evaluated programs by how much post-completion discretionary income former college students had to pay to meet their educational debt obligations.

To derive a college's PEP score, Third Way determines how much money a student pays out-of-pocket to attend a given institution (i.e., the net amount the student owes after scholarships and grants are factored in). Next, it calculates the average salary boost of students ten years after their college attendance compared to the average salaries of those with only a high school diploma within the same state where the college is located. Dividing net costs by the premium that college attendees earn vs. high school graduates gives the PEP quotient, which shows the number of years it takes for students to recoup the net costs of their education. Third Way also computes an Economic Mobility Index that allows students to compare how well different colleges help low- and moderate-income students recoup the costs of paying for their education by taking into consideration the percentage of Pell Grant recipients enrolled at each school.

Another measure of the economic value that students can expect on average from attending a given school has been devised by DegreeChoices, a relatively new college and career guide website.[11] Using public cost and earnings data from the Department of Education's College Scorecard and the Integrated Postsecondary Education Data System (IPEDS), DegreeChoices uses two metrics that are mathematically combined into an economic score that produces a ranking of colleges based on their economic value to students.

Payback measures how long it takes the average student to recoup the total cost of attending college (after subtracting financial aid) with their marginal earnings. Marginal earnings are the difference between what the average student would have likely earned before attending college and what he or she earns afterwards. *EarningsPlus* compares student earnings after college against a benchmark that DegreeChoices adjusts based on two variables that influence salary comparisons between different colleges—each school's unique mix of academic programs and the in-state/out-of-state composition of the student body.

Whether *Payback* or *EarningsPlus* is more important will vary depending on individual circumstances. *Payback* reveals how soon educational costs can be recovered on average, while *EarningsPlus* conveys relative economic advantages later down the road. To arrive at what is called an institution's economic score, a school's payback is divided by the percentage advantage/ disadvantage of its *EarningsPlus* factor. The lower the resulting quotient, the higher the school's ranking.

Every college, not just those confronting a possible financial exigency, should know how it performs on these and related measures of student success. Why? Simply because an increasing number of prospective students and their families are familiar with exactly such numbers. Not only are they familiar with them, but they may also base their college decision on what they show.

College leaders and faculty need to understand the impact that their institution's costs and economic benefits have on student choices and their ultimate educational success or failure. College costs drive many students away from college altogether; it leads millions to take out unmanageable loans to pay for it; and it causes millions of other students to drop out of college before ever earning a degree. It influences whether they will stay at a school or transfer, whether they will live on campus or off, whether they major in a subject in which they are truly interested or in a subject they believe will make them enough money to have made college be worth the expense.

Within the context of financial exigency, colleges are particularly likely to be interested in measures that tap students' trajectories from enrollment through departure. Over five or six-year periods, they might track:

- How many first-time and transfer students enrolled
- How many were retained from year to year
- How many earned a degree
- How many are now employed or attending graduate school, and what is their average annual income
- How many are still attending college
- How many have unpaid bills they still owe the college
- How many of those have been sent to collections

As one example, when Henderson State University calculated these numbers, it found 10,809 students that had enrolled between 2017 and 2022. Among those students, 47% had left the university without a degree, and 70% of them were included in HSU's student accounts receivables. Those student's delinquent bills represented more than $6 million in cash. While those numbers may represent an extreme example of poor student outcomes, many colleges in financial distress will discover that they have failed a distressingly large number of students, and that those failures are concentrated among low-income students for whom a college degree would have been key to economic mobility. Financial exigency is not merely an economic problem, it usually is also a problem of an institution failing to do a good job of educating students.

A Strategic Resource Allocation Model

We described the four key elements of a *Strategic Resource Allocation Model (SRAM)* in Chapter 3. Essentially, it shows how institutional resources could be allocated differently in the future to achieve the outcomes that should matter the most. It can serve as a roadmap for developing shared responsibility for executing a financial exigency by an institution's governing board, administration, faculty, and staff. It also informs external constituents like alumni, private donors, and lawmakers about the process.

A SRAM provides a lens that focuses an institution on the stewardship necessary to restore fiscal integrity and provide a sustainable financial platform. It offers a means of broadening and deepening a college's level of financial competency, raising it to a level required to move through exigency and emerge on the other side as a higher performing and more fiscally responsible institution. It focuses the institution on net performance—revenue and expenses—rather than on annual budgets. In the case of colleges whose main mission is teaching, which will be the case for most schools in financial crisis, it helps them look at expenditures with a new perspective—how much are they spending to enroll a student, keep a student, educate a student, support a student, and graduate a student prepared for a productive life.

A SRAM should help faculty and academic leaders (chairs, program directors, deans, and provosts) understand academic productivity and how every course offered, every program added or expanded, and every instructor and staff member hired affects a college's economic viability. It shifts the paradigm. No longer is managing the budget, collecting tuition, raising private donations, curbing expenses, and cultivating state appropriations someone else's job. Those duties become better understood by every member of the campus community. The SRAM enables a campus to understand how resources are developed and expended. It provides the framework to develop and execute a model of stewardship for the future.

THE TIMELINE FOR FINANCIAL EXIGENCY

Once a campus realizes that the financial crisis is real, that routine cost containments alone will not stop a downward spiral, and that the consequences of inaction pose a threat to its survival, financial exigency can be invoked. Preferably, the process would rely on existing policies and governance structures, but at institutions without such guidelines, a crisis management plan will need to be developed immediately.

The sequence and timing of a financial exigency plan will vary depending on the unique circumstances of a given college. There's no standard schedule or regular calendar to follow. In the case of Henderson State University, the process took about five months, which is a very accelerated period for a college to proceed through exigency, particularly a public college which is likely to have state policies, collective bargaining agreements, and legislative and gubernatorial oversight with which it must contend. Even within that compressed period, the sequence of events at Henderson State serves to illustrate the common steps and the order in which they will usually unfold at colleges going through a formal exigency process.

ASSESSMENT

The process begins with the assessment of the financial data and program outcomes that we previously described. In the case of HSU, that assessment started almost immediately after the new chancellor began his term on November 15, 2021. On December 7, he sent a memo to his Strategic Leadership team outlining the immediate steps that needed to be taken to improve Henderson's financial condition.

One of the first actions required in a financial exigency is to identify a leadership team that will be responsible for organizing and overseeing the process. Two options exist. One is to rely on existing governance structures such as a university budget committee or an administrative council to do the work. The other is for the president to appoint a special committee or task force to guide the effort. With either option, it's crucial that all key campus constituents—faculty, staff, students, and administrators—are represented. Some institutions also may decide to include one or more members of the board of trustees on the exigency committee.

Exigency plans should not be drawn up by a president with the help of a few cronies. Those are doomed to fail. While the president, with the approval of the governing board, is ultimately responsible for executing the plan, all key interest groups in a campus community need to be represented in the plan's development. Those representatives can either be elected to the steering group by their constituents or they can be appointed by the president from a slate of candidates submitted by each constituent group.

COMMUNICATIONS AND CONSENSUS

The second key component that should be in place when exigency is started is a thorough communications plan. The campus must have timely, accurate information about the process as it unfolds. Otherwise, rumors will swirl, fears will be stoked, and resistance to the process will be strengthened. The lack of constant, candid, and clear information is almost certain to derail or degrade any exigency plan. Similar attention needs to be given to communications with external groups, including the press, local and state government officials, an institution's accrediting body, and its alumni.

EXTERNAL ASSISTANCE

Early in the process, a decision will need to be made about hiring an outside consulting firm to help develop and analyze the data and make recommendations about potential solutions. While engaging such firms can be expensive, the failure to use their expertise can result in an institution overlooking key considerations and taking ill-advised actions. Expect criticisms about how much they're charging, particularly at colleges that have essentially just acknowledged they're going broke. Nonetheless, in most cases, we believe the cost of a carefully specified contract for consultant services will be worth it. They provide capabilities that most impoverished institutions simply do not have. And one other caution: don't expect to be able to hide the costs of external consultants. Their fee eventually will become public. Better to acknowledge it upfront than try to justify it later.

DEVELOPMENT OF THE MODIFIED CASH BUDGET

In January 2022, Henderson began to implement a modified cash budget—where expenditures had to be balanced against cash on hand—to achieve immediate cost savings for the remainder of the fiscal year. While that created enough temporary liquidity for the university to make payroll and debt service payments, it was not enough to put the institution on the road to a permanent financial recovery.

On February 3, 2022, the chancellor sent a letter to the HSU community indicating that he was beginning the process of declaring a state of financial exigency. The letter described the immediate steps that were being taken to curtail costs. It identified other short-term cuts that would be put in place, and it warned that termination of faculty and staff, large reductions in academic programs, and a significant restructuring of the university's administrative structure were likely. About the same time, Henderson State notified the Higher Learning Commission, its regional accrediting body, that it was declaring financial exigency. This is a crucial part of external communications that must not be neglected. It's much better for a university to disclose its exigency plans to oversight bodies before accreditors read about them in the press.

CAMPUS NOTICE

Consistent with university policy, HSU's Faculty Senate and its academic administrators, including the deans and department heads, were given 14 days to indicate whether they concurred with the chancellor's recommendation and to submit their own recommendations, along with the chancellor's, to the Board of Trustees. In addition, a Financial Exigency Committee was formed to provide its own recommendations for budget reductions and academic program restructuring. This Financial Exigency Committee would ultimately forward recommendations to the Board for cuts that were not as deep as those proposed by the chancellor.

COST CONTAINMENT AND CASH MANAGEMENT

On January 20, 2022, the HSU administration circulated a "Position Management Process" memo that specified that faculty and staff positions that were vacant or would become vacant would either remain unfilled or be eliminated. It also described a process for 1) requesting exceptions to the policy based on critical health and safety responsibilities, and 2) hiring temporary staff to perform critical functions.

FREQUENTLY ASKED QUESTIONS COMMUNIQUES

On February 11, the administration posted a Frequently Asked Questions (FAQ) memo that responded to several Faculty Senate questions about financial exigency. It explained the financial exigency process that was being followed, and it summarized the financial problems giving rise to it.

On February 11, 2022, the Chair of the HSU Faculty Senate submitted a letter affirming that a condition of financial exigency existed, a finding that also was supported by the provost and other academic administrators within the same week.

On February 15, a forum for students was hosted to explain the process. That was followed by a posting of FAQ from students on April 19. It assured them that they would be able to complete their degrees even in programs that had been tabbed for closing. It also informed them that their work study jobs would be continued and that spring semester classes would continue as scheduled.

PROJECTION OF POTENTIAL SAVINGS

On March 3, the campus was provided a written update on the anticipated savings that had been realized through furloughs, salary rollbacks, the elimination or consolidation of vacant positions and other spending cuts.

On March 9, the Campus Financial Exigency Committee was informed of the timeline for the work required from it between March – May. Throughout that period, the committee and the administration worked relatively independently to arrive at their recommendations for restructuring and reductions.

On March 15, the university released another FAQ memo, addressing questions pertaining to furloughs, salary rollbacks, vacation and sick leave, and eligibility for unemployment benefits.

As an aside, the routine and repeated use of a campus blog or FAQ memos is a very effective way to keep the campus well-informed about the status of the exigency process. They should be part of any college's communication plan during a period of exigency. They can serve to tamp down rumors, and they help dispel some of the worst fears that a campus community develops in reaction to an exigency declaration and process.

FORMAL EXIGENCY REQUEST AND RECOMMENDATIONS

On March 18, the chancellor submitted his formal request that the Arkansas State University System Board of Trustees approve Henderson State's declaration of exigency. On March 28, the ASU Board of Trustees voted to do so. On April 22, Henderson State's Financial Exigency Committee submitted its recommendations for program eliminations and reductions to the chancellor.

Those were submitted, along with the chancellor's own recommendations, to the Arkansas State University System Board of Trustees.

EXIGENCY APPROVAL FOR PROGRAM/FACULTY REDUCTIONS AND OFFICIAL NOTIFICATIONS

On May 5, 2022, just a few months after the initial warning to the campus in February, the Board of Trustees approved the chancellor's recommendations for restructuring HSU under conditions of exigency. As we indicated in Chapter 2, as a result of those recommendations, Henderson State University eliminated 25 degree programs. In addition, 88 faculty jobs were eliminated, 67 of which were filled, at the time, while 21 were vacant. Those faculty cuts would ultimately save about $5.3 million—$2.55 million in FY 2023 and another $2.78 million in FY 2024.

Under HSU's exigency policies, tenured faculty slated for termination were required to be given one year's notice and subsequently issued a terminal contract for their last fiscal year of service. By reducing its non-instructional staff positions, Henderson anticipated it would save an additional $1.5 million. Finally, by eliminating or restructuring dozens of administrative positions, it was able to achieve another $600,000 in cost savings.

With the Board's official decision came the hardest part of an exigency process—informing the faculty and staff who would be losing their jobs of those decisions. There really is only one acceptable way to communicate this news—it must be done personally and directly by the individuals responsible for the decisions, and it must be done prior to any program or staffing cuts being made public. In HSU's case, either the chancellor, the provost or the director of human resources called each of the affected individuals to explain that his or her position and academic program were being eliminated. In the case of tenured faculty, they were told they would be issued a terminal one-year contract. Everyone's employment status was triple checked for accuracy before any telephone calls were made. The list was separated randomly into thirds, and the three senior leaders made personal phone calls to each faculty member affected. Everyone was contacted within a single day.

With those calls, the steps necessary to affect a state of exigency had been completed at HSU. But, like similar scenarios at other institutions that have gone through exigency, those actions were far from the end of the story. Now, a new round of challenges loomed, important questions needed to be asked, and essential decisions had to made—how to deal with the pubic fallout from the exigency declaration, how to reassure students they would receive the education they needed and deserved, how to re-engage faculty and staff within a substantially different institution, and how to rebuild that institution into one that the public could trust to fulfill its academic mission and be financially secure.

In this chapter we've emphasized the sequence of steps that the key members of an institution embarking on financial exigency need to take for the process to be successful. But that understanding does not mean that everyone affected will accept or endorse the decisions that are made. Strong opposition, well-organized internally and repeatedly amplified externally, is to be expected. Financial exigency upsets the status quo in too many ways for it to be implemented without challenge. For administrators to stay the course and steer the institution through an exigency process to an effective outcome requires that they receive the backing from key stakeholders and policy makers, including their governing boards and elected officials in the state. We turn to these considerations in the next chapter.

NOTES

1. https://www.alaska.edu/news/system/august-21-message-rescind-financial-exigency.php

2. Leslie, D. W. (1977). Financial exigency and the future of the academy. In F.R. Kemerer & R.P. Satryb (Eds.). <u>Facing Financial Exigency</u>. Lexington, Mass: Lexington Books.

3. https://www.insidehighered.com/news/business/financial-health/2023/05/09/rare-debt-free-college

4. https://www.nacubo.org/Research/2021/NACUBO-Tuition-Discounting-Study

5. https://www.espn.com/mens-college-basketball/story/_/id/31402209/hartford-athletics-transitioning-division-division-iii

6. https://www2.ed.gov/about/offices/list/ocr/docs/interath.html

7. https://www.wiley.com/enus/Prioritizing+Academic+Programs+and+Services%3A+Reallocating+Resources+to+Achieve+Strategic+Balance%2C+Revised+and+Updated+-p-9780470559680

8. We recommend that institutions preparing an academic portfolio for the first time consider an external consultant. Several firms, such as Huron Consulting Group, Rpk GROUP, Mckinsey and Company, Bain and Company, KPMG, and AGB provide these consulting services.

9. https://collegescorecard.ed.gov

10. https://www.thirdway.org/report/price-to-earnings-premium-a-new-way-of-measuring-return-on-investment-in-higher-ed

11. https://www.degreechoices.com/best-colleges/

Chapter 5

The Freedom-Protection Coefficient

This chapter addresses higher education leadership and governance with a specific focus on the shared understandings and relationships that must exist between college leaders and their bosses. These relationships are important at any time, but they become even more critical when presidents and chancellors try to guide their institutions through tough fiscal times and help them achieve a new, sustainable business model. Without effective leadership and governance, fundamental changes in how colleges function are simply not possible. Entrenched interests are too forceful. Institutional inertia is too strong. That status quo will always prevail.

We concentrate on the dynamics between three sources of college leadership and influence: 1) presidents and chancellors, 2) institutional or system-level governing boards, and 3) key policymakers, including governors and state legislatures. What are the main responsibilities of these actors? How can they interact most effectively to help a college thrive, prevent it from suffering a financial crisis, or steer it out of one that's been allowed to develop?

In this chapter, we also introduce a concept that we call the *freedom/protection coefficient*. It's simply a short-hand way of describing how higher education leaders—presidents, chancellors, provosts, deans, and senior faculty—must first be given the freedom to take bold steps of leadership especially in times of crisis and then be supported and protected by their governing boards, elected officials, and other policymakers against the inevitable pushback and fallout that follow. Both the freedom or authority for campus leaders to act boldly and the protection or support from their bosses when they do are essential. When both are present, real change becomes possible. Without them, campus leadership will falter or even fail.

PRESIDENTS/CHANCELLORS

Most new college presidents and chancellors do not bring an expertise in budgeting or strategic finance to their job, and they rarely have much experience leading an institution through a real-time economic crisis that's so severe it might require a financial exigency to be declared. Some may not have even heard of that term prior to beginning their duties.

Although the road to becoming a college president has diversified a bit in recent years, the vast majority—more than 80%—of college presidents still come from within academia, according to the most recent American College President Study (2023), a comprehensive analysis conducted periodically by the American Council on Education.[1]

Among those insiders, the single most common pathway has been to move from being an academic administrator such as provost or dean—and before that usually a department chair—to a presidency. More than half of presidents (54%) took that insider's route. Deans and provosts are accomplished senior faculty who've developed a research and teaching expertise in their academic disciplines. They've been promoted up the professorial ranks, granted tenure, and at some point, they've decided to give administration a try, with many secretly or openly eyeing the job of college president as their ultimate destination.

However, unless their academic discipline is accounting, finance, or economics, most new presidents who've climbed up the academic leader to reach the C-suite in the Ivory Tower will begin their jobs with little or no knowledge about how to run a big, complex business, manage massive budgets, participate in bond markets, negotiate the state appropriation process, or direct capital construction projects, all of which they'll be expected almost immediately to do—and do well—as a president.

Most of their training for these tasks will take place on the job. Some may have attended one of the "new president" academies, like those offered by the American Association of State Colleges and Universities, Harvard University, or the Council of Independent Colleges. But the training in those boot camps is brief and doesn't cover any topic in detail let alone prepare presidents for the multiple complications encountered with complex financial matters.

A few might also benefit from the help of a mentor, either a retired president or an outside coach that might be retained to guide them. But most will learn in the crucible of the presidency itself, and their performance will be scrutinized on a daily basis by a host of highly opinionated observers and stakeholders, both on campus and in the broader community. In his highly personal account of serving as a university president at Hartwick College and Pacific University, M.A.F. Ritchie wrote, "If college presidents, like the turtle, must stick out their necks in order to make progress, also, like the turtle, they need a good thick shell to protect them from blasts of criticism that will surely come their way."[2]

Astute presidents understand their limitations, and that's why the most effective ones know the importance of building a senior financial team to help them develop a fiscally sound budget and a viable business model. Depending on the size and organization of the institution, this team will include some combination of the following: the provost, the vice president for administration, the chief financial officer, the head of procurement, the chief human relations officer, university counsel, an internal auditor, and perhaps the head of university development.

Regarding the members on this team, the provost has traditionally been seen as a "first among equals" in the senior leadership, but recently there's been a trend at some universities for the influence of VPs for Administration or VPs for Business or Finance to become stronger, rivaling or even surpassing the influence of the provost. Their growing importance may reflect the increasing complexity of higher education's financial affairs, but it can become problematic if the persons in those positions do not have an understanding and appreciation of the school's academic mission. That's one reason why a strong Faculty Senate, which at most schools can be counted on to represent traditional academic values, also needs to be part of regular budgeting and financial oversight processes. Faculty Senates often have faculty representatives with extensive budgeting and financial expertise, sometimes exceeding that of a president or provost. Their inclusion in financial decision-making is desirable, even essential, although we acknowledge that such involvement can be unnecessarily complicated by the faculty-administrator tensions that are prevalent at many institutions.

Appointing and leading a strong, cohesive financial team is a key responsibility for presidents/chancellors, and such teams are essential during both bountiful and lean times. The most effective presidents are those who have been able to recruit and appoint the right people to the right jobs in their administration. However, even with a strong senior leadership team in place, steering an institution through financial exigency will be a daunting challenge. Without one, it's likely to be an insurmountable task.

GOVERNING BOARDS

Presidents work for and with a governing board that has the final fiduciary and oversight responsibilities for their institutions. These boards of trustees (also called visitors, regents, governors, supervisors, or overseers) make the final decisions about an institution's policies, programs, and budgets that have been recommended by the administration. They also hire and fire the president and conduct annual reviews of his or her job performance.

Governing boards do not oversee or direct a college's day-to-day operations. That's the responsibility of the administration, but a governing board still has the final say on matters of financial significance—for example, approving tuition rates, giving the go-ahead on capital projects and other large contracts, authorizing salary and benefit increases, and approving major purchases and the issuance of debt. As the Association of Governing Boards (AGB) has observed, boards need to achieve a balance in their oversight, combining regular scrutiny with delegated responsibility—"noses in, fingers out," is AGB's pointed advice.[3]

In most cases, the members of the governing boards for public institutions are appointed by the governor, with input from the legislature. In some states, however, they are elected. For private institutions, which typically have larger boards than public colleges, board members are usually selected according to a process developed and approved by the institution itself. As an aside, we believe that board size often affects the level of careful fiduciary oversight they provide. Large boards can, on occasion, keep several members from knowing as much about the management of the institution as they should because they frequently delegate authority to an executive committee, a practice that can exclude too many members from being involved in crucial decisions.

What's important to recognize for our purposes is that board members may be selected for a variety of reasons that may or may not include any expertise in higher education or public finance. Geographic representation, a balance of political affiliations, alumni status, and a history of private contributions may—and often do—factor into board appointments. One hopes that financial acumen, legal knowledge, an appreciation for the value of higher education and solid business sense are also well-represented on any governing board, but often they're not, and their absence can be a major problem for institutions facing financial threats.

Governing boards typically use committees to accomplish much of their work. The most common committees are *academic affairs,* which oversees the curriculum and educational programs; *student affairs* with oversight of non-curricular student activities, such as residence life, health and wellness, and campus recreation; *audit,* which helps ensure that the institution's financial records are properly reviewed by a third party; *finance,* which reviews and approves the budget; and *an executive committee* that deals with important matters as they arise. Executive committees generally meet more frequently with the president than the board as a whole, typically to discuss critical issues like the budget or a personnel problem, to make timely decisions on matters of urgency, and to set the upcoming agenda for the board.

An engaged, competent governing board is crucial to the success of any college or university, and a solid working relationship between a president and the board, built on mutual trust, effective governance processes, open communication, and strategic alignment, is essential for both the board and the administration to lead the institution effectively.

We will have more to say about how boards and presidents should work together throughout the chapter, but for now we want to emphasize that a dysfunctional board-president relationship is frequently at the root of the kinds of mismanagement that have brought institutions to the brink of financial peril. The fear of learning the truth about an institution or a timidity about asking the tough questions about its future is often both a consequence of a fragile president-board relationship and the cause of a flawed financial strategy. Conversely, a board and a president that develop sound financial strategies and work hand-in-hand to implement them are key to managing scarcity and bringing an institution through even the most serious budget problems.

These concepts may seem elementary to some readers, and we acknowledge they are simple fundamentals—the blocking and tackling of university governance. Elementary though they may be, a breakdown in these fundamentals is often a major reason that a college's financial condition is allowed to deteriorate, sometimes bringing it to the breaking point.

GOVERNORS AND LEGISLATURES

The key policy makers in a state—the governor and the legislature—have a direct, recurring influence on the operation of the colleges in their state, particularly the public ones for which they establish the annual appropriations and pass legislation controlling many aspects of their operation. As we have described, in most states, governors also appoint the members of the public institutions' governing boards, giving them another opportunity for substantial influence over the mission, budget, and leadership of those institutions. And in those states that have a statewide higher education coordinating board, governors typically make appointments to that board as well, handing them another lever to affect higher education policy in the state. The focus of these coordinating boards, which, as we discussed previously in Chapter 3, were established by many states in the 1970s, is mainly on the public institutions in a state, but their influence and relationships with those schools is uneven. Flagship and land-grant universities tend to view them with suspicion and resistance, worried they will interfere with their autonomy or gradually shift state resources away toward the regional institutions.

Most states have a Department of Higher Education or a Department of Higher Education and Workforce Development as part of the executive

cabinet. Those agencies are statutorily charged with a range of responsibilities, including recommending higher education budgets, allocating state
financial aid, resolving disputes between institutions, and collecting data
about college enrollments, operations, and productivity. They also are subject
to considerable gubernatorial control and legislative oversight.

The participation of governors with public colleges generally falls along a
continuum of engagement. At one end of the continuum are governors who
choose to interact with the institutions largely through the state's coordinating and governing boards and the cabinet-level director of the department
of higher education. They prefer to work through existing executive branch
structures to achieve their educational agenda just as they work through other
executive agencies to influence policies concerning public health and safety,
child welfare, behavioral health, corrections, economic development, and
natural resources.

At the other end of the scale are governors for whom higher education is
a key policy and budget priority of their administration. They're much more
likely to interact directly with campus presidents, often bypassing the state
agencies that have been created to direct or coordinate the institutions. Our
sense is that this latter group has been growing in the past 10–15 years as
more governors link their state's economic development directly to policies
intended to increase the number of citizens who've earned a postsecondary
degree or credential of some type. Many governors have made higher education and workforce development the centerpiece of their policy agenda,
and they will work particularly closely with campus leaders to advance
that agenda.

For example, 48 states have now set goals for the percentage of their citizens who will have earned a college degree or other postsecondary credential
by a certain date. A common target is to call for at least 60% of working-age
adults to have earned a degree or high-quality postsecondary certificate by
2025 or 2030, an objective that's most often associated with the Lumina
Foundation, which began advocating for its must-publicized "Big Goal" of
60% higher education attainment back in 2008.[4]

As it turns out, at almost any time in history, American colleges could
have benefitted from a similar completion agenda. As higher ed historian
John Thelin has documented, a frequent practice over the years—even as
long ago as the early 1900s—has been for colleges to admit large numbers
of undergraduate students without fretting too much about whether they ever
earned a degree. This high attrition/low graduation pattern was found at many
non-elite institutions, but it also extended to historically prestigious colleges
such as Harvard, Yale, Princeton, Amherst, Brown, and William & Mary,
where administrators paid more attention to their annual student headcount
than to the percentage of students who persisted to graduation.[5]

Across the past 15 years, solid progress in educational attainment beyond high school has been achieved, bringing the "Big Goal" within reach. The percentage of U.S. adults ages 25 to 64 with college degrees, certificates, or industry-recognized certifications has steadily increased from 37.9% in 2009 to 53.7% in 2021, a gain of nearly 16 percentage points.[6] Governors and legislatures have been key to that progress. Many states have appropriated special funding incentives, passed new funding formulas, approved new transfer and admission policies, launched new institutions, and increased student financial aid to increase college completion rates.

One byproduct of the college completion push has been for governors and legislators to become much more involved in tracking the outcomes achieved by their state's colleges and universities. Can students still afford to attend college? Are more students graduating? Are they being prepared for the jobs the state's economy needs the most? Are they graduating with too much debt? How many have earned some college credits but dropped out before finishing their degree? How often are university research discoveries and new technologies being commercialized, leading to new business startups? These questions require that institutions view their missions through the wider lens likely to be used by key public officials. And they invite possible new partnerships between universities, employers, chambers of commerce, and other economic development interests in the state.

Elected officials are looking much more closely at how colleges spend their money and what they achieve with it. That scrutiny can become harmful when it serves purely partisan political interests, and recent events in several states illustrate the multiple hazards of politically motivated intrusions into campus operations. Freedom of inquiry can be stifled. Curricula can be dictated. Governors and the governing boards they appoint can run roughshod over anyone with whom they find disfavor.

The dangers of a governor targeting public universities to further a political agenda have become apparent in several states, but they are particularly well-illustrated by the quest of Florida Governor Ron DeSantis to overhaul and "recapture" that state's institutions according to his conservative ideologies. Bans against spending any state money on college diversity, equity, and inclusion (DEI) programs; the wholesale takeover of the New College of Florida's Board of Trustees; frantic objections to the dangers of concepts like critical race theory; and attacks on faculty tenure have all been part of the DeSantis crusade against higher education's supposed "trendy ideology." Whether his various diatribes have involved any legitimate concerns about campus curricula or leadership or have been just so much ruckus raising designed to generate publicity for his political ambitions can be debated. But what the DeSantis diatribes have made clear is that a governor who's prone to retaliation and strong arming can make the job of leading a college extremely difficult, constantly bogging it down in controversy and political turmoil.

Extra attention also can have an upside, however, when it comes from state officials who have a genuine interest in working with colleges to increase their impact. Most governors believe they have a stake in the success of their public colleges. They do not want them to fail, especially on their watch. Likewise, legislators will typically try to protect the funding for the colleges in their districts and will often work for a supplemental appropriation to help them survive through tough times.

When a college finds itself on shaky financial grounds, elected officials will usually try to support it, even when higher education hasn't been one of their policy priorities. As we discussed in Chapter 1, colleges and universities are often the major employer in a region, and they help keep a local economy humming. Even legislators who have been historically stingy when it comes to appropriating higher education funding do not want to see a public institution falter. They can—and frequently do—provide temporary relief through extra appropriations or loans that serve as a backstop against financial failure. That support is not usually available to private institutions, which, as we have already discussed, is one reason why the vast majority of colleges that close for financial reasons have been private schools.

That brings us to this fundamental point: A crucial task for any president/ chancellor taking a college through financial exigency—or any major downsizing and restructuring—is to enlist and maintain the support of elected officials throughout the process. That work can't be done with one phone call or a single office visit. It's not a job on the side or an isolated plea for help. It takes a candid, full, ongoing discussion of what's going to be required, how long it will take, what the fallout will be, and the prospects of success or failure. Chances are fairly good that conversations like that can convert key public officials into allies during a college's financial crisis. And, as some presidents have learned the hard way, neglecting to include these individuals in the process can lead to their indifference or opposition, adding one more burden to an already freighted financial exigency process.

The typical focus of presidential communications and outreach will be on state policymakers who determine the annual appropriations to public institutions and who also decide on the distribution of state financial aid to both public and private colleges within their state. But the federal delegation of a state—its U.S. representatives and senators—should not be neglected. Because so much student financial aid and loans are administered through the federal government and because of the interest they have in special categories of students, such as veterans and those with disabilities, federal elected officials can be valuable allies for institutions that are in dire financial straits, particularly if the president has been diligent in keeping them well-informed about the institution's problems and anticipated solutions.[7]

VOICES FROM THE FIELD

As we mentioned in Chapter 1, governors don't always come to the aid of a college facing financial struggles. In 2023, Alabama Governor Kay Ivey spurned Birmingham Southern College's request for state funds to help it keep its doors open. Her office also turned down at least two other requests from the college for pandemic relief money.

At Iowa Wesleyan University, school officials placed part of the blame on its decision to close in 2023 on Iowa Governor Kim Reynold's refusal to give it $12 million in federal Covid-19 relief funds it had requested. Governor Reynolds promptly responded with the following statement:

It wasn't until February 3, 2023, that my office received a request from the university for $12 million for ongoing operating costs. As I've said many times, we endeavor not to spend one-time federal dollars on ongoing expenses. To better understand their request and the financial health of the university, my office engaged an independent, third-party accounting firm to conduct due diligence. The firm reported that Iowa Wesleyan had a $26.1 million loan from the USDA, using their campus as collateral, that could be recalled in full as early as November 2023. Additionally, Iowa Wesleyan's auditor cited ongoing concerns about the university's fiscal health, stating "significant operating losses and reduced liquidity raise substantial doubt about its ability to continue as a going concern." The firm also highlighted that that while enrollment at Iowa Wesleyan has grown over the past three years, their financial health has continued to deteriorate over the same period.

Based on this and other factors, the independent accounting firm determined that providing one-time, federal funds would not solve the systemic financial issues plaguing the university. If the state would have provided the federal funding as requested and it was used to finance debt or other impermissible uses according to U.S. Treasury guidelines, the state and taxpayers could have been liable for potential repayment to the federal government. Moreover, the state has separately received $122 million in requests from other universities and community colleges across the state. With this information, I made the difficult decision to not pursue the university's funding request.

Governors have been willing to step forward and help a struggling institution. For example, when he learned about the financial plight of Henderson State University, Arkansas Governor Asa Hutchinson intervened at several critical points in time, including advocating for HSU to be integrated into the Arkansas State University system, facilitating a $6 million loan from the state to the school so it could meet its payroll and pay its past-due bills, and helping pay for the costs of an outside consulting group to advise HSU on its exigency process. He has a unique perspective on higher education and financial exigency, which we explore in his Voices From the Field.

VOICES FROM THE FIELD WITH GOVERNOR ASA HUTCHINSON

Businessman and attorney Asa Hutchinson is a two-term governor of Arkansas, elected first in 2014 and then again in 2018. In 2023, he declared his candidacy for the U.S. Presidency in 2024, running as a Republican. Hutchinson was governor of Arkansas when Henderson State University went through financial exigency, so we wanted to gain his insights about what he sees as higher education's current challenges.

Where did higher education fit in your overall policy agenda?
Higher education was high on my agenda. I campaigned on cutting taxes, promoting computer science in high schools, and making government more efficient. When I took office, I outlined specific priorities for the university presidents, including having them be part of the computer science initiative and developing a new funding model in Arkansas that would reward the institutions for success and effort.

My push for higher education was similar to what I wanted to see from state government overall—greater efficiency, which to me meant holding down tuition, reducing reliance on remedial education classes, shortening the time to graduation, and increasing the number of our folks who earned a degree. The presidents responded very well to those directions, and while the pandemic may have slowed us down a bit, we were still able to accomplish a lot. Arkansas ranked #2 in the nation for days of classroom instruction for K–12 during the pandemic. Now higher ed was more complicated because the tenured professors didn't want to go back in the classrooms so there was more pressure to stay virtual. Even at the higher ed level, however, Arkansas ranked high in classroom delivery of courses during the pandemic.

What type of relationship did you have with college presidents?

Overall, my relationship was excellent. I made it clear to the presidents that I respected higher education's independence, but I also wanted them to respect the leadership role of the governor. I can remember that one year I asked them to freeze tuition. I didn't issue an executive order or make it a mandate. I simply asked them to hold the line, and they responded very well, with all but one, I think, agreeing to freeze tuition that year.

When presidents would come to me with specific requests for funding, they typically would also let me know what steps they were taking to become more efficient, to cut their operating costs. And when we put in the new funding model for higher ed, the university presidents worked with us so that we could have an approach that we could all get behind.

What was your philosophy about making appointments to the governing boards?

Of course, board appointments are made within a political context, but I sometimes talked with presidents about the individuals I was considering for appointments because I was careful to appoint board members who would work in partnership with the university presidents. A good board of trustees backs the president, and if board members are in a position where they're not supporting the president, there's a breach that's hard to remedy. To have the right chain of command and the necessary checks and balances for an institution, it's essential to have the presidents and their boards be able to work well together. The key is to find a balance between respecting the independence of the institutions and accomplishing the state's mission.

What are the common mistakes that you think university presidents make?

The biggest problem is when a president and a board do not work well together. Now, sometimes, the problem is that a governor has made a bad board appointment, and that happens when you have an individual on the board with a personal agenda he or she wants to push, like getting rid of a coach or opposing a member of the university's administration. That kind of individualized aim can split a board and fracture an institution. I've seen it happen when you have a divided vote for the selection of a president or chancellor. And, of course, we had division on the HSU board concerning moving into the ASU system and the necessity of restructuring its costs. That proved to be a problem that we had to fix. When the Arkansas State University System said that an opportunity existed with HSU, I fully supported HSU joining the system, and I worked to make sure it happened.

Higher ed currently is facing a lot of financial pressures. How do you think presidents need to respond to those pressures?

First, presidents need to understand that they are operating in a competitive environment. Universities are not immune to competition. Cost, quality, and convenience all matter a great deal to students, who are the consumers of the product. Presidents certainly should know that, but faculty have to buy into this basic understanding as well. You are not guaranteed employment forever. There must be students in the classroom to support the institution, and if you are losing the consumer, you might lose your job. Higher education has to catch up with that.

There is a limit to the amount of support the state can provide to its colleges and universities so institutions need to look both at how they can become more efficient but also how they can generate other forms of revenue. Partnering with other schools to offer in-demand academic programs is one option, and—for those schools with a major research component—commercializing scientific and technological discoveries is another good avenue.

I also think there are advantages to university systems. They give institutions a solid foundation, particularly smaller ones, and their scale allows significant savings in terms of the services that can be shared. I also think there are positive implications for students in a university system, particularly in how it can facilitate easier, more seamless transfer pathways.

You were supportive of HSU going through its restructuring. What were your thoughts about that?

I knew it was very important to show confidence in the leadership of Henderson State and the ASU system as you went about making the decisions that were required. I knew you were making very tough decisions, and it was not easily accepted by some within the campus. I especially wanted to give students confidence that they weren't going to a shaky institution, and I wanted the public to know that Henderson State was implementing the changes that had to be made and that it would do so successfully. When you look at the private sector—mergers and acquisitions—there are always changes and efficiencies that have to be made. There's some pain in the initial phases, but in the end, if done for the right motive and not all about profit, then the changes are worth that pain.

I knew the university had gone through the process of learning the truth about where it stood financially, and while I wonder why the problems had not been detected earlier, the immediate job in front of us was to go through the process quickly and to adopt changes. There is an important lesson to be learned in the Henderson State story and that is the importance of digging deep enough to detect the early warning signs of financial trouble. Presidents always need to be ahead of the curve.

THE FREEDOM/PROTECTION COEFFICIENT

The effective interplay between presidents, governing boards, and elected officials involves two key dynamics—trusting presidents enough to give them the *freedom* to make hard decisions and take decisive actions and then *protecting* them from the fallout that inevitably ensues. These two elements are particularly important when an institution must confront and cope with a financial crisis, but they cannot be developed only when a crisis occurs. They don't happen with the flip of a switch. They need to be cultivated on an ongoing basis, starting whenever a president is hired and then continuing throughout his or her term of office. We use the term "coefficient" here not so much in its modern mathematical sense of being a numerical multiplier but more in the sense of its original use as a noun describing cooperation in the interest of producing a result. We mean it to represent the joining of freedom and protection to empower leaders to bring about significant levels of systemic and structural change.

The responsibility for building an effective working relationship with a governing board rests primarily with the president. It's the president who should initiate regular calls to the board, typically via the executive committee, the board chair or, with the board chair's blessing, the chair of the board's finance committee. It's the president who should arrange for a thorough introduction and orientation to the institution for every new board member. It's the president who must assure that board members are never surprised by

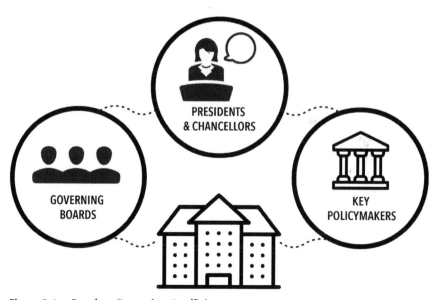

Figure 5.1.   Freedom-Protection Coefficient

either good or bad news from the college. It's the president who should alert the board to internal and external risks and make certain that risk assessments are regularly conducted for the institution. And it's the president who should help the board develop confidence in the institution's senior administrative team and faculty senate leadership.

How often does the president need to communicate with the board? The regular rhythm will need to be worked out with board leadership, but it's wise to error initially in the direction of communicating too frequently, rather than not frequently enough. Better to have a board chair want to taper down a communication schedule than indicate it needs to be ramped up. In our collective experience with more than a dozen board chairs over our careers, multiple calls per week became the norm. Simply put, those calls helped nurture the vital partnerships that can make or break presidential leadership.

At institutions that are part of a university system, the president will need, of course, to channel board communications through the system head, but the main principle remains the same—boards need to be informed as soon as possible about significant campus developments and issues. Whenever a college board chair learns about an institutional controversy or problem from reading it in the press first, that college's president has failed a test of leadership and has undercut the board's trust in his or her abilities. Most presidents don't get the chance to repeat that mistake.

A healthy president/board relationship is the foundation of the freedom/protection coefficient. It's the basis for a board understanding the need for constructing an academic portfolio, for conducting an analysis of program costs and productivity, and for trusting the process of strategic resource allocation. It's why a board will be willing to have the back of a president who recommends difficult measures to avoid exigency or who decides that proceeding with financial exigency has become necessary.

A similar dynamic needs to be cultivated between presidents and elected officials. Part of the job of a university president is to understand the educational priorities of governors and legislators and, assuming those policies reflect an appreciation for the value of higher education, to help them achieve those priorities. Accepting that responsibility is the cornerstone or an effective government relations strategy, and it's the beginning of a relationship with policy makers that combines the freedom of presidents to lead their institutions with the protection they will occasionally need when they do so.

An illustration of the freedom/protection coefficient at work with a governor took place in Missouri, when following the depths of the 2008 recession, the legislature warned the state's public colleges and universities to prepare institutional impact statements in anticipation of possible reductions of anywhere from 15% to 25% in their fiscal 2010 state appropriations. Those cuts were avoided when Governor Jay Nixon brokered the following budget deal with the presidents of the state's 13 public universities—if they agreed to freeze their tuition rates, he would recommend that no cuts be made to their state funding. Lawmakers subsequently approved that *quid pro quo*, and all the institutions were spared any cuts in their appropriations. At the same time, Missouri's college students saw no increases in their tuition during a period where large tuition hikes were becoming the norm in many other states.

That deal became the basis for subsequent budget bargains between the university presidents and Nixon as he established a fuller higher education agenda during his second term in office. For example, in 2016, Nixon pitched the following deal to the campus heads: freeze your undergraduate tuition for the 2016–17 school year in exchange for a 6% increase in state funding, a substantial portion of which would be doled out through a new performance funding formula that awarded larger state appropriations to universities if they hit various improvement goals for outcomes like better student retention and graduation rates. Although the legislature subsequently reduced the increase to 4%, the deal still held, and the universities proceeded with the promised tuition freeze. (For more, see Voices from the Field with Governor Jay Nixon.)

Implicit in each of these agreements was the expectation that university presidents had to reign in institutional costs. Even with the appropriation increase, the tuition freeze meant their overall operating revenues would decrease unless the universities realized large enrollment gains, an outcome that none of them thought was at all likely. The deal required the institutions to reevaluate many aspects of their operations and trim expenses. We know because we were both parties to those deals.

As part of the Missouri higher education agenda, universities clamped down on expenditures, and several restructured the organization of their academic departments. The state initiated a comprehensive review of academic programs. Several universities reallocated money internally to boost programs they had identified as high performers, and almost all of them placed a new emphasis on improving student outcomes as part of the state's commitment to college completion goals. A leading example of these initiatives was

VOICES FROM THE FIELD WITH
GOVERNOR JAY NIXON

Jeremiah W. (Jay) Nixon was first elected governor of Missouri in 2008, following four terms as the state's attorney general. He was re-elected to a second term as governor in 2012. Both authors worked with Governor Nixon when we were university presidents in Missouri (Ambrose at the University of Central Missouri, and Nietzel at Missouri State University), and we both had the opportunity to be part of what became his well-recognized higher education policy. Based on our long-term relationship with him, we asked Nixon to share some of his perspectives on higher education leadership and the relationships he sought to form with university presidents.

How important was higher education in your overall policy agenda?

When I began my first term in 2009, the nation and the state of Missouri were in a recession. My first concern was to balance the state's budget, which, at the time, was facing a deficit of more than $250 million. Unemployment was at 8%, tax receipts were way down, and people across the state were suffering and worried about their future. We were forced to make deep cuts in almost every area of state government, but eventually—through fiscal belt-tightening and assistance from a federal stimulus package—Missouri was able to gets its economy back on its feet.

In addition to steering the state's continuing economic recovery, my top three policy priorities were strengthening public education, including both K–12 and higher education; enhancing the state's mental health facilities and services; and promoting environmental conservation and the state's outdoor economy. I also wanted my state to develop a strong emergency management capacity, which it did. That asset later proved invaluable to the city of Joplin's recovery, after it was hit with a devastating EF5 tornado in 2011.

Initially, my primary interest in higher education was to keep tuition rates down. I wanted Missouri's public universities to be among the most affordable in the nation, and we were able to work with the institutions to put in place three tuition freezes during my time in office. However, my higher education agenda broadened over the years, and frankly, part of that evolution grew out of my decision in 2010 to hire you (Nietzel) to become my senior policy advisor focused on public education, after you retired from Missouri State University.

Working with the presidents, we were able to introduce a new funding model based on institutional performance; conduct a statewide review of academic programs, resulting in the elimination of dozens of duplicative or low-enrollment programs; launch Western Governors University-Missouri, giving working Missourians another affordable option for continuing their education; support the creation of the Missouri Innovation Campus, which became a model early college program; rejuvenate Jobs For America's Graduates, an academic recovery program to prepare high school students for college and careers; and expand several university programs for training more mental health professionals.

What sort of relationships did you seek with the university presidents?

For a couple of reasons, I wanted to establish direct, personal relationships with them. I preferred that to working more indirectly with the institutions through agencies like the Coordinating Board for Higher Education or the Department of Higher Education. First, I personally liked talking to the presidents; they're interesting people with important jobs. I wanted us to develop confidence in each other, and that required having frequent opportunities for frank conversations and free-ranging debates among ourselves. I tried to meet with the presidents as a group in my office at least three to four times a year, in addition to making at least one annual visit to each of their campuses. These visits enabled the presidents to keep me abreast of the big issues facing their campuses and brief me about any major initiatives or controversies they were anticipating. They also gave me the chance to let the presidents know what I was counting on them to accomplish for the state.

Second, I cultivated these relationships because I wanted to be in a stronger position than the legislature when it came to shaping education policy. My view is that unrelenting political partisanship combined with term limits significantly degrades the policy competence of many state legislatures. They control the appropriations to be sure, but I wanted the governor's office to be the place where presidents could trust that decisions would be based as much as possible on objective data and sound policy. That's also why I empowered several of my senior staff to talk and work directly with the presidents. I wanted them to see my team as a reliable resource and sounding board.

What qualities define an effective university president from your point of view?

I looked for two qualities. First, the ability to move forward, with an eye trained on the future. I didn't like to see presidents getting bogged down reacting to every campus controversy. There are plenty of those, arising all the time from disgruntled faculty, impatient students, and unhappy fans. University campuses are renown for disputes and differences of opinion. Presidents who allow themselves to be dragged into too many of these brouhahas are wasting their leadership in my opinion.

Second, I really liked to see presidents develop strong relationships with students. I think that's time very well-spent. Students are why public universities exist, and the presidents who are most effective are strong advocates for their students. That's one reason, by the way, why I was drawn to those presidents who understood the importance of keeping tuition in check. I didn't like seeing presidents trying to balance their university budgets on the backs of students, just as I didn't like them calling an increase in state funding the only way their institution could be successful.

What were the most common mistakes you saw us presidents make?

I think some presidents don't protect and project their power enough. Some are too easily intimidated by some state senator or representative who threatens their funding. Others are too worried about offending their faculty or alumni by making tough financial decisions. Presidents should take principled, data-driven positions regarding their institutions and be willing to defend them publicly in front of all kinds of audiences. And by the way, a good governor should stand up for presidents when they do that.

I also think some presidents want to have too much influence on a governor's appointments to their governing board. They want someone they already know or someone who has donated money to the school. They sometimes lobby for or against an appointee based on whether they think the person will be sufficiently friendly or generous toward the institution. Governing boards should work closely with their president, but they should not simply be cheerleaders. They need to attend to their fiduciary responsibilities with the utmost seriousness—challenging a president who they believe is going down the wrong path and supporting a president who they know is making hard, but necessary, decisions.

the Missouri Innovation Campus at the University of Central Missouri, a dual enrollment program that we describe more fully in Chapter 8.

THE NEED TO BE STRATEGIC

The goals of a robust freedom/protection coefficient are to 1) enable college leaders to ask the right academic and fiscal questions about their institutions and 2) encourage them to act courageously on the answers to those questions and 3) design a business model that's sustainable for the future.

As we previously described, the tendency in higher education over the years has been to believe that finding more resources is the answer to most financial problems. The pattern has been to plan to increase tuition, enroll more students, and/or expand programs and services, without paying too much attention to the eventual costs or returns on investment from those policies. But the past two decades have shown that belief to be less than realistic in many instances. Scarce resources are now more common than abundant ones at many institutions. As a result, college leaders need to think differently about how their institutions can prosper in an era where being more selective and strategic about resource allocation has become essential.

What's increasingly needed is a perspective that connects a college's mission with the higher education market forces that are likely to be dominant for some time to come. Understanding the limits of an institution's current business model can prompt it to make better decisions about resource allocation, financial risk management, and its future place in the higher education marketplace. It's that opportunity we explore next.

ALIGNING AN INSTITUTION'S MISSION WITH ITS RESOURCES

How can colleges and their governing boards become more strategic? How can they develop and practice healthier financial habits? How can they best respond to a changing higher education marketplace in which declining enrollments are expected and public funding is unlikely to be able to keep pace with inflation?

To begin, each institution needs to develop a business model that is aligned with its fundamental mission and that focuses the investment of resources in programs that are most likely to attract students and address workforce needs. For institutions whose mission is primarily focused on teaching, which is the case at many institutions now facing financial problems, this will require a hard look at how much they are spending on research and service activities and possibly cut back in those areas. Rather than trying to support the full range of scholarship and outreach often associated with major universities, financially strapped colleges need to understand where they have the best opportunities for enrollment growth and then carefully evaluate the academic programs, student services, and administrative organization at their institutions, followed by the reallocation of funding to strengthen those efforts.

In order to evaluate its business model and consider other alternatives, a college needs a comprehensive review process that, according to higher education financial expert Rick Staisloff,[8] includes:

1. Collecting baseline data. College leaders must be able to answer the threshold "Where are we now?" question. As we've discussed in previous chapters, that assessment requires reliable institutional data on enrollment trends at the institutional, school/college, department, and

academic major levels. It also demands trustworthy data on revenue and expense trends, and both the historic and projected demand for various academic programs and student services.

Data like these are even more valuable when they are benchmarked against a group of institutions considered to be peers or aspirant schools. These baseline data are strengthened using an academic productivity portfolio that bundles the fundamentals of costs, student success and outcomes into one management tool. As we noted in the previous chapter, we recommend hiring an outside consulting firm to help with the process of gathering, validating, and analyzing these data and beginning to develop strategic business model alternatives for the institution to consider.

The engagement of these outside intermediaries can be expensive, but probably not as expensive as the mistakes or missed opportunities that are likely to occur without their expertise. A decision to engage outside professionals will often result in the criticism that if the institution has enough money at its disposal to afford an expensive consultant, it should have enough to avoid financial exigency. This is largely an exercise in sophistry, but hearing such outcries might tempt some presidents to avoid or to not disclose their engagement of outside consultants. That's a mistake for two reasons. First, as previously mentioned, the employment of the consultants will not remain a secret for long; it's better to acknowledge it up front than to have to explain it away later. Second, the consultant can provide independent, third-party verification of both the institution's financial condition and of the likelihood of success from a revised business plan.

2. Identifying stakeholders and determining who is on the leadership team. When forming the team, it's crucial to differentiate between those team members who will provide input and those who will make decisions. Input should be obtained broadly from the board, top administrators, faculty leaders, and perhaps alumni and student representatives. A smaller group, however, should be charged with the decision-making. In most cases, this group would be formed from senior administrators, which, as we suggested earlier, might include the president; provost; VP for administration; the chief financial officer; the heads of procurement, the human relations office, and internal audit; university counsel; and perhaps the head of university development. It's essential, however, that there be no confusion about how final institutional decisions are made—it's the governing board acting upon recommendations made by the president.

3. Developing a communications plan. Reviewing a business model will involve asking hard questions around the number and type of

programs and services necessary to accomplish the institution's mission. Accompanying the review, the institution will need a clearly defined internal campus communication plan that outlines its purpose, process, timeline, and participants. If boards and campus leaders are not transparent about a change process, its chances of success are seriously compromised.

4. Gaining board support. An institution's governing board must support the institution's decision to move forward with a comprehensive review of its business model. The board needs to pressure test the review process, ensuring that it has accurately portrayed the institution's current business model and the higher education market in which it will compete. Finally, after the board approves the process, it's responsible for holding senior leadership accountable for implementing the plan.

5. Determining program strengths. Although the review of its business model might lead an institution to reconsider its mission, creating a new mission is not the primary purpose of the review. The main purpose is to require the institution to define a future that's built on strategic strengths and that's financially sound. And yes, that requires some hard-nosed calculations about which programs and services are best positioned to drive revenue. These so-called "signature" or "spire" programs enable a college to establish a positive brand. They help distinguish the institution from competitors in unique ways.

Colleges sometimes identify their signature programs based on a reputational history or a conviction that they have no choice but to be very good in a certain area to be respected. That type of justification won't do. As Figure 5.2 illustrates, an evaluation of academic program strengths needs to consider three outcome performance metrics.

First, the evidence for program quality must be based on tangible results, like student enrollments, graduation rates, accreditation reviews, post-graduation assessments such as licensure exams, and the positions of influence that graduates assume in their careers.

Next, a college's program strengths need to be compared to what the higher education market is demanding. High-quality programs do not automatically mean there is sufficient interest among students or employers for those programs to be promoted. While market demand is not the only reason to protect or invest in an academic program, an institution must find a sufficient number of academically strong programs that respond to public demand to be able to generate the student enrollment necessary to support its operations.

Finally, as we detailed in Chapter 4, an institution's programs and services must be evaluated in terms of the net revenue they generate. Historically, higher education has focused on gross, rather than net,

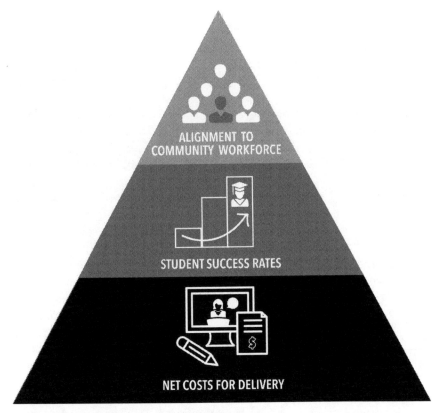

Figure 5.2. Outcome Performance Metrics

revenues. That is no longer a sufficient analysis. Institutions, especially those in financial trouble, must develop a fully allocated cost model and academic portfolio, where they determine those programs that either add to or subtract from the bottom line.

6. Evaluating a new business model. Once an institution identifies what it believes should become its strategic business model, it will also need to establish a process and set of measures to monitor its implementation and progress. The metrics selected for this kind of evaluation are often referred to as "key performance indicators" (KPIs) that are displayed on institutional "dashboards" summarizing the progress that's been made. Examples might include the percent of total revenues contributed by various programs, student enrollments, graduation rates by different types of instructional delivery—in-class, online, or hybrid—and the net costs per student credit hour and degree program.

These kinds of metrics help an institution translate numbers into effective storytelling, allowing it to communicate complex financial data to both the campus and external stakeholders in an understandable and compelling manner. Strong narratives help build a consensus for changes, and they provide a "north star" where the institution hopes to go because of those changes. While data-informed storytelling is a vital leadership tool in normal times, in the context of financial exigency it becomes essential to fortifying the institution's resolve to see the process through to its conclusion.

Even when it's described by a well-constructed, finely tuned narrative, however, a major campus restructuring, particularly one involving financial exigency, will be met with strong opposition and counternarratives. "You're gutting the soul of an institution," "you're turning us into a trade school," "enrollment is going to tank," "get rid of athletics before you lay off faculty," "exigency is just your excuse to fire people you don't like," "you can't expect staff to pick up the slack without a raise," and "I'm never giving your institution another dime" are just some of the reactions an exigency declaration will evoke, no matter how well it's described or how much it's necessary.

The level of change involved in a financial exigency is a traumatic experience for everyone involved. That kind of upheaval always exacts a significant emotional cost. Lives are disrupted, friendships are ended, dreams are ruined. And much of this turmoil unfolds in full public view, causing the personal attacks and inevitable wounds to hurt even more and their ramifications to be felt in many quarters. Anticipating and coping with this kind of fierce resistance is the topic of our next chapter.

NOTES

1. https://www.acenet.edu/Documents/American-College-President-IX-2023.pdf

2. Ritchie, M.A.F. (1970). *The College Presidency: Initiation into the Order of the Turtle*. New York: Philosophical Library.

3. https://agb.org/collaborative-leadership-for-higher-education-business-model-vitality/boardroom-conversations-what-are-the-roles-and-responsibilities-of-our-leadership/

4. https://www.luminafoundation.org/stronger-nation/report/#/progress

5. Thelin, J.R. (2004). *A History of American Higher Education*. Baltimore: Johns Hopkins University Press.

6. Some of the increase is due to the subsequent counting of sub-baccalaureate certificates, which were not originally included in Lumina's goal.

7, P, Beverly (2018) Politics, governmental advocacy and fighting for funding. In S. Green (Ed.) *Declaring Financial Exigency in Higher Education: How Do You Recover*. New York: Nova Science Publishers.

8. https://agb.org/trusteeship-article/how-to-review-your-business-model-some -best-practices/

Chapter 6

The Resistance

This chapter explores the multiple forces that make it so difficult for colleges to change how they operate even when they teeter on the brink of financial collapse. The playbook that's been written to resist all types of change in higher education is well-established, drafted by strong campus constituents, each guarding their own interests and each siloed in their own realities. These protected interests are quite adroit in generating narratives intended to defeat or delay major changes. Some of these narratives convey legitimate concerns that need to be carefully considered. Others are largely false, but confronting their underlying myths is difficult nonetheless, particularly given the ability and willingness of critics and the media to amplify them.

A culture of resistance is embedded in every college campus. It stems from an appropriate questioning of all things by an accumulated group of experts who enjoy a level of independence and autonomy seen in few other organizations. Faculty have been trained to challenge authority and be openly skeptical of "official" views and positions. They are particularly inclined to be suspicious of administrators, who are often ridiculed as carpetbaggers with personal ambitions that constantly need to be monitored and kept in check or as deceitful characters who cannot be trusted. (J. Mckeen Cattell, an eugenicist and controversial professor of psychology at Columbia in the early 1900's, was quoted thusly: "I once incited one of my children to call her doll Mr. President, on the esoteric ground that he would lie in any position in which he was placed.") As a result, examples of resistance through personal attacks, intellectual arguments, legal challenges, and governance disputes are rife across the history of higher education. Resistance to major college reorganizations is certainly no exception, and it may reach its apex when the changes are as extensive as those involved in financial exigency.

Our discussion of resistance to financial restructuring is organized around three topics.

- First, what are the most common objections raised against a college scaling back its academic programs and retrenching its faculty? Understanding and answering the typical arguments made against exigency or near-exigency procedures are essential tasks for college leaders about to embark on a significant downsizing of an institution.
- Second, what methods are typically used to convey this opposition? The methods of resistance range from uncoordinated, ad hominem attacks to well-organized protests, legal challenges, and formal actions by the faculty. In most cases of institutions going through financial exigency, all possible tactics should be expected.
- Third, how should leaders respond to this resistance? Organized opposition and scattershot expressions of condemnation cannot be prevented; indeed, peaceful forms of protest remain the right of those affected by a major reorganization, and that right should be respected and protected. However, their potentially harmful effects can be limited with the right combination of anticipation, determination, data, and empathy.

COMMON ARGUMENTS AGAINST FINANCIAL EXIGENCY

The arguments against the necessity of invoking financial exigency vary depending on the unique history and current circumstances of each institution, but here are seven of the most common objections along with our perspectives on each of them.

"Incompetent administrators caused the problem, now they want faculty and staff to be the ones who pay for it."

When a financial exigency is declared, campus constituents often place the blame on administrators who "let the problems fester," "were asleep at the switch," "didn't listen to the warnings," "have moved too hastily," "blew it all on athletics," "ignored the faculty," or "spent money we didn't have on things we didn't need." All these claims may be accurate to some extent. In our review of institutions on the brink, we've found that some had reached their breaking point through a series of bad financial decisions, risky investments, unchecked growth in institutional debt, and poor budget oversight by their leaders and boards. That's true whether the administrators invoking the financial exigency are the same ones who helped create the problems and/or let them accumulate.

However, while the premise of administrative incompetence may be accurate in some cases, using that accusation as a basis for opposing a major restructuring or a declared state of exigency is not a reasonable conclusion.

First, blaming specific individuals for causing a problem does not mean that they or their successors should be disqualified from trying to solve it. That's especially true when the perceived "culprits" are no longer in office, and new leadership has been brought on board with the explicit charge of righting the ship, as is often the case with colleges that are in financial disarray.

Second, college administrators are not eager to fire faculty and staff. In fact, they try to avoid it for as long as possible and may often wait too long before taking what they realize has become a necessary step. They know the trauma and drama that retrenchment will cause, and in most cases, they have attempted to shave costs through every nonpersonnel action that's available. But they cannot change the numbers, and when it comes to what usually breaks a college's budget, the math is brutal.

In cases of financial exigency, the numbers have become so bad that it is difficult, if not impossible, to fix them without significant personnel and program restructuring. At every college, at least 70% of overall operating costs are in compensation—the wages, salaries and benefits paid to faculty and staff, and the bulk of that expenditure is attributable to faculty.

The reality is that achieving the cost savings necessary on a recurring basis to correct unaffordable institutional budgets almost always requires employee layoffs. In addition, faculty retrenchments are seldom done in isolation. They're usually accompanied by other cutbacks in staff positions and administrators. And when colleges and departments are combined, as they often are during exigent circumstances, the number of people who are paid add-on stipends for administrative duties is also reduced.

Finally, when faculty and long-term staff are let go during a restructuring, most colleges attempt to give them severance packages to mitigate some of their economic damages. For example, the full-time, tenured faculty who were terminated because of Henderson State University's financial exigency were given a one-year terminal appointment under the terms of their current faculty contracts.

In the exigency at Southeast Missouri State University, the administration negotiated severance packages with the Faculty Senate that included providing health insurance for up to five years for all faculty who were discharged. Ken Dobbins, the president of Southeast Missouri State University at the time, credited that single provision as a primary reason that the exigency declaration was accepted by the institution as well as it was.

Severance packages present their own difficulties, however. First, many institutions in a financial crisis cannot afford them, even though they exchange a one-time payout for a continuing obligation. Second, the cumulative cost of a severance package adds to the total amount that a restructuring must ultimately save, resulting in deeper cuts than might have otherwise been necessary without them. In Henderson State's case, the amount spent on the one-year terminal contracts exceeded the amount saved in current year reductions, meaning that the total savings from academic restructuring could not be realized until one full year later.

"Our problem is not too many academic programs, it's administrative bloat."
Faculty often point to the fact that the number of administrators hired over a certain number of years outstrips—on a percentage basis—the number of faculty who've been added during the same interval. The implication is that administrative "bloat" is "out of control" and should be the first target for cutbacks, not instructional faculty.

Up to a point, we don't disagree. New mandates from both the federal government and state agencies have resulted in colleges hiring more non-instructional staff to oversee those mandates. In addition, student demands for greater support in areas like information technology, behavioral health, disability accommodations, and other student services have led institutions to hire more professionals working in those areas.

A recent study of more than 1,500 colleges and universities by the American Council of Trustees and Alumni (ACTA), found that, between 2010 and 2018, growth in non-instructional spending—including for student services (29%) and administration (19%)—increased more than instructional spending (17%). The report, titled *The Cost of Excess,* also found that while the number of full-time faculty increased by 5% (and the amount spent for their salaries increased by 10%) during this period, the number of full-time, non-instructional staff increased by 9%, and their salary costs rose by 15%.[1]

Breaking down those numbers further, the ACTA study found that the number of managers increased by 9%, and business and financial operations staff increased by 25%, while their salary outlays rose by 15% and 33% respectively. In contrast to the increase in administrative professionals, the number of office and administrative support staff fell 10% between 2012 and 2018. If anything, the Covid-19 pandemic may have exacerbated this trend toward colleges employing more expensive administrators while the number of lower-paid general support staff have declined.

The point is that any institution going through financial exigency should place a priority on reducing expenditures for administrative staff. Either through attrition, position combinations, salary rollbacks, or layoffs, institutions should be diligent in eliminating administrative duplication or excess. In many cases, an institution's overall administrative payroll has grown well beyond its ability to fund it. Put simply, it employs too many relatively high-priced people to serve the number of students it's enrolled.

Having acknowledged that priority, it will still be the case that faculty compensation will comprise two-thirds or more of total institutional salaries and benefits. While institutions facing a severe financial crisis need to cut their costs in all areas, they will usually be able to make the level of reductions required only if reducing faculty positions remains on the table.

"Exigency is just an excuse to get rid of disfavored tenured faculty."

While we cannot speak to the motives involved in every single exigency declaration, a targeted attack on specific faculty members is not likely to be one of the goals. Tenured faculty are affected by financial exigency because most institutions follow a policy of terminating their appointments under only two conditions: reasons of cause specific to a given faculty member or financial exigency. In contrast, nontenured faculty can be let go for any of several reasons, and they often are, with less notice and fewer rights for appealing their dismissal.

For institutions needing to achieve large reductions in expenditures, tenured faculty members in departments that serve relatively few students are a logical group to consider. Reducing their number is not a vendetta nor an attempt to target specific victims; it's a matter of focusing on one of an institution's largest category of expense. In most instances it will not be possible to achieve the millions of dollars of cuts required by institutions in serious financial peril without retrenching some tenured faculty. In the most severe crises, it may require the elimination—not just the reduction—of entire programs and all their personnel.

Practicalities aside, matters of exigency also pose fundamental questions about the nature and future of faculty tenure. Long regarded as an essential protection of faculty members' academic freedom and their ability to study and speak about controversial issues, tenure is an increasingly hot-button issue in higher education. It's our third rail. Talking about or tinkering with it is sure to set off all kinds of alarms in academic quarters.

Contentious as tenure continues to be, little disagreement exists about one fact: it's gradually disappearing. In 1975, 45% of instructional faculty were either tenured (29%) or on the tenure track (16%). By 1995, the percentage had dropped to 35% (25% tenured, 10% tenure-eligible). By 2015, only 21% of college faculty were tenured or on the tenure track (8%).[2] According to a recent AAUP report, 73% of instructional positions were off the tenure track as of 2016.[3] That means that the traditional protections and benefits of tenure are not enjoyed by most teachers now employed at American colleges and universities. These numbers parallel a marked decline in full-time faculty regardless of their tenure status.

Whether you survey university administrators or talk with newer faculty members, they agree on this: tenure's days look to be numbered. In a 2011 survey conducted by the Pew Research Center along with *The Chronicle of Higher Education*, fewer than a quarter of university presidents said they'd prefer full-time, tenured professors to make up the majority of faculty at their schools,[4] Instead, 69% would prefer that most of their faculty work under long-term or annual contracts. Forty percent of the presidents of four-year private colleges responding to the survey preferred faculty with long-term contracts, while 30% favored tenure. Among the presidents of public colleges, half said they preferred tenured faculty while 36% would like to have their professors on long-term contracts instead.

In a 2023 survey of chief academic officers, conducted by Hanover Research for *Inside Higher Education*, 52% of provosts indicated they would prefer a system of long-term faculty contracts over the current tenure system. Although the provosts endorsed the importance of academic freedom, many of them believed there were other ways besides tenure that could protect it.[5]

The financial fallout of the pandemic coupled with a spate of legislative attacks on tenure by conservative lawmakers in several states constitute new threats to tenure's endangered status. What was once seen as an iron-clad commitment might eventually become merely a paper-thin promise or a remnant of history. For example, late in 2020, in the depths of the pandemic, an administrator at the University of Colorado proposed converting 50 tenure and tenure-track faculty lines in the university's College of Arts and Sciences to 25 non-tenured instructors who would be expected to teach more classes but earn less money.[6] Few higher education leaders expected Colorado to be the sole example of this type of proposal in the post-pandemic future, but budget-conscious college administrators are probably not tenure's biggest menace, it's the increasing number of attempts by state legislatures to end or restrict tenure that constitute the biggest risk.

After several attempts to end tenure in states like Iowa, Texas, and South Carolina failed in recent years, it appeared that the anti-tenure fervor had cooled. But in 2023, the anti-tenure movement was revived.

- In Texas, Senate Bill 18, filed by State Sen. Brandon Creighton, who was chair of the Texas Senate's Subcommittee on Higher Education at the time, prohibited that state's public higher education institutions from offering tenure or "any type of permanent employment status" starting on Sept. 1, 2023.[7] The bill also would have permitted the Board of Regents to establish "an alternate system of tiered employment status for faculty members provided that the system clearly defines each position and requires each faculty member to undergo an annual performance evaluation." No post-tenure review, no reforms, and no process improvements were viewed as necessary in Texas. The bill, which passed the Texas Senate, would have accomplished what many conservative politicians, including Texas Lt. Gov. Dan Patrick, have wanted all along—the complete elimination of college tenure.

Eventually, however, the Texas House of Representatives refused to go along with Senate Bill 18; instead of prohibiting tenure, it substituted a version of the bill that requires universities to conduct regular performance reviews of tenured faculty and that gives university boards more leeway in dismissing faculty who hold tenure. In what was viewed by many close Texas observers as a surprise, the Senate agreed to that version, preserving many of the tenure practices currently in place at Texas institutions.

- The North Dakota legislature took up a particularly bad proposal in 2023 called the "tenure with responsibilities" act. HB 1446 would have created a four-year pilot program for tenured faculty at Bismarck State College and Dickinson State University giving the presidents of those universities the authority to review any tenured faculty member "at any time the president deems a review is in the institution's best interest."[8] What made the bill even more alarming is that Stephen Easton, the President of Dickinson State University, helped draft it. It was ultimately narrowly defeated in the North Dakota Senate, but it came very close to becoming law, a signal of how strong anti-tenure attitudes have grown.
- Of course, Florida was not about to be left behind in the rush to curtail tenure. House Bill 999, introduced by Republican Rep. Alex Andrade, was a dreadfully ill-advised bill that would—along with mandating several other big-government intrusions into university operations—give governing boards in Florida the power to review the tenure status of college faculty anytime they find reason to do so.[9] That provision was ultimately stripped out of the bill, but no one will be surprised if it resurfaces in some form in future Florida legislative proposals or in another state that puts the end of faculty tenure in its sights.

Defenders of tenure—both among administrators and the faculty—are beginning to focus not so much on whether it will continue to exist in its current form, but how it could be modified so that its most important elements can be preserved. Reasonable answers to that question need to recognize the pros and cons of the present system, as well as the realities of campus politics and the external forces taking dead aim at ending tenure entirely.

Tenure does protect faculty who espouse unpopular ideas. Given the intent of many politicians to dictate campus policies, put classroom gag orders in place, control academic curricula, and ban tenure outright, it's essential to guard faculty from threats and harassment and protect their academic freedom. Ideally, tenure also promotes intellectual leadership and encourages shared governance. It strengthens the faculty's hand in the give-and-take of university decision-making. Tenured faculty can give wise direction to academic programs, sage advice on hiring new faculty, and seasoned counsel on university budgets and priorities.

However, tenure also can sometimes protect ineffective faculty, providing job security to a few individuals who no longer deserve it, but who continue in their jobs to the detriment of both students and institutions. Another problem is that tenure too often imposes intellectual orthodoxy, stifling—rather than safeguarding—academic disagreements. It also enforces a faculty caste system—a tenured upper class who enjoys their entitlements and untenured part-timers and adjuncts who struggle with their daily disenfranchisement.

Tenure, in its present form, is too blunt an instrument to accomplish the faculty protections that are needed without the excess baggage that's sometimes encumbered. Among the heaviest of that baggage is the loss of hiring and financial flexibility experienced by tenure-heavy institutions. Although tenure does not guarantee endless employment nor was it designed to be a lifetime sinecure, the process of terminating tenured faculty at most universities is so complicated that it's a step rarely taken.

Reasonable reforms to tenure are possible. It can be revised in ways that maintain most of its advantages and minimizes its occasional, worst abuses. Three options for reform—a reinstatement of mandatory retirement, a limit of the total length of tenure, and the use of renewable, multi-year contracts—are summarized in Textbox 6.1.

The future of tenure is likely to take one of two directions. Either it will continue to erode, dying from a thousand cuts or killed off in one state after the other by hostile legislation, or it will be replaced with various approximations involving tenure-like contractual protections. We recommend the latter course. It preserves most of the essential protections afforded by traditional tenure, it balances faculty independence with institutional flexibility, it allows expenditures to be adjusted as demanded by revenues, and it has the additional benefit of allowing more adjunct faculty to be appointed into well-protected and better compensated, full-time faculty positions, thereby reducing the exploitation of part-time faculty that the tenure system has long countenanced.

Tenure has become a benefit that protects a shrinking minority of academicians, leaving the majority of untenured, contingent faculty to suffer the competitive hard knocks of academic capitalism that underpays them, excludes them from shared governance, and denies them most of the protections that are of greatest importance to college faculty.[10] It doesn't have to be this way. A rethinking of tenure is in order, but it will be better if faculty are at the forefront of that discussion. It does no good to merely decry the demise of tenure, condemn administrators for hiring too many adjuncts, bemoan society's under-appreciation of the academy, complain about tenured faculty being

TEXTBOX 6.1. THREE OPTIONS
FOR TENURE REFORM

Reinstate mandatory retirement at age 70. The combination of tenure with the current ban against mandatory retirement for university faculty allows retirement to be deferred as long as faculty choose, blocking opportunities to hire new scholars with fresh ideas and locking in the high salaries of a college's most senior faculty. The federal ban against mandatory retirement could be lifted for university faculty, but post-retirement appointments could still be offered to productive faculty older than 70, providing an earned extension of their employment that recognizes their value to students and society.

Limit the total length of tenure. Another way to transition from the current system of tenure would be to allow faculty members who currently hold tenure or who are on the tenure track to retain that same status. Eliminating tenure or the eligibility to earn it for these individuals would be unfair and probably illegal. They should be "grandfathered" into the tenure system status quo.

Here's the change: New faculty hires could still earn tenure, but its total length would be limited to a finite number of years that would also involve periodic post-tenure reviews. A term of 35 years would be sufficient to cover the professional lifetimes of most faculty, although arguments could be made for shorter terms. After that period, whatever its length, institutions and individual faculty could negotiate annual or multiyear post-tenure contracts as they see fit. The end of the tenure term would not preclude extensions of appointments.

Offer renewable multiyear contracts. A more aggressive change would be to grandfather in tenured faculty and allow current tenure-track faculty to earn tenure but offer renewable multi-year contracts (with due process protections, for-cause requirements, and performance reviews) to new hires. These contracts should be long enough for faculty to establish or maintain their teaching acumen and scholarly expertise and give sufficient time to insulate them from external pressures and internal disputes.

Seven-year contracts seem about right. That's the same length as the initial probationary period prior to most tenure/promotion decisions. It's long enough for faculty members to prove their mettle, but not so long as to entrench bad decisions. More important than the length of the contract, however, is that it can continue to be renewed—or not. Good performance can be rewarded and sustained; poor performance earns a timely termination.

retrenched during financial exigencies, or dismiss out of hand any change in the terms or conditions of the current tenure system.

Those strategies have been in play for some time, and they've not worked. Instead, they've helped prompt extremist legislative proposals to throw tenure out completely, gut its basic protections, and make it subject to the whims of administrators. A more productive approach would be for faculty to come to the table and put their ideas on it in the way of tenure reforms or other alternatives that could be negotiated with university administrators and governing boards.

"It's an attack on the arts and humanities."

It's true that colleges that have reduced academic programs or majors have often, although certainly not exclusively, included disciplines in the arts and humanities among the cuts. The justification for those reductions has been market-based—enrollment in arts and humanities majors has dropped steadily over the past several years. This decline is a prolonged national phenomenon, well-recognized by everyone in higher education, including humanities faculty, who've championed various initiatives to revive student interest in their disciplines, often by adding internships or other practical experiences to the major or by combining courses in business with a standard humanities curriculum to enhance job prospects for humanities graduates.

The most complete data on the majors declared by college graduates are reported by the National Center for Education Statistics, which charts the number of bachelor's degrees awarded by U.S. colleges and universities in 32 different degree fields. In the 2015–16 academic year, 1,920,750 baccalaureate degrees were awarded in the U.S. By 2020–21, that number had grown to 2,066,445, representing a 7.6% gain, equal to 145,695 more graduates.[11]

However, the overall increase masks very different trajectories for specific majors. Engineering, health professions, computer science, psychology, biological and biomedical sciences, and business all saw healthy increases across that five-year period, but majors in English and English literature, foreign languages, the liberal arts and general studies, and visual and performing arts saw declines of 16%, 16%, 4%, and 3%, respectively. In addition, the total number of students graduating in 2020–21 with degrees in foreign languages (15,518), English (35,722), and liberal arts and general studies (41,909) was dwarfed by the number of graduates majoring in business (391,375), health professions (268,018), and biological and biomedical sciences (131,499).

A financially strapped college that eliminates majors in any field—including the arts and humanities—is not mounting an ideological attack, and it's not accusing the liberal arts of being broken. It's making a rational reallocation of scarce resources that reflects student demand. In addition, eliminating a major in Spanish or art history does not mean that students will no longer be required to take classes in a foreign language or the arts. The decision to eliminate a major is not the same as eliminating that subject matter from the core curriculum. Colleges have generally maintained the same level of liberal arts requirements in their general studies core after financial exigency as they had in place before it.

If anything, the reduction of humanities majors means that senior faculty could be more available to teach lower- and mid-division courses to a greater number of students than was the case when their typical teaching assignments were concentrated in upper-level classes and seminars. Claims that colleges that are forced to downsize are "demoting" the humanities have probably done more to harm these disciplines than protect them. A more productive approach would be for faculty to embrace a greater involvement in remaining or reimagined courses where they can acquaint more students with the value and rigor of the humanities.

"The administration wants to turn us into a trade school."

This argument is a corollary of the "they're gutting the humanities" line of attack. It speaks to the fact that a pullback in the humanities is frequently combined with an enhancement of instructional resources in more practically oriented, high-demand fields of study like computer science, business, health professions, and STEM departments, the disciplines to which more students have been migrating in the past decade.

The "trade school" allegation is largely hyperbole. As we have already discussed, academic restructuring seldom involves a degrading of the humanities in the core curriculum. Regardless of whether humanities departments are consolidated, downsized, or ended, all the students in any major are usually still required to complete the same set of liberal arts courses.

If what critics mean by "we're becoming a trade school" is that the institution will no longer be graduating students who majored in German, philosophy, linguistics, or other humanities, the complaint is undercut by data showing the de facto decline of those majors has already taken place through student's choices. They've voted with their feet. How much of a real difference is there between a major that's no longer offered and one that enrolls and graduates few, if any, students over the years?

There is probably some loss of prestige, at least temporarily, for an institution that shuts down several majors. And there is no denying the fact that such institutions become less comprehensive in their intellectual breadth. Those are real losses to be sure. But an institution in financial jeopardy must answer the question of whether it can afford to maintain departments and programs that are serving a dwindling number of students just to retain its claims to academic comprehensiveness. The reputational and intellectual consequences of closing majors must be balanced against the repercussions of the entire institution going broke and being forced to close.

"The cutbacks mean larger classes and therefore poorer student learning"
Of all the criticisms leveled against faculty retrenchments, the claim that it will result in larger classes and therefore poorer student learning is probably the one with the greatest resonance among the public. It's just intuitive to believe that smaller classes are better for students than larger ones. "Big is bad, small is all" is such an article of faith in the general community and among teachers that reducing class size may be the one policy most likely to be seen as the magic bullet for educational improvement.

In fact, the data about the relationship between classroom size and student performance are much more mixed and nuanced than most observers assume. Even in K–12 classrooms, where the bulk of the research has been performed, any advantages of smaller over larger classes are moderated by a host of other factors including teacher experience, student readiness, and the subject matter involved.

At the collegiate level, the data are even more equivocal. Some studies have found that an increase in collegiate class size leads to an increase in dropout rates and a reduction in on-time degree completion, but no change in long-run degree completion. A large, well-designed study at Temple University explored the relationship between class size and course grades in more than 8,000 undergraduate courses. The results indicated that after controlling for instructor experience, the effects of class size were not consistent and interacted with various student variables as well as the academic discipline involved.[12] That's consistent with other research showing that any effects of collegiate class size on student learning are often confounded by differences in teacher experience, teaching style, student motivation, and the difficulty of the course material.

In addition, the research on the effects of class size may have little to do with the actual changes that students experience at a college that's eliminated low-enrollment classes. As an example, an institution that eliminates several classes with small enrollments will see its average class size increase, leading to the corollary charge that students are going to be short-changed in the process. But for most students, who were never enrolled in those small courses anyway, the size of the classes in which they continue to be enrolled may not change at all. The number of students in a calculus or composition class does not change just because the institution eliminated its advanced classes on Dante, Heidegger, or Steinbeck.

Finally, whether an increase in class size might be detrimental to student engagement or performance depends on the range of increase that's involved. It's one thing to increase a class's size by 10–20 students when its current subscription is 100 or 150. It's another matter when an addition of 10–20 students would double the number of students in the class.

"It's not an expense problem, it's a revenue problem"

This claim is an illustration of the "if only" sentiment that's so often used to argue against or delay major reductions. If only we had more money from the state, . . . if only our enrollment would pick up, . . . if only a big donor would come through, . . . if only we had a bigger endowment or spent more of it. . . . These appeals are almost never realistic, and individuals who cling to lack-of-revenue arguments are often the ones who may be the most resistant to change.

Although college presidents should—and will—advocate for larger state appropriations and look to create new streams of revenue wherever they can, they also need to educate their campuses that more revenue is more of a dream than a strategy. Legislators are hesitant to appropriate more money to universities that can't balance their books. Student enrollments seldom turn around quickly enough to reverse years of stagnant or falling numbers. Major donors give to causes near and dear to their hearts, not to underwrite day-to-day operations. And most institutions in financial peril don't have large endowments they can tap, and even when they do, most funds in those endowments are restricted to specific purposes designated by donors.

Nonetheless, the "we need more" argument is one that many college leaders advance, preferring to ask for funding increases rather than require spending decreases. For example, in 2023, the flagship Twin Cities campus of the University of Minnesota announced that its tuition revenue would come in at $17.3 million less than what it had expected. How did the university respond to that discovery? It requested a $302 million increase in its appropriation from the state. In a March 15, 12023 letter to legislators,[13] the University of Minnesota system (with campuses at the Twin Cities, Morris, Rochester, Duluth, and Crookston) said it needed $135 million for core mission support, $48 million to make up for the system-level tuition shortfall, and $40.5 million to allow it to freeze tuition for resident undergraduate students. According to the University of Minnesota, Twin Cities, if the state didn't come through with the full increase, it would look to increase tuition for in-state undergraduates by 6.5% to 7.5%. At a time when more young people are questioning the value of college, we question whether increasing what it costs for them to attend or demanding that the state pay more for them to attend is a sound, long-term strategy.

METHODS OF RESISTANCE

Opposition to a financial exigency or similar finance-driven restructurings can take several forms, ranging in size, intensity, organization, and duration. In this section, we review six of the most common forms of resistance, beginning with those that are the most formal or highly organized and concluding with those that are less coordinated, but are often the most kinetic and emotionally traumatic.

No Confidence Votes

A vote of no confidence in a campus president/chancellor is one of the most organized and highly visible means available to faculty who oppose restructuring through financial exigency. Although votes of no confidence by the faculty carry no legal or official authority, they're not without their consequences. Intended to publicly upbraid a president, criticize a governing board, or call for the firing of other administrators, they are an effective way to publicly dramatize a faculty's dissatisfaction with an institution's leadership. If not a knock-out punch, a no-confidence vote still can give a leader a black eye.

According to the *Chronicle of Higher Education*, at least 24 institutions took no-confidence votes in their leaders in 2021, the highest number in recent history.[14] In a 2021 AAUP survey, 7.4% of 396 respondents reported that a no-confidence vote had been taken about an administrator at their institution in the last three years.[15] The reasons for no-confidence votes vary, but in several cases—for example, at the University of Tulsa, the University of La Verne, Henderson State University, South Carolina State University, West Virginia University, and the University of Evansville—the votes were prompted by faculty displeasure with large-scale academic and financial restructuring overseen by a president or provost.

How effective are no-confidence votes? While some observers are prone to dismiss the action as merely symbolic, or just an acute symptom of chronic faculty unrest, no-confidence votes are often followed by a president's decision to step down from office. A no-confidence vote is not a triviality. According to the *Chronicle's* analysis of more than 235 no-confidence votes from 1989 to the present, about 51% of the presidents who had been the subject of a vote of no confidence exited their office within a year. A separate study of 57 no-confidence votes reported similar results—within six months of the vote, the campus leader was removed from office in 32 of those cases.[16] As we know in the case of Henderson State University, even though it involved only an executive committee vote with a limited number of faculty, almost all of whom had been notified they were receiving a terminal contract, a no-confidence vote by the faculty can add to a president's conclusion that a new campus leader will be needed to lead the institution in the future as it rebuilds its academic programs and administrative structure.

Some institutions have formal guidelines for how to conduct a no-confidence vote, but most do not. They define the process—including how the resolution is drafted, who gets to vote on it, and how the vote is taken—as they go along. Some no-confidence votes demand that the president be terminated. Others stop short of that and instead cite what's perceived to be the administration's incompetence and call for a change in governance processes that would strengthen the faculty's role in future institutional decision-making. One advantage of the ad hoc nature of the process is its flexibility—it allows a segment of the faculty to respond more quickly to presidential actions deemed to be harmful than might be the case with a well-defined governance process. A main disadvantage of an ad hoc process is that the vote may not be truly representative of an institution's overall faculty sentiment, many of whom may not participate in the vote.

Even though a no-confidence vote may be one of the more influential, albeit non-binding, forms of faculty resistance, faculty might still be reluctant to use it. They may fear retribution from the board, other faculty members, or the administrators they're condemning. They may be concerned about rupturing a relationship with the president that had been functional, if not cordial, up until the dispute giving rise to the vote. And they may worry that a no-confidence vote might reflect poorly on the institution, causing alumni, the public, and policy makers to lose their confidence in it, worsening an already bad problem.

Lawsuits

Faculty or staff whose appointments are terminated during a financial hardship can file lawsuits alleging wrongful termination, age discrimination, breach of contract, or other causes of action. The success of this type of litigation depends largely on the facts specific to the retrenchment, but typically the cases involve a balancing contest in which the ability of a college to manage a financial crisis is weighed against the need to protect employees from being arbitrarily dismissed or being terminated contrary to legal obligations set forth in official policies. Colleges with collective bargaining agreements will need to honor the legal requirements concerning faculty layoffs and program discontinuations that such agreements typically include. For institutions without collective bargaining agreements, the controlling obligations concerning employment will usually be found in the faculty or university handbook of policies.

One commentator put it this way: "Courts faced with the dismissal of a faculty member for reasons of financial exigency must determine in each case (1) whether a financial exigency exists and (2) whether the dismissal represented a good faith effort to alleviate that exigency. In addition, courts will also be faced with the allocation of the burden of proof on each of the questions."[17]

When an institution proceeds with financial exigency, one of the most critical resources is the guidance and support provided by its human resources staff and legal counsel. Every personnel decision must be vetted in terms of possible negative impacts on a protected class of employee and on its consistency with contractual obligations. When the financial situation is dire, the elimination of programs in their entirety versus the selective reduction of individual faculty lines can minimize the risk of legal charges that the actions were discriminatory.

AAUP Censure

As we described in Chapter 2, faculty who believe their university has not followed proper retrenchment procedures can take their claims to the American Association of University Professors (AAUP) and request an investigation. Those investigations are conducted under the auspices of AAUP's committees on Academic Freedom and Tenure or its committee on College and University Governance. In such instances, investigating committees made up of faculty from other institutions are appointed and charged with determining the relevant facts of the situation before rendering a written report with its conclusions about what's transpired at the college under investigation.

In the past, AAUP investigative committees have often concluded that an administration failed to consult adequately both before and after declarations of financial exigency or through retrenchment of faculty without an exigency declaration. They're likely to question whether an exigency was justified, whether there were departures from AAUP principles and standards when invoking it, whether individuals were treated fairly, and whether the process was flawed in other ways.

After their investigative work is completed, the committees publish case reports detailing their findings. When they find what they believe to be major departures from AAUP-supported standards, AAUP staff may communicate with an institution's administration to try to achieve a resolution consistent with those standards. Occasionally, however, when those efforts fail, AAUP may start a process that can lead to its censure of the institution, meaning that AAUP has decided that conditions for academic freedom and tenure are unsatisfactory at that institution.

A list of censured institutions is published "for the purpose of informing Association members, the profession at large, and the public that unsatisfactory conditions of academic freedom and tenure have been found to prevail at these institutions."[18] According to AAUP, "placing the name of an institution on this list does not mean that censure is visited either upon the whole of the institution or upon the faculty, but specifically upon its present administration. The term 'administration' includes the administrative officers and the governing board of the institution." As of 2023, 58 higher ed institutions were on the AAUP censure list.

Like faculty votes of no-confidence, AAUP censure has no legal impact or governing authority over an institution. It's a public scolding of an administration, meant to nudge it into compliance with what AAUP judges to be necessary standards of shared governance and satisfactory conditions for faculty's academic freedom. Even though it lacks any ultimate authority, censure threatens enough bad publicity and generates other unwanted attention that most institutions will try to prevent it or work to be removed from the published list. That gives the process some teeth as a means of resistance.

Presentations to the Governing Board

Many governing boards routinely include the opportunity for individuals to comment on agenda items under consideration by the institution's board. For example, it's common for students to appear before a board and urge it to vote down a tuition increase. Faculty may come before the board to lobby for pay raises or a new academic program. Members of the local community may request that the board allow them to speak for or against a university's plan to build new residence halls or acquire property in a neighborhood. The number of individuals offering comments may be restricted, and the board also may limit the amount of time allocated to each presenter. Presenters are usually required to give advance notice to the board of their intention to appear and offer comments, subject to the board's approval.

When a board votes on the administration's plans for financial exigency, program reductions, or faculty retrenchment, it should extend the opportunity for the campus community and the public to offer formal comments on the proposal. It's important to give opponents an official platform to air their views and complaints about the process and to request that the board reject or modify the administration's recommendations. While such testimony is unlikely to sway the board's final decision, giving students, staff, and faculty a chance to have a voice in the formal proceedings increases transparency and the perception of fairness.

Petitions, Protests, and Marches

Campus petitions, protests, sit-ins, marches, mock funerals, and boycotts are common forms of expressing resistance to a major financial restructuring. These are time-honored ways of protesting unpopular actions on America's college campuses. Not only should demonstrations and protests be expected following a declaration of financial exigency, but administrators should defend the right of their detractors to engage in such protests. Nothing will mobilize opposition to a campus leader or a controversial decision faster than an attempt to shut down debate or muzzle peaceful protestors, particularly when they include students and their family members. Critics of an administration have every right to speak out against what they deem to be unfair treatment or inept leadership.

Campus demonstrations can be effective in drumming up sympathy for the cause in the short run, but their long-term impact is usually negligible. They are intended to put campus leaders on the hot seat, making them squirm. And they often achieve that aim. At Henderson State University, demonstrators marched in front of the chancellor's residence to protest his financial exigency plans, many of them holding signs as they chanted, "You know what I know? Chuck's gotta go!"[19]

Letters to the Editor and Social Media Campaigns

Letter writing, Facebook posts, tweets, blog entries and comments to the press—both on and off the record—are popular ways of expressing opposition to campus financial overhauls. Sometimes this messaging takes the form of an organized media campaign. In other instances, it's more of a free-for-all, where just about anything goes. The messages run the gamut from the persnickety to the profane, the rude to the menacing. Somewhat akin to the well-known stages of grief, they often express disbelief, anger, and sadness over the institution's plight. But they also frequently descend into name-calling and ad hominem attacks. We know of one financial exigency where the local police advised the chancellor's wife to leave the area for a while out of concerns for her personal safety.

Social media is especially prone to such excesses and abuses. As illustrated in this chapter's Voices from the Field, it's been social media rather than coverage in traditional media where the most angry, destructive forms of communication have typically occurred in response to a financial exigency process.

Of course, traditional media also affords opportunities for some hard knocks against administrators who lead an exigency process. Here are a few excerpts from a May 2022 letter to the editor of the *Democrat-Gazette*,[20] a statewide Arkansas newspaper that covered the Henderson State exigency story:

- "Henderson is burning. Again."
- "I imagine this must be what a hostile corporate takeover feels like; everything Ambrose has done so far has been by administrative fiat."
- "We were hopeful at first, but we realize now that we are victims of bait-and-switch tactics. Little from his initial interview with the search committee would have suggested the draconian changes Ambrose had in mind."
- "But now he has the matches set to burn HSU down once more so he can remold it in a corporate-style model concocted at KnowledgeWorks, his previous realm. There is no evidence that he has concern for the human collateral damage nor the harm to HSU's reputation as he proposes to eliminate most of the programs in the arts, humanities, and sciences that lie at the academic heart of HSU."
- "Ambrose initially seemed like an affable sort of fellow in spite of his edu-business jargon. He has convinced many that he can balance HSU's budget while transforming higher education to better meet the needs of our region; however, he is simply cutting costs by amputation rather than skilled surgical reductions."

Presidents leading an institution through exigency have been called "dictators," "autocrats," and "tyrants." Accusations of incompetence, impropriety, vindictiveness, dishonesty, favoritism, and collusion are common. Here— and in Figure 6.1 — are a few verbatim quotes from individuals taking to X (Twitter), Facebook, or other social media to voice their disapproval and dismay with the invocation of exigency:

- "Here at the end, it feels like we've been blindsided, and I'm not alone in that. It's been very quick and brutal and demeaning on so many levels."
- "The craziness just doesn't stop."
- "My alumni heart is broken."
- "Apparently I am not worth employing."
- "From a numbers and alignment standpoint, it makes complete sense. But that's very different from how it impacts individual lives and the campus community and society as a whole, and my heart just breaks, it really does."
- "Budgets are moral documents. If university administrators believe in the humanity of their classified staff, they can find the money."
- "If you're planning to be an incoming freshman, go somewhere else."
- "Academia is now reduced to making a few people rich."
- "Save time and just close."
- "The whole thing sucks."
- "#FuckChuck."

Henderson State U @HendersonStateU

Henderson State students are being treated to a late night breakfast tonight by faculty and staff as final exams continue this week. Good luck to all our Reddies with their remaining finals! #BreakForBreakfast

9:44 PM • May 3, 2022

7:38 PM • May 5, 2022

Breakfast for dinner - nice savings chuck. It kinda looks like dinner smells like tasty financial exigency and at least he hasn't yet said "let them eat cake"

Henderson State U @HendersonStateU

Are you interested in a career in the arts? Learn more about Henderson State and how we can help you earn a bachelor's degree within our Arts and Humanities learning community - http://hsu.edu/...

11:13 AM • Oct 25, 2022

9:32 PM • Oct 25, 2022

This is shameless and misleading. Let's be real. The current leaders at Henderson care nothing about arts or humanities.

2:39 PM • Oct 26, 2022

@DrChuckAmbrose @chuckiwelch Arts and humanities WITHOUT ENGLISH AND OTHER RELATED DISCIPLINES! C'mon, Henderson. Get real. If you are interested in this area (and most other subjects, actually), you MUST go elsewhere. Ambrose and company: stop selling snake oil!

Henderson State U Retweeted
Henderson Greek Life @HSUGREEK

🔥Greek week is coming up next week 🔥 Who will be the Survivor? #hsugreek #bereddiegogreek

9:41 AM • Oct 24, 2022

3:07 PM • Oct 24, 2022

Lip sync battle makes sense. Without a performing arts or any liberal arts programming - students should just learn how to become tik-tok stars as this also does not require a degree from an actual university

---

Henderson State U @HendersonStateU

2022 Henderson Alumni Class Notes are now available to view online - https://hsu.edu/pages/alumni/a...

Send us your life updates, to be included in our next class notes, by visiting http://bit.ly/3VYQMVy.

9:13 AM • Dec 15, 2022

1:48 PM • Dec 16, 2022

Alums should realize their alma mater no longer represents or cares about them ...

Henderson State U @HendersonStateU

Within Henderson State's education programs, you can expect personal attention from expert faculty, real-life learning experiences, and high-quality programs.

Learn more at bit.ly/HSU-TeacherEd.

10:11 AM • Mar 7, 2023

4:15 PM • Mar 8, 2023

Yes, for now...as of next year, you are getting rid of programs necessary for the training of future high school teachers!!! That leaves a huge gap, does it not?

Henderson State U @HendersonStateU

Henderson State students [...] presented their research at the state capitol yesterday!

11:27 AM • Feb 9, 2023

9:32 PM • Feb 9, 2023

It's a shame future HSU students won't have the same opportunity because their majors were cut and their professors were fired.

Henderson State U @HendersonStateU

Today's career fair is just another way we are connecting school to work and getting students to be #ReddieForWhatsNext.

10:12 AM • Nov 2, 2022

3:08 PM • Nov 2, 2022

What about the 67 careers you destroyed when you UNFAIRLY fired dozens of highly qualified TENURED and tenure track PROFESSORS? What about the COUNTLESS career options dashed when you CANCELLED STUDENTS' MAJORS? Fair? No way!

Henderson State U @HendersonStateU

Join us for the Captain Henderson House's official ribbon-cutting this Friday, August 12 at 1:30 pm! hsu.edu/news/2022/aug/10/...

8:21 PM • Aug 10, 2022

9:44 PM • Aug 10, 2022

Ironic that this beautiful antique house (and I hope it does well under new management) is tied to a university whose history and integrity have now been destroyed by egotistical opportunists.

Henderson State U Retweeted
Student Engagement Center @HSU_SEC

Congratulations to our 10 finalists and our Henderson Got Talent Winner 2022 ... #LiveReddie #Reddie4WhatsNext

9:44 PM • Oct 19, 2022

1:22 PM • Oct 19, 2022

Henderson['s] Got Talent....leaving this school in droves.

Figure 6.1. The Resistance

HSU Alumni
@HSUAlumni

Register for the Texarkana Area Alumni Reception on Thursday, January 19. Click the link below to register. https://bit.ly/3uYDZGU #ReddieAlumni

10:30 AM · Jan 9, 2023

11:20 AM · Jan 9, 2023

Wait, you're still a university/college?

Henderson State U
@HendersonStateU

Are you interested in a career in business? Learn more about Henderson State and how we can help you earn a bachelor's and/or master's degree within our Business, Innovation, and Entrepreneurship learning community - http://hsu.edu/pages/future...

11:39 AM · Oct 13, 2022

6:54 PM · Oct 13, 2022

Hey, potential Reddies: I would bypass the marketing campaigns and just go right to the source. Ask current STUDENTS and FIRED FACULTY if THEY would recommend Henderson.

5:10 PM · Oct 13, 2022

Are you interested in being part of a community where learning and education are truly valued? Don't go to Henderson.

Henderson State U
@HendersonStateU

It's Battle Week!

Game Day/Ticket Info: bit.ly/3DTPDXA
Live Stream: youtu.be/vraEU9GPkx4

0:24 PM · Nov 9, 2022

1:22 PM · Nov 10, 2022

Speaking of battles: biology students are dissecting Halloween candy in their ONLINE BIO LABS. Why not show solidarity with the horrible academic situation and play this weekend's game on a baseball field using a beach ball?

Henderson State U
@HendersonStateU

Welcome Week 2022 activities begin in exactly 12 days! #WelcomeWeek #LiveReddie

4:15 PM · Aug 1, 2022

4:11 PM · Aug 2, 2022

Reddie to learn a trade and nothing else!

12:39 PM · Aug 7, 2022

Reddie to find out your classes don't have teachers!

11:34 AM · Aug 3, 2022

And, to add to Mary's comment, get Reddie to take classes from exploited adjuncts who are making far below minimum wage. @DrChuckAmbrose is reimagining Henderson State as a factory obsessed with checking random, questionable "competency" boxes and not actually educating you.

Henderson State SGA
@HendersonSGA

Our @HendersonSGA reps are here at the Little Rock Capitol to kick off Save AR students week. Join us throughout this week as we raise awareness towards education and prevention of substance misuse. #SaveARStudents2022 #LiveReddie

9:41 AM · Oct 24, 2022

8:07 PM · Oct 24, 2022

Yes, Reddies, fight for your right to a real education. Fight to undo the cuts of your current Chancellor.

7:47 PM · Oct 23, 2022

Raise awareness about the destruction of the liberal arts and the cutting of programs at Henderson State University.

Chuck Ambrose
@DrChuckAmbrose

It's #FamilyDay and #ReddiesDay @HendersonStateU

@HSUAdmissions_
with a great group of students and their families who are #ReddieforWhatsNext.

1:19 PM · Sep 17, 2022

2:53 PM · Sep 17, 2022

If you didn't fire a majority of your most qualified faculty, then maybe these seats would be filled.

12:31 PM · Sep 19, 2022

#fuckchuck

VOICES FROM THE FIELD

Campus leaders who have served during the age of Twitter, MySpace, Facebook, Instagram, Snapshot, YikYak, TikTok, and LinkedIn etc. know both the benefits and the risks of communicating through social media. Many presidents have successfully embraced these tools to elevate their institutions with a much larger and more diverse audience than they could reach with more traditional media. They celebrate their students' success and champion faculty and staff achievements. They tell inspiring stories about their institutions, debate Jay Bilas about intercollegiate athletics, thank donors for their gifts, and even go back and forth with students about whether to call for a snow day or not. Posting on social media became part of their workday, and for many presidents it became a way not only to portray their schools in a favorable light but also to share details about their personal lives.

But as the world has become more divided along political, social, and cultural lines, social media has taken a nastier turn. It's often functioned to widen gaps, rally competing forces, and sometimes convert disagreements into intimidation and harassment. It's become a source for heat, more than for light. Personal information that presidents might have disclosed through social media has sometimes been turned against them.

Within the context of financial exigency, social media can stir up the emotions of students, alumni, faculty, and staff and become a very effective means of organizing resistance. It can spread rumors, spark emotions, and spur impulsive behavior. It can change the dynamics of the typical campus debate, increasing tempers rather than generating ideas.

The use of social media to spread misinformation during campus disputes can provoke several bad outcomes that may even include shortening the tenure of campus leaders who manage to make their own missteps public or who decide the grief they're experiencing makes the job no longer worth it. Because of reactions like these, several of our former colleagues have told us that they now question whether the benefits of a strong social media presence outweigh its disadvantages.

Although these kinds of statements seldom lead to significant changes in the ultimate outcome of a major institutional restructuring, they illustrate how intensely emotional the process will often become. People are afraid. They are bitter. And they feel abandoned. Financial exigency and its analogues inevitably leave a trail of trauma and hurt for both those directly impacted as well as the decision-makers that cannot be overstated.

COPING WITH RESISTANCE

College leaders who take institutions through a financial restructuring should expect it to be one of the most difficult personal experiences in their professional careers. Every decision will be scrutinized and second-guessed. Old friendships will be lost, as new enemies are made. The conflicts will be public and protracted. Presidents have told us they know they've become a *persona non grata* in academia because of their attempts to manage financial crises. "What university would ever hire me after I decided to cut academic programs and terminate tenured faculty?" is a question we heard more than once from those who've gone through the process. One president's spouse gave this blunt assessment of her husband's status after exigency: "You're toxic."

The negative repercussions from directing a major financial reset cannot be prevented, but they can be anticipated and moderated to some degree. Here are six strategies to consider.

Anticipate the Worst

Coping with the blowback that ensues from a financial exigency begins with campus leaders accurately anticipating how angry and intense the opposition will be. As we have already discussed, the criticisms will often be very personal, they'll come from all directions, and they'll be repeated over and over again. Presidents should not make the mistake of assuming that past campus friendships will insulate them from attack or that rational arguments will convince critics that an institution's financial vulnerabilities have reached a breaking point. Once a financial exigency begins, the gloves will be off.

So, our first piece of advice is simple: Presidents and their loved ones should expect the worst. While that expectation won't prevent traumatic events from happening, it may help take some of the emotional sting out of them. And, while we wish it were not the case, campus leaders also need to be prepared that their personal safety and security might become real concerns during a financial crisis, representing one of the most severe threats they're likely ever to encounter in their careers.

Develop a Confidant

Leading an institution through financial exigency can be a lonely experience. To combat that isolation, presidents need to cultivate a confidant to whom they can turn throughout the ordeal. Whether with a colleague, a mentor, or an outside-of-the-profession friend, the opportunity to vent about one's deepest feelings is key to coping with intense stress. Family members offer this kind of support, but we recommend that someone else outside the president's intimate circle also serve the role of the trusted counselor. Those closest to the decision maker typically do not know all the dimensions of the crisis or who the main antagonists are. They should be shielded from these sources of conflict as much as possible.

Rely on the Data

All the data that we described in Chapter 3 detailing an institution's budget history, its debt, its net costs and productivity, and its cash flows will be called upon again and again as the organized resistance to restructuring takes shape and proceeds. That's one more reason why having these data in hand is so important. They are the ground on which specific terminations, reductions, and reallocations must be defended.

Presidents must know these data inside and out and be ready to respond to challenges by using them to describe—clearly and factually—the institutional conditions giving rise to financial exigency. Presenting these data to different audiences in the most effective way possible is another reason we favor the use of external consultants who have an expertise in framing narratives involving the implications of serious financial crises.

Rebut Inaccuracies

As part of their resistance, opponents of restructuring often make false assertions about the institution, its students, its budget, or its academic programs. Left unchallenged, these inaccuracies can become part of a narrative that's accepted as credible and frequently repeated in the press. Although it is neither possible nor productive to fact-check every erroneous statement, it is advisable to address gross distortions or misstatements, so the public record is as factual as possible. The president should not be the only person making these corrections or clarifications. Other senior administrators, such as the provost, the vice president of administration, the budget chief, and the campus communications team also need to step forward and rectify major falsehoods as promptly as possible.

Don't Respond to Personal Attacks

While fact-checking and record-clearing are effective strategies for dealing with fallacious assertions about the institution, responding to personal attacks is not. Granted, it's very hard to ignore name-calling and mudslinging when you're the target, but responding to such ad hominem attacks will just further fuel the fire and often do more harm than good. Reacting to individual tirades usually accelerates their volume and frequency. Better to let those who engage in smears embarrass themselves before their peers. The most vicious dissenters usually manage to discount themselves as people grow weary of their constant carping. Put simply, when it comes to social media attacks, do not engage. On this score, we agree with a former First Lady, who famously said, "when they go low, we go high."

Focus on the Future

Presidents need to remember that financial exigency is not an institution's ultimate goal. It's not an end in itself. It's a means of not merely preserving an institution, but improving it, making it into a better college, designed to serve students and society more effectively.

Therefore, presidents need to keep their exigency messages focused on the future of the institution—how it will achieve its mission better, how it will enhance the education of its students, how it will reward its productive faculty and staff, how it will make discoveries that improve lives, and how it will become a stronger engine for economic prosperity. We turn to the visioning of that future in the next two chapters.

NOTES

1. https://www.goacta.org/resource/cost-of-excess/
2. https://www.aaup.org/sites/default/files/Academic%20Labor%20Force%20Trends%201975-2015.pdf
3. https://www.aaup.org/sites/default/files/10112018%20Data%20Snapshot%20Tenure.pdf
4. https://www.chronicle.com/article/most-presidents-prefer-no-tenure-for-majority-of-faculty/
5. https://www.insidehighered.com/news/survey/provosts-views-tenure-gen-ed-budgets-and-more
6. https://www.insidehighered.com/news/2020/12/04/boulder-arts-and-sciences-dean-wants-build-back-faculty-post-pandemic-one-non-tenure
7. https://capitol.texas.gov/tlodocs/88R/billtext/pdf/SB00018I.pdf#navpanes=0
8. https://legiscan.com/ND/text/HB1446/2023

9. https://www.myfloridahouse.gov/Sections/Documents/loaddoc.aspx?FileName =_h0999__.docx&DocumentType=Bill&BillNumber=0999&Session=2023

10. Tenured faculty usually retain that status when they become administrators, and when they step down from their administrative post, they often return once again to the ranks of the faculty. That arrangement can introduce compensation excesses when the "retreat" to the faculty is accompanied by former administrators retaining a large percentage of their administrative salary. This is an issue of both fairness and expense, and it can be avoided by a policy that limits post-administrative salaries to some benchmark, such as the median of a department's senior faculty.

11. https://nces.ed.gov/programs/digest/d22/tables/dt22_322.10.asp

12. https://journals.sagepub.com/doi/10.3102/0013189X20933836

13. https://www.house.mn.gov/comm/docs/8YbwMp5jv066hvxWwS7-mg.pdf

14. https://www.chronicle.com/article/whats-behind-the-surge-in-no-confidence -votes

15. https://www.aaup.org/article/2021-aaup-shared-governance-survey-findings -demographics-senate-chairs-and-governance#.ZCbzV-zMKqB

16. https://collegepresidentresearch.uark.edu/2017/12/power-of-the-faculty/

17. https://www.repository.law.indiana.edu/cgi/viewcontent.cgi?article=3160 &context=ilj

18. https://www.aaup.org/our-programs/academic-freedom/censure-list

19. https://arkadelphian.com/2022/05/04/video-chucks-gotta-go/

20. https://www.nwaonline.com/news/2022/may/08/fighting-hsus-financial -firestorm/

Chapter 7

Year Zero

Year Zero begins when an institution that's declared exigency and implemented most or all of the ensuing cost reduction recommendations begins to put itself back together. It represents the starting point for an institution to follow through with its plans to redefine its workforce, reallocate its resources, and redesign new pathways for student success. Year Zero is the time when a college begins to move from what it's been to what it needs to become.

As a result of proceeding with a financial exigency, institutions will have made major cuts in their recurring costs. Academic programs have been closed, tenured faculty have been terminated, the number of administrative and support staff has been reduced, and entire departments may have been eliminated or reconfigured. Now comes the crucial test—how will an institution that's just been through an exigency move forward? What will it define as priorities? Will it be able to recruit new students and retain its current ones? Will donors provide enough gifts to get the institution out of financial trouble? How will it reallocate resources to the educational outcomes that matter the most? Can it overcome its recent crisis? Will its leadership stay in place? How can it partner with other institutions to leverage improvements?

This chapter addresses these and other Year Zero questions, and it reinforces the message that financially imperiled institutions should not wait too long or hesitate to use all the tools available to address a financial crisis. Doing so often increases the risks of financial problems becoming deeper, perhaps precipitating a school's ultimate downfall.

As illustrated in Figure 7.1, the Purposes of Year Zero are for a college to:

- *Recover* from the shocks and emotional turmoil associated with a declaration of exigency.
- *Renew* its mission commitments to students, faculty and staff, and all other constituents.
- *Reallocate* resources to its academic and scholarly priorities.
- *Restructure* its academic programs and reorganize its administrative offices.

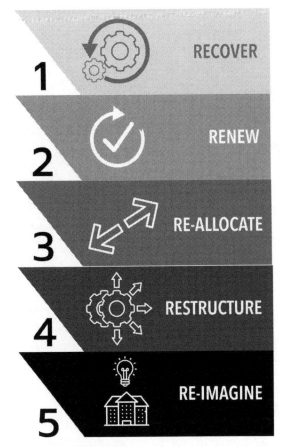

Figure 7.1.   Five Purposes of Year Zero

- *Reimagine* a future where it achieves better outcomes for its students and serves the community more effectively.

Harkening back to our discussion in Chapter 4, Year Zero is when a college emerges from exigency, prepared to realign its resources for long-term success. Financial exigency is not a college's end state, nor its ultimate goal. Financial exigency doesn't solve the high costs of college. It doesn't enhance student learning. It doesn't increase retention or graduation rates. It doesn't lower debt. And it doesn't guarantee that students are any better prepared for life or work after they graduate.

Financial exigency should be understood as a means to an end. Correctly conducted, it begins to balance an institution's academic programs and services with the resources it has available. It's led to difficult decisions to eliminate or reduce operating costs down to a level that balances overall revenue with expenditures. Financial exigency amounts to finding an institution's financial floor. Hitting that floor can hurt. As one president admitted to us, "I knew we were going to hit the floor, and I knew it was going to hurt."

Year Zero is a fragile time. The pre-exigency institution has been changed in multiple ways, and the post-exigency institution has yet to take full shape. The doubters and the critics have not all left. They are working side by side with faculty and staff who are relieved that exigency's tough decisions have been made and now are ready to move the college forward. Many of the faculty whose positions were eliminated will still be on one-year terminal contracts during Year Zero. They remain in place to continue to condemn the exigency decisions and try to undermine them. Some of these faculty will actively discourage new students from enrolling in the institution, and they may advise current students to transfer to another college as soon as they can. Despite these detractors and distractions, college leaders must keep their eyes on the prize and use Year Zero to develop an agenda that's focused on new and renewed priorities. Here are the considerations that we recommend be placed on the front burner.

YEAR ZERO PRIORITIES

Keep a Modified Cash Budget in Place

First and foremost, Year Zero institutions should continue to use a modified cash budget, requiring their expenditures to be balanced with their revenue. They need to keep cash the king. They must continue to focus on cost containment measures and make certain that the first steps of rebuilding don't require spending money the institution doesn't have.

For an institution emerging from a financial exigency, an initial temptation will be to make up for the painful cuts it's just gone through. It's easy to fall back to higher education's traditional ways of staffing institutions, particularly at a school that has recently cut back its staff, resulting in the remaining employees having to shoulder a bigger workload. But that "old normal" workforce model is exactly what helped lead many institutions down the primrose path to their financial brink. Most colleges employ more people than they can afford, and charging students ever increasing tuition or beseeching the state to appropriate more funds to pay for them is not the answer.

Year Zero is the time to validate that an institution has found a sustainable financial floor. Our advice is to keep a hiring freeze in place throughout it, approving only the most well-justified exceptions involving health, safety, and revenue generating activities. No one should be hired or rehired, no academic programs should be added, no additional tuition discounts should be

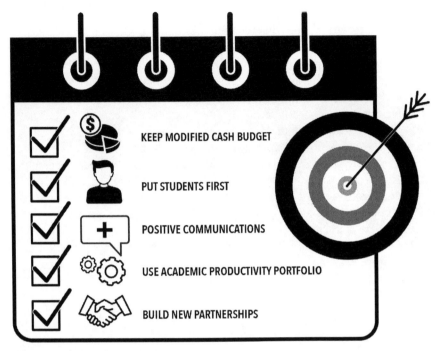

Figure 7.2. Year Zero Priorities

offered, and no new administrative offices should be created without a careful analysis of what each will cost and an understanding of how it will fit within a strategic finance model.

Two questions will inevitably arise in Year Zero. First, will the institution increase its tuition? And second, will continuing employees be given raises? On the tuition question, we recommend against an increase. An institution that's just gone through what is probably its most extensive cost-cutting process in history undercuts its message of greater efficiency and stringency by immediately requiring students to pay more tuition.

The question about raises is more complicated. We caution against giving across-the-board raises because they're incompatible with a state of exigency, and they're sure to cause long-lasting resentments not only among staff who lost their jobs but also for some employees who were retained. Nonetheless, for those remaining employees who have been required to take on additional duties because of a smaller workforce, moderate pay increases, accompanied by a job reclassification, are fair and justified. Those raises will still be criticized and used to argue that the institution was never in a state of true exigency. However, we believe they represent smart investments in a smaller, but hopefully more productive, workforce.

Put Students First

When institutions end academic programs, whether through exigency or other means, they owe their students thorough, timely, accurate information about how the closures will affect them and what their options are for continuing and financing their education.

Most institutions understand this obligation and have guaranteed students that any programs slated for closure because of a financial emergency will be continued for as long as necessary to allow students currently enrolled in them to finish. Usually, the programs are left intact until all current students have completed them. In other instances, a few of the program's requirements will be changed or even waived to accommodate completion more easily. Another common "teach out" arrangement is for the college to negotiate transfer agreements that allow students to re-enroll at nearby institutions to finish their degrees, often at the same tuition rate and accompanied by a special, streamlined process for transferring.

The failure to provide a teach-out plan is one way that a financially faltering institution can lose its accreditation, further imperiling its future. According to a recent discussion of how institutional accreditation can intersect with financial exigency, federal regulations pursuant to the Higher Education Reauthorization Act require that an accredited institution must submit a teach-out plan when "the staff of the accrediting body determines that the institution is at risk for a sudden closure or suspension of its operations because it is in financial distress, under government investigation or facing significant challenges."[1] Those teach-out plans are then subject to approval by the institution's regional accrediting agency.

"Teach out" guarantees are a necessary, but not sufficient, protection of student interests. Students also need policies that allow them easy access to their transcripts and other records that may be necessary for employment or transfer purposes. They need to know if their financial aid will remain in place, if work-study options will be continued, and if their housing and dining contracts will be honored. How will students who want to transfer and are seeking refunds be treated? Will students be able to continue their participation in intercollegiate athletics and other extracurricular activities? Faculty and staff will need to assist students find alternative pathways to completion and help arrange the supports essential to getting them there.

College students demonstrate a strong resilience, resulting in a commitment to their home institutions that often exceeds that of the faculty and staff that serve them. Many students will enroll and remain at an institution they know is in financial trouble. They will stick with it even after accreditors have placed it on probation, and they will persevere through campus scandals and leadership upheavals. To some extent, this loyalty is born from necessity.

Many students are bound by a job or family obligations, requiring that they attend a college near where they live. In other instances, a local institution is simply students' only practical option or their most affordable one, allowing them to pursue their education while living at home or keeping their current job.

What happens to students when a college closes an academic program in which they were enrolled? Do most of them remain at the institution? Do they switch majors or transfer to another college? Or do the majority drop out, adding to the list of casualties from their institution's financial difficulties? The short answer is that we don't know. Very little research exists on this topic. The closest approximation to an answer may come from data showing what happens to students enrolled at institutions that close altogether.

A 2022 study conducted by the National Student Clearinghouse Research Center and the State Higher Education Executive Officers Association provides the most comprehensive answers about the fate of students attending colleges that shut their doors.[2] The study's sample included 467 institutions of higher education that closed between July 1, 2004, and June 30, 2020. Nearly half (49.9%) were in the private, for-profit two-year sector, followed by 28.1% in the private, for-profit four-year sector, and 17.8% in the private, nonprofit four-year sector.

More than two-thirds (68.5%) of the closures took place through a relatively orderly process, meaning that the institutions had teach-out agreements and student record-retention policies in place, and provided adequate notice of the upcoming closure to students. These "orderly closure" institutions tended to be small, enrolling an average of 134 students compared to the schools that closed abruptly without providing teach-out agreement or timely notice, which had an average of 682 students. Compared to institutions that remained open, institutions that closed enrolled larger proportions of students of color (55.0% compared to 46.4%), female students (69.5% compared to 66.1%), and students receiving Pell Grants (54.7% compared to 45.8%).

A total of 143,215 students were attending those institutions that closed. The largest percentage of them were pursuing associate degrees (42.0%), and the majority were enrolled full time (51.5%). Most of the students (82.9%) who experienced a school closure were attending for-profit institutions (46.4% at four-year institutions and 36.5% at two-year institutions).

What happened to students who experienced a college closure? Less than half re-enrolled in another postsecondary institution after the closure (47.1%). Of those who did reenroll, 29.7% did so within one month of the closure, while 26.0% stopped out of college for at least one year. Over one-third of students who re-enrolled managed to earn a postsecondary credential (36.8%); an additional 10.4% were still enrolled when the study concluded. However, most re-enrollees stopped out without earning a credential (52.9%).

Students who re-enrolled within one to four months were the most likely to earn a credential eventually (47.6%), while those who stopped out for more than one year were the least likely to do so (18.7%). Students who had re-enrolled within one to four months took six years on average to complete a degree, while those who stopped out for four to 12 months required 6.9 years to finish their degrees.

Seven out of every 10 students experienced abrupt closures, and they had worse re-enrollment and completion rates than students whose closure experience was more orderly. For example, among students attending private, for-profit four-year schools that closed abruptly, 42.4% re-enrolled at another institution, while 70.1% of students who went through an orderly closure subsequently re-enrolled. Completion gaps by race/ethnicity also were exacerbated by abrupt closures, with larger gaps in degree attainment among abrupt vs. orderly closures, especially for Hispanic (26.4% vs. 43.0%) and Black students (25.3% vs. 39.4%).

These numbers paint a bleak overall picture. Fewer than half of students attending a college that closed ever re-enrolled at a different institution. And of the students who did re-enroll eventually, only 37% had earned a credential. Add it all up and only 17% of students whose education was disrupted by a college closure go on to earn a degree or certificate.

Although the problems for students caused by a financial exigency are not likely to be as severe as those following an outright college closure, the policy implications are still clear. First, the particularly poor outcomes for students experiencing an abrupt institutional closure point to the fundamental need for institutions to monitor their financial status more closely so that students are not suddenly thrown into risk. Second, regardless of whether it involves an institutional or an academic program closure, providing students with complete information about their options and offering them as much academic and personal support as possible are a college's moral duties.

Finally, keep in mind that one of the contributing factors to many financial exigencies like that encountered at Henderson State University is a low student retention rate, reflecting the significant number of students who are at academic risk. In Year Zero, those same students are now being educated in an environment with fewer faculty, staff and student support services. If anything, Year Zero will pose an even larger risk to their academic success. Consequently, it increases the institution's obligation to offer as much guidance and support as possible to those continuing students.

Develop a Positive Communications Outreach

An effective communications strategy is just as important to navigating Year Zero as it was to the original declaration of financial exigency. Many of the same objections to exigency will continue to be aired, and new criticisms will emerge.

- "How can you call yourself a university after you eliminate math, chemistry, and art majors?"
- "You need to get out of that place and come work for us."
- "We've turned into a community college."
- "We're just a trade school now."
- "Who would ever want to enroll at a college that's about to close?"
- "It will be impossible to ever hire new faculty at this place."

Contending with these criticisms will consume a significant amount of Year Zero time and energy, but they must be addressed. Three audiences will require special attention—students; faculty and staff; and outside groups, including business leaders, alumni, local officials, and K–12 school administrators.

Communications with Students

The most immediate, pressing challenges will be to keep current students enrolled and recruit new students to enroll. Detractors and competitors will try to use financial exigency as a reason why students should avoid or flee a college. To counter those messages, the institution must develop a coordinated communications strategy that clarifies financial aid policies and teach-out plans for current students and reassures prospective students about the stability of the institution. This is not a mission impossible. Many colleges that have gone through an exigency or major downsizing find that students are much more inclined to remain loyal to them than anticipated.

Another major push in Year Zero should be to re-recruit and readmit former students, many of whom have withdrawn or "stopped out" of college. Often, they will have done so for financial reasons. In fact, many have been forced out by policies that prevented them from registering for classes because they had unpaid bills. They are included in the college's accounts receivables; at some schools, their names have been sent to collections agencies. In other cases, they've dropped out because of academic problems. And some have left because work or family obligations have required it.

Year Zero is a time for a college to consider various forms of academic redemption or recovery to help these "stop out" students resume their education. These efforts can include college completion grants, which are small awards, often funded by private donors, that enable students who are close to graduation to pay off their outstanding bills and return to school to finish their degree. These grants are ideal for those students who've dropped out because of unpaid balances that in a surprising number of cases do not involve a large amount of money. We discuss them and related policies further in the next chapter.

For other students, offering them what's known as academic bankruptcy may be the right intervention. Academic bankruptcy, sometimes called "academic amnesty," is a policy that allows students who've earned poor grades in one or more semesters to remove some or all of those grades from their academic record. It offers a reset, enabling students to repair a bad cumulative GPA that's resulted in them being placed on probation. Academic bankruptcy affords students a chance at a fresh start and a way to get back on track in their academic career. Institutions have different policies for how and when students can petition for academic bankruptcy, but Year Zero colleges might consider making their policies as accommodating as possible to those students who've been academic casualties during the school's financial struggles.

Finally, some institutions might turn to third parties like ReUp Education, who specialize in finding and re-enrolling former students who've stopped out of school for various reasons.[3] These companies help institutions tailor their messages to encourage adult students to return to school, and they also provide coaches who encourage and advise students about the steps they need to take to access financial aid and re-enroll.

To be most effective, student recruitment and recovery efforts cannot just be the job of the president. They require all hands to be on deck. Faculty involvement is key. Whether it's through their regular advising duties, in-class discussions, or informal interactions, faculty need to show entering, continuing, and returning students that they're committed to their educational success.

The environment for recruiting students is growing ever more competitive as institutions turn to artificial intelligence (AI) and marketing research to refine their outreach and pitches to students. College leaders have learned that AI can do much more than churn out routine prompts and helpful tips to students. They're now using the technology to address some of their major bottom-line problems, such as declining enrollments and high levels of student attrition. Schools emerging from financial exigency can be particularly well-served by such tools.

According to Arijit Sengupta, founder of Aible, a San Francisco-based AI company, colleges and universities are starting to catch up with other industries like banking and health care in using AI to impact key performance indicators.[4] They're turning to these tools to increase their enrollment yield, prevent first-to-second year attrition, target financial aid more specifically, and optimize their fundraising appeals to potential donors.

The approach is straightforward. Once an AI model sorts through the complexity of a large amount of data and detects previously hidden patterns, an institution can focus on how to change their practices to take advantage of what machine learning has suggested in the way of predictions and recommendations. As an example of particular relevance to any Year Zero institution, one private, mid-sized university wanted to increase the percentage of applicants who eventually enrolled at the institution. It was spending thousands of dollars to purchase student prospect lists, and devoting hundreds of hours to calling the students on those lists. But the end result was disappointing—fewer than 10% of the applicants ever officially enrolled in the university.

Instead of "carpet bombing" all the names on the list, Aible was able to generate a model that guided the university toward more precise targeting of students. It identified a subset of applicants who—based on their demographic characteristics, income levels and family history of attending college—were most likely to respond to well-timed recruitment phone calls from the faculty. It also identified the amount of financial aid it would take to influence their enrollment decisions.

It then advised the university to make personal calls to those students along with tailored financial aid offers. The time this intervention took—from identifying and collecting the relevant data, developing the algorithm, and recommending the intervention strategy—was only about three weeks. Preliminary results indicated that the university would see about a 15% increase in its enrollment yield. Likewise, if a college wanted to use its data to improve undergraduate retention, it could rely on an algorithm to identify students who were most likely to leave at specific junctures. The school could then deploy its advisors and counseling center staff to prioritize retention efforts for the most at-risk students.

Student recruitment and enrollment at Year Zero colleges also needs to be informed by the research that shows the most effective ways to contact and communicate with prospective students. While Year Zero institutions are not likely to be able to afford an AI firm or the services of for-profit enrollment management powerhouses like EAB, Ruffalo Noel-Levitz or Niche, they can learn what recruitment techniques work best from the surveys these firms have repeatedly conducted with large numbers of college prospects.

For example, Niche regularly conducts a Senior Enrollment Survey about the process high school students follow when applying to college. As part of its survey in 2022, it received completed responses from 21,866 high school seniors who had registered a profile on its platform.[5] The survey covered several areas, including when and how students went about applying to college, how successful they were in gaining admission, how they approached standardized admissions tests, what kind of financial aid they received, and what factors were most important as they decided where they would attend college.

Among the results are several findings that should interest colleges that have just been through a crisis like financial exigency and now face the challenge of encouraging students to apply despite the negative publicity the college has probably recently received. Here are key examples:

1. *The majority of students begin their college search process after their junior year;* 24% started during the summer before their senior year, 27% during the fall semester of their senior year, and 7% during the spring semester of their senior year. Only 17% of students started their college search before their junior year.
2. *Most students make an in-person visit to at least one college.* Prior to the pandemic, only 7% of students said they had made no in-person visits to a college they were considering. That percentage jumped to 28% in 2021, during the peak of the pandemic. After the pandemic, about 80% of students said they were making at least one in-person campus visit. Even among students from low-income backgrounds, 75% made at least one campus visit.
3. *Emails (75%) and letters (64%) were the communication channels cited by most respondents as influential in their application process.* More than a quarter (26%) of students said they applied to a college they previously hadn't been aware of because of a prospect email they received. Text messaging was the third highest-rated communication, with 40% saying it was influential. Video chats were the fourth highest-rated. Postcards were the least likely to be rated as influential forms of communication.
4. *College websites were the most important source of information used to research colleges* with 90% of respondents reporting them as important. The next most used resources were college search platforms like Niche at 78%, net price calculators at 71%, a visit to the college at 68%, virtual tours at 55%, and virtual events at 51%. The heavy reliance by students on college websites offers an effective, low-cost opportunity for institutions in Year Zero to showcase the messages and data needed and used the most by students.
5. *Family members were cited most frequently as sources of influence on student's college applications (75%).* The next most influential groups were current students at a college at 64%, friends at 61%, and online reviews at 55%. This spells both good and bad news for colleges in Year Zero. On the one hand, students and faculty who've taken and maintained a hostile view of exigency can continue to spread their discontent and discourage students from applying to the institution. On the other hand, many others are eager to move on and build a better college. They can be a persuasive group with prospective students.

6. *Over half of students said that admissions counselors influenced their decision.* Counselors were significantly more influential for Native Hawaiian/Pacific Islander, African American/Black, and Hispanic/ Latinx students. They were also more influential for first-generation students, low-income students, and students reporting a GPA below 3.0. The message is clear: focused outreach to high school counselors needs to occur throughout a financial exigency.

7. *Institutional prestige carries considerable weight with students,* with 62% saying a college's brand and name recognition influenced their decision; only 5% said that it didn't matter to them at all. This factor obviously spells some trouble for colleges suffering from years of financial scarcity. Those that ultimately declare exigency are likely to suffer a degree of reputational damage that will matter to many applicants. That damage may be magnified at institutions that have historically enjoyed a prestigious brand, but now are forced to acknowledge their troubled finances.

8. *Campus diversity matters—a lot.* Diversity was the most important campus community factor, with 84% saying that a diverse student body was appealing, and 46% of those saying that it was a "must-have." Diversity among faculty and staff was also important, with 81% wanting it, and 40% of those saying it was a must-have feature. Matters of diversity were important to students from underrepresented groups (89%) as well as those who were not from underrepresented groups (79%).

9. *Campus distance from a student's home is a factor.* Over half of the students said they considered colleges further than four hours from their home, while 18% reported they only considered colleges within an hour of home. Only 38% of first-generation college students reported considering a college more than four hours from home, compared to 53% of their peers. Family income mattered on this score as well—58% of low-income students considered enrolling in a school more than two hours from home compared to 86% of students from households earning more than $130,000 per year. Geographic proximity can be a positive factor for regional institutions as they begin a Year Zero renewal with a strong focus on recruiting students from nearby communities, coupled with emphasizing their relatively low tuition rates.

10. *Safety was another major concern.* More than 9 in 10 respondents (97%) indicated the importance of on-campus safety, and 96% cited the safety of the town or community around the campus as an important factor.

11. *Applicants are very sensitive to sticker price.* Among the respondents, 81% said they eliminated colleges from consideration and did not apply because of the "sticker price." That's a substantial increase from 73%

who said the same thing in 2021, and the 68% in 2020, and 56% in the pre-pandemic era who eliminated schools based on sticker price. "As college prices go up, so do the scholarships used to make it more affordable for students," said Will Patch, Niche's Senior Enrollment Insights Leader. "However, the pricing for college is so different than anything else that the majority of students are choosing to eliminate colleges from consideration based on the sticker price rather than waiting to see how much aid they receive. Every time the total cost increases, a college eliminates more potential students." First-generation and low-income students are more likely than their peers to say that they would only consider colleges whose total cost was less than $10,000 per year.

Other recent research confirms some of these same considerations as important factors to students making their choices about where to go to college. According to a survey of 2,000 16–19-year-olds conducted in 2023 by *The New York Times* and Morning Consult,[6] the top five most important factors were:

1. Affordable tuition
2. Graduates' high earning potential
3. Low student debt
4. A safe campus
5. A campus near family or hometown

The kinds of four-year colleges that have been most prone recently to severe financial crises are public regional universities and small private institutions that are not highly selective in their admissions policies. These schools tend to charge lower tuition, are often located in small communities known for low crime rates, enroll a high percentage of first generation-to-college students, and are highly familiar to students, families, and employers in the region.

Given how well these characteristics map onto several of the factors highlighted by students as important to their college decision-making, they suggest a recruitment strategy for Year Zero institutions: emphasize affordability, safety, familiarity, and graduates' job placements with local employers. Focus on nearby high schools and two-year institutions, pay special attention to family members, cultivate relationships with high school counselors, use email to communicate with prospects, and emphasize a low tuition sticker price.

One word of warning. Be careful about increasing the amount spent on institutional financial aid. As we've pointed out, an increase in tuition discounts to lure more students to attend is one of the strategies that has contributed to financial problems at many institutions. Year Zero is not the time to double down on a losing tuition discounting proposition. Instead, it requires a careful balancing of financial aid and net revenue, with the goal being to improve an institution's overall cash position with a stabilized enrollment.

Communications with External Groups

Reassuring external audiences about the institution's stability must also be a Year Zero priority. Business leaders, alumni, local officials, and K–12 school administrators all want to know if and how the institution will survive its financial exigency. Are rumors of an imminent closure accurate? Is the college still able to hire faculty and staff? Are faculty fleeing to other schools? How are enrollments holding up? What's happening with fundraising? Where's the college headed?

These are all reasonable questions, and it's imperative they be answered in a forthright manner. Year Zero presidents need to devote a significant percentage of their time to public messaging about the future of the institution. Meetings with the editorial boards of the area's newspapers, appearances on TV and radio, talks to chambers of commerce and service clubs, and visits with groups of alumni should be front and center on the president's calendar. The script for these meetings is clear: "we've made the tough decisions that were necessary, and the college is now much better positioned to move towards a sustainable, better future."

One question that inevitably arises in the aftermath of financial exigency is its impact on fund-raising strategies. Is it a good time to make a push for more private gifts? Or will recent exigency cause donors to hesitate and worry that they shouldn't "throw good money after bad?" The answer to this question depends on institutional specifics, but there are a few rules-of-thumb to bear in mind. First, small private colleges typically have a stronger donor base to turn to than do regional public universities. Second, emergency fundraising is less likely to be successful if it comes on the heels of a recently completed capital campaign rather than being the first campaign to be organized in several years. The correct framing of the campaign is another key consideration. For example, will the theme be to "save the college," or will it be to "make college affordable for all our students."

In Chapter 1, we identified several small, private colleges where last-ditch fundraising proved insufficient to save them from closing. But there have been notable exceptions. Perhaps the best known occurred at Sweet Briar College, a private women's liberal arts college in Virginia, which announced in 2015 that "insurmountable" financial problems and "intractable" enrollment declines would force the college to close, ending its more than 100-year history. Before calling it quits, Sweet Briar's board had considered several alternatives, including merging with another institution and the controversial step of admitting men, but in the end the board decided that none of those options would work. It elected to close the institution.

However, Sweet Briar's alumnae, who claimed they were blindsided by the board's action, fought back. They formed an organization called "Saving Sweet Briar."[7] They filed a lawsuit to keep the school open. And they immediately began to raise money. In three years, they raised $57.3 million, setting new annual records each of those years. Finally, a settlement was worked out based on the Saving Sweet Briar alumnae providing an immediate infusion of $12 million and the Virginia attorney general giving permission for $16 million of restricted money in the endowment to be released for operating funds. The board was replaced, a new president was hired, and Sweet Briar was resurrected.

Sweet Briar's success may be an aberration, however. Its special mission and its extraordinarily loyal alums lent a special resonance to its appeals for money that other schools will probably find difficult to duplicate. Far more common we believe will be those schools whose financial hole is simply too deep to be filled with private donations. While college leaders will be expected to beat the bushes for more private support, fundraising will seldom be a panacea for financially imperiled institutions. At best, it will offer some stopgap support and protection.

Communications with Faculty and Staff

A Year Zero campus community will consist of a mix of faculty and staff who remain divided about the imposition of financial exigency. Some will remain determined to resist it. Others are relieved that the decision was made and are committed to helping the institution rebuild. These are the people who've weathered the crisis, maintained their commitments to students and are resolved to improve their school. While it will be easy to be drawn into disputes with the former group, that temptation should be resisted. Our advice is to focus on the group that's ready to rebuild and rally around the institution. Identify a group of faculty and staff who will be empowered to lead the solutioning process and rely on them to make key restructuring decisions and oversee their implementation.

There are at least two advantages to using such campus "champions." First, it turns their survival mentality into a force for solutions. After years of turmoil and crisis, these individuals often have excellent ideas for how to operate the institution more effectively, and they are eager to see what can be accomplished now that the institution has finally made difficult financial corrections.

Second, institutional changemaking at schools with ample resources is different from changemaking at institutions that are strapped for money. As leaders, college presidents are not inclined to be patient. They want to fire up the engines and start to rebuild the college as soon as possible. They prefer to schedule by a clock, not a calendar. But when they push too hard, expect too much, or accelerate too fast, they risk exhausting people and breaking the institution before it has a chance to be put back together. A leadership group of faculty and staff can act as a restraint on presidential impatience, helping to find the pace of recovery that their institution can tolerate.

Use the Academic Productivity Portfolio

An academic portfolio was a vital tool to move an institution through a financial exigency. It provided a unit cost basis for what programs to keep, change, or eliminate. It charted student demand and quantified program outcomes. In Year Zero the academic portfolio can identify the programs that should be elevated based on student interests and market demand. It also gives colleges the opportunity to reconsider how they organize their curriculum and academic departments and to identify what learning experiences other than traditional classroom instruction they want to emphasize. A comprehensive academic revisioning should involve the following three themes, each of which holds promise, we believe, for institutions that are emerging from financial exigency.

Interdisciplinary Clusters or Meta-Majors. Many institutions that restructure their academic programs have replaced departmental or college silos with a smaller number of units organized around interdisciplinary themes. While such reconfiguring typically saves only a modest amount of money, it does create—at least in theory—a leaner academic structure better attuned to the complexity of human knowledge and understanding. There are dozens of examples of colleges that have consolidated academic departments. Usually, they cite three goals for such institutional flattening: 1) achieving a more integrated curriculum, 2) increasing opportunities for interdisciplinary teaching and research, and 3) reducing administrative costs.

In some cases, the reorganization is as simple as consolidating two or more colleges. For example, as part of a strategy to reduce $5 million in annual operating costs in 2023, Missouri State University combined two colleges—the College of Humanities and Public Affairs and the Judith Enyeart Reynolds College of Arts and Letters—into one college, the Judith Enyeart Reynolds College of Arts and Humanities. Scores of colleges have done something similar in recent years, eventually producing savings from the fact that fewer faculty are being paid for administrative duties like chairing a department or serving as an associate dean of a college and that fewer support staff are necessary to help run the smaller number of remaining units.

- At Marymount University in Virginia, four schools and 26 academic departments were consolidated into three colleges and 10 interdisciplinary units, resulting in 47 faculty no longer having to be paid stipends for administrative work.[8]
- The University of Akron reduced its number of colleges from 11 to five, as it looked for ways to save $65 million in operating costs after the pandemic.[9]
- Generally, when a college restructures its academic programs, it intends for the new organization to achieve a greater coherence among a set of programs that were previously housed separately. As part of the financial exigency at Henderson State University, more than 50 disciplines and programs, many with their own administrators, were consolidated around four "meta-themes": Applied Professional Science and Technology; Arts and Humanities; Business Innovation and Entrepreneurship; and Health, Education, and Social Sustainability.
- HSU modeled its plan on a similar reconfiguration designed at Plymouth State University, one of the public universities in New Hampshire. Facing a 16% decline in its enrollment, Plymouth State reorganized all its academic units around seven clusters:[10] Arts and Technologies; Education, Democracy and Social Change; Exploration and Discovery; Health and Human Enrichment; Innovation and Entrepreneurship; Justice and Security; and Tourism, Environment, and Sustainable Societies.

Project-Based Learning. Institutions looking to restructure their academic portfolio also can reexamine their traditional reliance on classroom instruction and replace or supplement some of it with more immersive, active forms of learning. An excellent example is project-based learning, an inductive form of teaching where students learn concepts and skills by studying and solving real-world questions and problems. While project-based learning has usually been associated with elementary and secondary education, most frequently in STEM disciplines through such excellent curricula as Project Lead the Way,[11] it has now made inroads into undergraduate education as well.

In the past, higher ed tended to dismiss project-based as merely "learning by doing," but that trivialization is giving way to an appreciation that problem-based pedagogy can help college students develop both conceptual abilities and practical skills. Frankly, these purist objections to project-based-learning strike us as highly odd. Who, for example, objects to the fact that their dentist or internist "learned by doing" throughout their clinical training and internships?

Project-based learning is at the core of the curriculum at the highly respected Worcester Polytechnic Institute (WPI),[12] where first-year students take a two-term Great Problems Seminar that requires them to study and come up with solutions to global problems such as infectious diseases, energy shortages, and urban growth. Later in WPI's curriculum, an Interactive Qualifying Project has students work as multidisciplinary teams to solve specific problems.

Other institutions like Purdue University, Iowa State University, and the University of Wisconsin have all expanded their use of problem-based methods. The University of Illinois partnered with EduSourced, a software platform specializing in project-based learning, to launch a public health collaboration between students, alumni, and officials from the World Health Organization/Pan-American Health Organization. Housed at the University's Center for Health Informatics,[13] the collaboration focuses on assisting public health agencies address local health problems by matching them with students who have the requisite analytic and data science skills to study such issues.

These examples illustrate a larger point—an academic restructuring need not only be concerned with putting an institution on a firmer financial footing. It can also be the time when a college explores new educational ground and many new forms of pedagogy such as hybrid classes, flipped classrooms, learning cohorts, and service-learning communities, all of which have been found to be cost-effective ways to boost student learning at many institutions, regardless of their financial standing.

Internships, Apprenticeships and Capstone or Competency-Based Experiences. Year Zero gives institutions a chance to survey how often their students have opportunities to engage in" high-impact learning practices," a term that comes from the National Survey of Student Engagement (NSSE), which has been administered periodically to ask college students about how often they participated in activities such as internships, study abroad, and capstone experiences.[14]

NSSE's founding director, George Kuh, promoted the concept of student engagement as an important factor in student learning and an indicator of educational quality. According to Kuh, student engagement involves a family of activities requiring students to devote more time and energy to educationally purposeful activities than what often occurs in the typical college classroom. These activities modify the role of faculty members, replacing the "sage on the stage" with the "guide at the side." Properly conducted with active guidance and frequent mentoring from faculty, high-impact experiences like internships, apprenticeships and capstone projects increase the active engagement of students in their education, and because they usually carry academic credit, they can substitute for some course requirements, thereby easing the increased teaching loads that Year Zero faculty would otherwise be forced to shoulder. The evidence suggests that students who engage in an active learning experience outside of the classroom will be more likely to persist year-to-year and complete their degree.

A shift to competency-based education could be facilitated by greater acceptance of assessments that evaluate what students know how to do and whether they have the skills that today's employers are looking for—the ability to communicate clearly, think critically, and work collaboratively. Just such a move is underway, exemplified by the Carnegie Foundation for the Advancement of Teaching and the Educational Testing Service announcing in 2023 that they were teaming up to develop new ways to evaluate competency-based learning.[15] The partnership between these two well-respected organizations aims to work with practitioners and policymakers "to create a robust, scalable suite of assessment and analytic tools that captures the full range of skills required for American students to succeed in K–12, postsecondary education and beyond."

Since 1906, the Carnegie Unit or "credit hour" has defined what counts as learning and determined the basic organization of secondary and postsecondary education. Although "seat time" has served as the time-honored, primary definition of student learning in college, it's becoming ever clearer that mere time on task is not a good measure of students' content knowledge or skill mastery. As Carnegie Foundation President Timothy F. C. Knowles acknowledged, "Current assessments fail to capture what we know matters most, and do not provide key stakeholders—students, parents, and educators—with the insights they need to accelerate learning. How we demonstrate progress must become competency-based, and families and educators should be supported by assessments that capture learning whether it occurs in the classroom, after school, on a farm, in the workplace, or in an internship."

Year Zero institutions should be the among the first to welcome an emphasis on skill-based rather than time-based learning. To be sure, such a shift will take time to penetrate various higher education traditions, but it affords colleges a long-term strategy not only to improve their financial bottom line, but also to increase their graduate's competitiveness for good jobs.

Build New Partnerships

Institutions cannot move through Year Zero on their own. It's very difficult to put all the pieces back together to arrange for sufficient staff coverage, build a class schedule, offer a full curriculum, and fulfill the teach-out obligations owed to students without the help of partners. It's next to impossible to eliminate dozens of academic programs along with many of their personnel within an academic year or less without partnerships to fill in the instructional and student support holes that were created. The following five types of partnerships can help bridge many of those gaps on an immediate basis, and in some cases, they offer longer-term solutions.

Explore becoming part of a university system. A potential system partner can provide resources and support that are very difficult to afford as a stand-alone institution. (A related option for private institutions is to pursue a merger or acquisition partner.) While this option exists only in states where at least some of the public institutions are organized into a system, it opens the door to many new resources through other universities that are already predisposed to work together with common systems and structures. Shared courses and instructors are the immediate academic partnerships that a system can provide. But legal, financial, procurement, and HR services are the other types of administrative support that can be gained by joining a system. They are also areas where Year Zero institutions are most likely to have lost significant capacity by virtue of attrition, retirements, and/or staff reductions.

Find a partner with significant online resources. A larger institution with a significant online portfolio of courses and instructors and the technology necessary to deliver virtual instruction is a very cost-effective solution to the immediate gaps in a curriculum that are caused by financial exigency. We are aware of the limitations and mixed reactions associated with the various forms of virtual instruction that reached a peak as a necessary measure during the Covid-19 pandemic.

As with any instructional method, online learning comes with positives and negatives, and researchers are starting to learn more about it, particularly the conditions under which it works well or poorly. According to one summary, "Much of the pre-pandemic research into online higher education concluded that students in online programs did worse than students in in-person courses, with lower grades, higher dropout rates, and poorer performance in subsequent classes. On average, outcomes were especially bad for men, Black students, and students who had fared poorly in their earlier educations."[16] However, much of that research also suffered from various confounds that made it difficult to draw firm conclusions. For example, prior to the pandemic, students who took courses online were more likely to be part-time rather than full-time, and they were also more likely to be employed than students taking in-person classes. Those differences raise the possibility of a significant self-selection bias that could affect the results.

The pandemic eliminated much of any self-selection bias since almost all college students were forced to go online for their classes. Some preliminary post-pandemic research results about virtual education have tended to be a bit more positive. For example, online instruction appears to be most effective in large introductory classes perhaps because the technology allows students to engage in chatrooms and other virtual interactions, facilitating more engagement with the material than occurs in many large lectures. On the other hand, students in small classes like online instruction less, believing that it deprives them of the personal interactions that should be—but are not always—a hallmark of such classes.

While there is still a lot of skepticism about online classes by both faculty and students, there is also a recognition that its quality should not be judged based on its use and reception during the pandemic, when learning with any modality was jeopardized by multiple kinds of disruptions and chaos. We expect that the use of online instruction will increase, and we expect that acceptance of it will improve as both faculty and students become more adept at it. Colleges of all sorts have had lots of experience with blended learning formats where basic content is provided online and discussions and lab sections are conducted live. Those kinds of hybrid learning environments are likely to become more common at all kinds of institutions.

Develop a partner in close geographical proximity. Neighboring institutions often have a history of sharing resources. In the case of Henderson State University, instructional resources were immediately offered by its neighbor across the street—Ouachita Baptist University. In its first Year Zero semester, HSU had 80 students enroll in courses at OBU. HSU's financial crisis had opened the door for the two institutions to develop a deeper partnership that proved to be a win-win for both schools. Both universities benefitted from reducing their instructional costs and eliminating some duplication of services.

Technology enables partnerships to extend beyond institutions that are located close to one another. For example, dozens of private institutions have formed a collaboration called the Lower Cost Models Consortium. It allows small colleges across the country to partner and offer high-demand majors that they would otherwise be unable to offer by sharing online access to the courses necessary for degrees in fields like computer science or public health.[17] Hundreds of other small institutions are using technology to share courses through organizations like the Council of Independent Colleges.[18]

Work directly with a two-year college partner. Four-year institutions have much to learn from community colleges about delivering cost-effective curricula and providing support to students from all sorts of backgrounds. They are adroit at accomplishing a lot with scarce resources. A Year Zero partnership between two-year and four-year schools offers opportunities for course sharing, shared advising, the creation of seamless transfer opportunities and several other kinds of articulations.

We will have more to say about collaborations between two-year and four-year institutions in the next chapter, but for now we want to emphasize that the new ecology of higher education favors more and more inter-institutional interactions. An increasing number of students take courses from both community colleges and four-year schools, interspersed throughout their higher education journeys. The wise Year Zero college administrator will try to maximize those numbers as well as search for other ways to leverage the resources of their colleagues in the two-year sector.

Develop new partnerships with employers. An effective and affordable way for a restructured college to build back a curriculum is to form new educational collaborations with private employers. This kind of partnership enables a Year Zero college to combine traditional degree offerings with industry-directed training that's tied directly to internships and employment opportunities following graduation.

An excellent example is TechWise an 18-month virtual program offered by Talent Sprint and supported by Google.[19] The program is intended for students pursuing tech majors or minors at community colleges and minority-serving four-year institutions. It's fully funded by Google, including all tuition for the program plus a scholarship of $5,000 to help cover basic expenses while a student is in the program. The curriculum, which emphasizes preparation for entry-level positions in software engineering, consists of three courses—Computational Thinking, Web Basics, and Advanced Data Structures and Algorithms—plus three immersive projects conducted under the supervision of Google mentors. Upon completion, students earn a TechWise certificate in addition to whatever traditional degree they complete.

The initial TechWise cohort consisted of only 120 students nationwide, but the potential for curricula that are co-designed by universities and employers to attain a much larger scale is obvious. National employers can build large networks of university providers, and smaller companies can put together partnerships with local or regional institutions.

This merger of work and education has been in the making for several years and now there are countless examples of traditional college curricula being successfully supplemented with skill-specific training at the same time. These partnerships demonstrate that the question of whether it's better for high school graduates to obtain a college degree or earn an industry certificate is a false dichotomy. Year Zero colleges need to move toward a "both/and" solution rather than clinging to an "either/or" position, and partnerships with employers offer one vehicle for doing so.

There are challenges to designing such partnerships to be sure. Faculty and employers speak difference languages about education and workforce readiness, and there are important questions about the ultimate responsibilities for designing and delivering partnered curricula, selecting and evaluating students, and predicting and filling talent gaps. All these matters can be resolved, however, if three simple principles are followed: 1. The partnership has the backing of the university president and the business's chief executive officer from its outset. 2. Both parties put student interests first when designing all elements of the collaboration. 3. The curriculum—including both formal course content and practical, hands-on experience—is based on empirical data about workforce needs.

In this chapter we've described the key issues and tasks facing institutions as they emerge from a financial exigency. Year Zero is the time when an institution begins to find its footing on a new financial floor, discovering what it needs to discontinue and what it needs to emphasize as it steps up from that floor. Using Henderson State University as an example, even though its leadership changed, it emerged from Year Zero repositioned to be a productive, public residential college that had proven its capacity for innovating and for making the hard financial decisions now facing many institutions. It was ready for its next chapter.

Year Zero can be thought of as a bridge from an institution that could no longer afford its total academic portfolio to one that focuses on the education it can deliver effectively and efficiently. In the next and final chapter, we extend that discussion further and examine several educational policies and practices that can help financially stressed institutions become better colleges, designed to serve their students and communities well.

NOTES

1. S. Green, P. Boyles, and C. Wright (2018). Accrediting and degree authorization during financial exigency: Communicating with state and regional agencies. In S. Green (Ed.), *Declaring Financial Exigency in Higher Education; How Do You Recover?* New York: Nova Science Publishers.

2. https://nscresearchcenter.org/wp-content/uploads/SHEEO-NSCRCCollegeClosuresReport.pdf

3. https://reupeducation.com

4. https://www.forbes.com/sites/michaeltnietzel/2022/10/01/colleges-are-turning-to-artificial-intelligence-to-improve-enrollment-and-retention/?sh=4e42342d1285

5. https://www.niche.com/about/enrollment-insights/2022-niche-senior-enrollment-survey-the-new-normal/

6. https://www.nytimes.com/2023/03/27/opinion/problem-college-rankings.html

7. https://sbc.edu/news/defining-leadership/

8. https://narratives.insidehighered.com/academic-restructuring/index.html

9. https://www.uakron.edu/oaa/initiatives/redesigning-ua/final-report

10. https://www.plymouth.edu/academics/our-learning-model/

11. https://www.pltw.org
12. https://www.wpi.edu/project-based-learning
13. https://research.illinois.edu/researchunit/center-health-informatics
14. https://nsse.indiana.edu/nsse/index.html
15. https://www.ets.org/news/press-releases/carnegie-foundation-ets-partner-to-transform-the-educational-pillars-they-built.html
16. https://hechingerreport.org/what-researchers-learned-about-online-higher-education-during-the-pandemic/
17. https://www.thelcmc.org/
18. https://www.cic.edu/member-services/online-course-sharing-consortium
19. https://techwise.talentsprint.com/faq.html#faq10

Chapter 8

Beyond Exigency

BECOMING A BETTER COLLEGE

Financial exigency need not be the deathblow to a college. Contrary to the common wisdom, institutions can cut their spending and still achieve educational success if they rebuild smartly at the same time. The long-term goal is to develop a new financial model that puts student success first and that's sustainable for a future where the demand for and the funding of many institutions remain uncertain at best. Although this model might originate in the severe financial emergencies experienced by colleges on the brink, we believe it can be replicable at many other institutions that need to reduce their expenditures, albeit not at the extreme level involved in financial exigency. As an example, we point to E. Gordon Gee, president of West Virginia University, who told his campus in 2023 that as its enrollment dropped, it needed to brace for budget cuts as large as $75 million in the near future. "When we put our students first, it brings everything into context," according to Gee. "It crystallizes our priorities. And it shines a light on those things that may no longer be relevant."[1]

For years, higher education has focused on the importance of students being "college-ready." In this concluding chapter, we suggest that the script needs to be flipped to the need for colleges becoming more "student-ready." The question then becomes how do we re-imagine a college that's financially stable and that works for all students? How do we promote student access to the education they and their communities need and, at the same time, help them succeed?

Building a "better college" will require several changes, including a constant focus on how resources are allocated, an emphasis on making the university a learning community that works for all students, greater attention to student success, more effective use of educational technology, and the expansion of partnerships with K–12 educators and private employers.

This kind of turnaround requires internal capacity, external support, and determined leadership. With those elements in place, important improvements in how colleges operate are possible. Now, as we suggest in this chapter, the task becomes one of persuading colleges—both those that are facing immediate financial problems and those that are relatively financially secure—to face up to that challenge.

THE STUDENT-READY COLLEGE

What are the qualities of a student-ready college, and how can all institutions serve students better? We define a student-ready college as one that achieves excellent outcomes for students in a timely manner and does so equally for all of them, regardless of their background. Therefore, the business model for higher education should no longer be defined primarily by how many students enroll in college. Instead, as we've argued in previous chapters, student success should be understood in term of how well colleges perform three basic jobs that students hire—and society pays—them for:

1. Opening the doors of access to advanced education
2. Providing students with the support necessary to complete their degrees
3. Equipping students with the knowledge and skills they need to be effective citizens who are also economically successful.

Colleges in financial difficulty are likely to be experiencing difficulties in each of these areas. Their enrollments have declined. Too many of their students are dropping out before earning their degree. Many have taken on educational loans, leaving them saddled with debt they cannot afford to pay back. And prospective employers are often dissatisfied with the skills of recent graduates, finding them to be lacking the basic competencies needed for entry-level positions and long-term career success.

Although these problems are not confined to colleges that are in, or near, financial exigency, they can be expected to be most severe in those circumstances. In this chapter, we discuss ten policies and practices that we believe can help all colleges put student success at the forefront and that can help institutions improve their financial standing. We organize these policies around the three basic imperatives we've previously identified for every college: increasing access, helping students earn their degrees, and making sure students learn what they need to know to become effective and productive citizens.

INCREASING ACCESS

Financially endangered colleges face a serious dilemma. Almost all of them have suffered steep declines in enrollment and desperately need to turn those numbers around, but they don't have many resources to invest in solutions. They won't be able to hire a large cadre of new recruiters or admission officers. They can't afford to increase institutional financial aid to "buy" more students; and often, that's the exact strategy that precipitated or aggravated their financial downturn. They won't be able to finance fancy new residence halls or recreation centers to attract students. And they are not in a position to add new undergraduate programs or graduate degrees to broaden their missions. Despite these limitations, colleges emerging from financial exigency have several options for recovering enrollments. Here are four relatively low-cost, low-risk strategies to consider.

Expand K–16 Pathways

One of the most promising approaches for a college to regain enrollment is to increase the opportunities for high school students to interact with its faculty and students. Building early interest in and identification with an institution can give it an advantage when it comes to students' eventual enrollment decisions. Another advantage of "early college" experiences is that they're not very expensive either for students or colleges. In fact, because students can accumulate a substantial number of college credits while still in high school, early college programming can achieve a double win: decreasing students' total costs of attending college, while at the same time lowering an institution's instructional expenditures.

Dual enrollment is the best-known example of a program that allows high school students to take a college course and simultaneously earn both high school and college credit.[2] In general, the evidence suggests that dual enrollment has a positive impact on a range of outcomes, including high school graduation rates, college enrollment, college success, and college completion rates. Its use is widespread. Approximately 88% of high schools offer dual enrollment, and 34% of U.S. students take at least some college courses in high school.[3]

Historically, however, dual enrollment opportunities have been less available at schools that serve lower-income communities and communities of color. Even when they are available, students from these communities tend to participate in them less often. Emphasizing outreach to those same communities could enable struggling institutions to close disparities in educational access at the same time they enlarge their recruiting base. One national program has already shown how to do it.

The Education Equity Lab is the brainchild of Leslie Cornfeld, a former federal civil rights prosecutor and later an advisor to New York Mayor Michael Bloomberg and two U.S. Secretaries of Education. Since its founding in 2019, Ed Equity Lab has become one of the nation's leading models for preparing low-income and underrepresented minority students to enroll and succeed in college. It follows a simple plan: deliver and support college credit-bearing courses taught by faculty from leading colleges and universities in teacher-led high school classrooms, at no cost to the students.[4]

Here's how it works. Local school districts are invited to participate, and they select Title I schools to host the courses. Principals pick the high school teachers who will assist the college faculty offer the course, and they also select the students—typically about 25 per course. Many Ed Equity Lab high schools offer multiple courses—meaning students can graduate with a semester or more of transferable credits under their belts, resulting in substantial tuition savings. The students—mostly juniors and seniors, but sometimes exceptional sophomores—are selected based on their academic record as well as teachers' nominations of those believed to have the potential to succeed.

The courses are offered as dual enrollment classes where students receive both college and high school credit. They are taught by 1) the college faculty member, who delivers the lectures asynchronously via video, and holds office hours via Zoom; 2) a high school teacher who co-teaches the course; and 3) a graduate or undergraduate student who functions like a college teaching assistant responsible for leading a weekly live discussion section and helping the professor grade exams and other class requirements.

Ed Equity Lab delivers and supports all aspects of the model, including onboarding schools and universities, conducting orientations and trainings for teachers and teaching fellows, and organizing virtual events and career and college advising sessions. Students can take the courses for free. School districts pay $250 per student per class, a discounted rate that's made possible by the universities' generous pricing and the considerable underwriting that Ed Equity has been able to attract from private foundations and individual donors.

As of 2023, Ed Equity Lab's partners included Morehouse College, Princeton University, Stanford University, Georgetown University, Cornell University, Wesleyan University, Barnard College, the Wharton School at the University of Pennsylvania, Spelman College, Brown University, Howard University, Arizona State University, and the University of California system. Since launching its first course — "Poetry in America: The City From Whitman to Hip-Hop"[5] taught online by Harvard Professor Elisa New, Ed Equity's program has expanded dramatically. By the end of 2023, it will have reached over 15,000 students in more than 100 school districts across 29 states. The program's goal is to be in 25% of the nation's Title 1 high schools by 2025 and to reach more than one million students in the next decade. The curriculum has expanded as well, with more than 30 courses offered so far. For example, students can enroll in a Personal Finance course offered by Wharton faculty, an Introduction to Computer Science by Stanford, Environmental Studies from Howard, or a Psychology course at Penn.

Through the Spring 2023, 80% of students completing a Lab course have passed it, making the courses eligible for college credit at most colleges. Many students take—and pass—multiple classes, giving them a strong start on their college degrees. Early results show that Ed Equity Lab alumni are better prepared to succeed in college. "Our preliminary data show our students are enrolling in four-year institutions and going out of state to attend at higher rates than similarly situated students," said the Lab's Chief Academic Officer, Ariel Murphy Bedford.

Michaell Santos, a student from the Bronx and president of the Ed Equity Lab Alumni Society, is a great example of the program's impact. After completing five Ed Equity Lab college courses, Michaell was accepted to Yale University, where he plans to major in political science. According to Michaell, "since my junior year, the lab has given me countless opportunities and has allowed me to grow as a student and person . . . The National Education Equity Lab made me realize that I could be successful outside of my South Bronx bubble."

Another example of a well-designed high-school-to-college pathway is the University of Central Missouri's Innovation Campus, a program that former President Barack Obama lauded as a laboratory for innovation when it launched in 2012. A partnership between the University of Central Missouri, the Lee's Summit R-7 School District, Metropolitan Community College and dozens of local business partners, the Missouri Innovation Campus (MIC) illustrates a model for an accelerated pathway to college that integrates secondary and postsecondary education and focuses on student outcomes and workforce needs.[6]

Beginning in their junior year in high school, students in the MIC take specific college courses offered either through the University of Central Missouri or Metropolitan Community College in addition to their regular high school courses. This dual enrollment enables them to earn an Associate's Degree shortly after they graduate from high school, and it puts them on an accelerated schedule to earn a Bachelor's Degree in just two years after high school, allowing them to enter the workforce and start their careers sooner.

Six academic programs are offered:

- Bachelor of Science in Design and Drafting Technology—Associate Degree: Engineering Technology
- Bachelor of Science in Computer Science—Associate Degree: Computer Science and Information Systems, Software Development emphasis
- Bachelor of Science in Cybersecurity
- Bachelor of Science in Software Engineering
- Bachelor of Science in Business Administration—Big Data and Business Analytics
- Bachelor of Science in Business Administration—Computer Information Systems

During their enrollment in the MIC, students also complete a three-year, paid internship at one of the dozens of Kansas City area businesses that are partners in the program. Students begin their internships the summer after their junior year of high school with a paid, eight-week, 40-hours-per-week internship. The internship occurs each summer, as well as two days a week during the fall and spring semesters, until the student graduates from the university. The internships serve a dual purpose. First, they give students real-world training and supervised experience that's fully integrated with their academic curriculum. Second, the MIC business partners benefit by being better positioned to hire well-educated employees with skills aligned to the needs of the individual company. Through the internship experience, business partners can interact with students, shape their skills, and determine if they would be a good fit for the company, reducing their training and hiring costs.

Offer Direct Admissions

An increasing number of colleges and universities are experimenting with a new admissions strategy to boost enrollments and increase student diversity. It's called direct admissions, a process where colleges make offers of admission—sometimes with promises of financial aid, sometimes without—to students without requiring them to go through a lengthy admissions process first.[7] Think of it as a flipped system, like receiving notice of a pre-approved mortgage. Here are the basics. A student first creates and posts a profile, including information like grades, test scores, location, interests, and other college-relevant information. Participating colleges then evaluate those profiles and extend admission offers without requiring students to go through the traditional admission hassles of obtaining letters of recommendation, writing an essay, and filling out multiple application forms.

A company named Concourse, founded in 2016 and subsequently acquired in 2022 by education consulting firm EAB, was one of the first to enter this market. It created an online platform for students to submit their

VOICES FROM THE FIELD: JEFFREY SCARBOROUGH AND QUINN COSGROVE

Jeffrey Scarborough is a 2020 graduate of the University of Central Missouri (UCM), with a BS in cybersecurity. He's currently working on his MBA at UCM. An early participant in the Missouri Innovation Campus (MIC) program, Scarborough is a Senior Security Analyst with Cyderes, a cybersecurity company headquartered in Kansas City. We interviewed him about his impressions of the MIC.

When did you first learn about the MIC?
I first heard about MIC when I was a freshman in high school, although I think my parents might have heard about it sooner. I attended an open house at Summit Technology Academy with the Lee's Summit School District and heard Stan Elliot (the director of the MIC) talk about accelerated degree programs. I remember him saying this won't be easy, and it's not for everyone. I had always been interested in technology in general, but when I heard about the new programs available through the MIC, that's when I really started to fall in love with that career path.

How did MIC change your college and career plans?
My family had always expected me to go to college, but which degree and what major was not clear at the time. I knew I wanted to study technology, but being able to dive into all the broad fields of IT and learn more about specialties in IT really helped define what I wanted to focus on. Today, there are so many options within IT.

How did the internship play into your plans?
It was absolutely an enticement to join the program. It gave me real-world experience early on. I had a chance to interview with several companies in the Kansas City area, an opportunity to have a three-year internship, and the chance to learn first-hand from the professionals on the team. I never expected to have a paid internship in high school, and it changed my ideas about the traditional college route that required four years to complete a degree.

What were the best and worst features of the MIC program?
The best feature was the internship and the chance to learn real-world experience with my mentors about cybersecurity. I had the

chance to work on contracts for a federal department during my internship, and that was a unique opportunity for me.

The downside was that I missed out on some of the usual high school and college experiences that you have when you go through the traditional four-year high school, four-year college sequence. But having said that, I also made lifelong friends through the MIC. Our cybersecurity cohort still hangs out often.

What do you think you saved as a result of the MIC?

Well, it saved me financially for sure. Having the paid internship helped me afford college, along with the scholarships I received. But what it really saved me was time. Being able to work and go to school in parallel saved me a lot of time compared to what it would have taken to do them one at a time. I graduated from college and entered the workforce at age 20. I had the fundamentals of IT under by belt, but, in addition, with my three years of internship experience, I was ready to work with people who had spent years in the field.

Can you describe the quality of learning you experienced at MIC?

I really valued being able to take college classes taught in person by college professors while I was still in high school and have those classes count for both high school and college credit. I had never heard of that possibility before. It was such a unique way to learn. The workplace was our classroom too because I worked on government contracts with five to six security professionals, each one with their own specialty. For me to be able to bounce around between each of them really helped me learn about all the issues in cybersecurity—from fundamentals to governance to policy.

What are you doing now?

I was an intern for three years, working on one contract with SAIC. I graduated from UCM in 2020 and started working full time on the same contract. I was able to work on another contract, but once it was complete, I joined Cyderes, Cyber Defense and Response. That's a local cybersecurity organization in the Kansas City area, and I'm working in a global security operations center and training our new analysts. I'm very optimistic about what else I can do with my cybersecurity skills in the future. I couldn't be more excited to see what the future holds, maybe something more technical, maybe something managerial.

I remember my first impression of the MIC program was being nervous about whether I would be able to do it. I was worried it might be too hard, but now after completing the program, I can look back on it and think, "I shouldn't have been worried."

Quinn Cosgrove was in the first cohort of students that entered the Missouri Innovation Campus (MIC). He is a 2016 graduate of the University of Central Missouri, majoring in systems engineering, following his earning an A.S. degree in computer and information sciences from Metropolitan Community College in Kansas City. He currently works as a principal technology consultant for ProActive Solutions in Mission, Kansas.

Quinn, do you remember the first time you heard about the MIC?

I do remember it. I was a junior at Lee's Summit West High School. I remember thinking, "It's too good to be true." It hit me that if I joined the program, I was going to get a subsidized education and that it would give me a chance to get into a career field that was growing all the time. I also remember that I could avoid the four-year college hamster wheel and earn a degree along with a lot of work experience at the same time. And I remember you, President Ambrose, telling us that the MIC would give us a chance at going to college without any debt, and you weren't lying. Here I am ten years later, without any student debt to pay.

Did you have any hesitation about joining the MIC?

It was really a no-brainer for me. I had always been interested in technology so being able to fast-track my education in something I was already drawn to made a lot of sense. I was ready to rock and roll.

What were the pros and cons of the MIC in your view?

There were both, but the pros definitely outweighed the cons. On the pro side my education was being paid for, and I was able to gain all this hands-on experience at the same time I was going to school. Those were clearly the most positive benefits and what swayed me to stick with it.

On the negative side, it takes a lot of work. Going to school at night and working in the internship is not what every 17-year-old kid dreams of. That was difficult. It can be daunting. I vividly remember a point in time when I wanted to drop out and be with my friends who had gone away to college and were partying and having a lot of fun. But I had a conversation with someone at Metro Community College who sat my ass down and let me know what was important. So I stuck with it, and now I'm glad for that decision.

One other big positive is that I got to shake hands with President Obama when he came to visit the program. I will never forget that moment. It was one of the coolest experiences of my life. I don't think I've ever looked so stone-cold, straight-faced for a handshake in my life.

Do you remember what President Obama asked you?
I don't.

He asked you if you were going to work at DST for the rest of your life, and you said "I don't think so but I'm going to be a lot more competitive with this experience." That's quite an answer for a high school student to the President of the United States. It was probably one of my (Ambrose) most favorite moments as an educator to be honest.

What do you think the MIC saved you?
Oh man, in monetary terms you're looking at six figures, because not only do you have to consider the money you saved, there is also the money you're generating. I think at the peak of my internship I was making about $20 an hour, and then I got a full-time job while my friends were still in college trying to finish out their degrees. To know my friends were digging a hole of $60–80K in college debt, and I didn't have any, I felt like the richest guy in the world. It was invaluable, really.

How would you describe the balance between learning in the classroom and the internship?
Like most things in life, you can learn something but until you've experienced it or touched it you don't have the full appreciation or understanding of it. No offense to the education system, but I learned more on the job than in the classroom. I learned a ton of the foundational or conceptual aspects of technology in the classroom, but then I show up for work on Tuesday and run into a problem that correlates to what I learned in the classroom. Having those two things tied together amplified the quality of information I acquired.

I also volunteered to help with the internship program after I completed my degree. In a very short period of time, I was on both sides of the education/work spectrum. Many times, I was younger than the new interns I was talking to.

What are you doing now?
After graduating, I joined DST Systems as a general systems administrator. I left there in 2018 and went to Cerner where I first worked as a systems engineer, doing a lot of automation and then cloud computing. And then almost out of nowhere I got an opportunity to move to ProActive Solutions, where I now do presentations for potential customers. So I've moved from the backend of IT to the business side of IT. I started in a corporate environment when I was 17 so I was able to learn early and get polished sooner than most graduates. And all the other MIC students I keep in touch with have their bearings about them and are excelling.

profiles, which are certified by the students' counselor, a teacher or principal. Universities are then presented with anonymized versions of the profiles that match their admission criteria, and they decide whether to make proactive offers of admission and financial aid to prospects who meet their criteria. While universities sign a commercial agreement with Concourse to participate, there is no fee charged to high schools or counselors. Students are charged a fee to create a profile, but that fee can be waived based on financial need. Colleges participating with Concourse also waive their application fees. If they are accepted, students are under no obligation to accept the offer.

As of 2023, Concourse had about 125 colleges making direct admission offers, and now other companies are introducing their versions of direct admissions, joining a handful of states that also have experimented with a direct admissions policy. Idaho was one of the first states to introduce a direct college admissions program, rolling it out in 2015.[8] Initial evaluations show that it yielded an increase in first-time undergraduate enrollments by more than 8% and in-state student enrollments by almost 12%.

The Common Application (Common App) began piloting a direct admissions program in 2021, offering admission to students who create a Common App account but have not yet completed all their open applications. In an early version of the pilot, six participating colleges offered admission to 18,000 students, and over 800 students accepted the offer. The impact of the pilot was strongest for Black, Latinx, and first-generation students, according to Common App. In 2022, the Common App launched a third round of its direct admissions pilot, with 14 colleges participating, reaching nearly 30,000 students with direct admission offers.[9]

In fall 2022, SAGE Scholars launched its FastTrak[10] program to match highly qualified students with colleges and universities that best suit their interests before they apply. By uploading key pieces of information to their student portal, including high-school transcript, GPA, and activities, students can be considered for direct admission at dozens of FastTrak colleges. Niche also started a direct admissions project in 2022 with 13 institutions.[11] In the state of Minnesota, over 50 colleges and universities have participated in that state's version of a direct admissions program, including a full range of community, technical, tribal, public, and private institutions.

How much might direct admissions help struggling institutions change their admissions trajectory? Could it be a game-changer, or is it just a flash in the pan? Initial evidence suggests it can boost applications but has only small effects on enrollment. And we still don't know how students enrolled through direct admissions perform academically once they are in college? Those are key questions still to be answered. Direct admissions will probably never be embraced by highly selective colleges, which engage in an annual ritual of publicly touting the high percentage of applicants they turn away. But the majority of institutions are not highly selective; they admit the majority of the students who apply. Direct admissions may offer struggling colleges in particular an effective tool to address some of their enrollment challenges.

Increase Transfer Agreements

Another strategy for enrollment recovery is to form stronger partnerships with two-year colleges. Transfers from two-year schools to four-year institutions have been on the wane since the pandemic. From the fall of 2020 through the fall of 2022, the number of students transferring from a two-year to a four-year college was down by 14.5%, or about 78,500 students.[12] This decline is best explained by the overall loss of students enrolled in community colleges, particularly since the pandemic. Between 2017 and 2022, total enrollment in community colleges decreased by more than 1.5 million students, representing an astounding 25% decline.[13] Admittedly, these declines have thinned out the two-year transfer pipeline to a significant degree, but here are three strategies institutions could pursue to pump up their transfer numbers.

First, to strengthen their appeal as an affordable route to an eventual four-year degree, institutions should continue to ease transfer pathways as much as possible through strong articulation agreements that maximize the block transfer of course credits, rather than requiring students to go through a confusing and cumbersome process of having each individual course evaluated for its transferability. A related strategy is to sign agreements with nearby institutions that would allow community college students access to campus activities and amenities at the 4-year school. Institutions that are willing to cut through the academic red tape that often ties up the transfer process stand to gain students. Eliminating policies that hold students back rather than move them forward is a key to becoming a transfer destination.

Second, guaranteed admission agreements can be negotiated between community colleges and the receiving four-year institutions. An example of such a plan has been proposed by the University of California, which would assure community college transfers in that state admission to one of the campuses within the UC system.[14] Under the plan, students would need to complete a set of general education courses with a minimum grade point average, but after they do, they are promised admission to the system.

A third option is to develop an arrangement called *reverse transfer.* Reverse transfer is a process for awarding an associate of arts degree to students who transfer from a two-year to a four-year institution prior to completing the associate of arts (AA) degree requirements at the two-year institution. Through reverse transfer students can combine the credits they earn at their four-year school with those they had previously earned at community college and retroactively be awarded an AA degree. It gives them a second chance to earn their first degree.

Each year thousands of community college students transfer to four-year colleges without having finished their AA. Many of these students ultimately drop out of college, exiting, despite years of study and a mountain of debt, without any formal higher education credential to their credit. Reverse transfer changes that equation. Instead of going 0 for 2 in the degree column, students can "reach back" and earn an associate of arts degree, and those who persist can add a BA to the final ledger. This recover-your-degree strategy can be a focus of an outreach by colleges that are intent on increasing enrollment by transfer students.

In 2012, 16 states joined the Credit When It's Due initiative and developed policies to implement reverse transfer agreements between their public colleges. After the first three years, more than 15,000 students had taken advantage of reverse transfer and earned associate of arts degrees while working toward their baccalaureate degrees.[15]

A similar, multi-state reverse transfer program was Project Win-Win, sponsored by the Lumina and Kresge foundations and organized by the Institute of Higher Education Policy in partnership with the State Higher Education Executive Officers.[16] Sixty-one associate degree-granting schools in nine states were initially recruited to find former students who were no longer enrolled and had not been awarded a degree but whose records documented they were very close to qualifying for an associate's degree. The institutions found almost 130,000 eligible students and completed degree audits for about 42,000 of them. More than 4,500 students were awarded degrees, and another 1,700 who were within 12 credits of graduation returned to college to finish their degree. Several states, including Colorado, Florida, Maryland, Michigan, Missouri, Oregon, and Texas have now passed legislation implementing reverse transfer policies, often as part of an overall statewide strategic plan that establishes a goal for the number of citizens who have a college degree by a certain date.

The halls of academia have a reputation for being crowded with foot-draggers who can offer all kinds of reasons to oppose policy innovations. The growth of reverse transfer is a welcome exception. It shows that a smart policy can overcome such resistance, an example of initiative overcoming inertia with students coming out the big winners. Even with this success, however, most college faculty and many administrators have never heard of reverse transfer, creating a space that a college on the financial rebound could fill by offering students the chance to finalize the credentials they've worked to earn.

Partner With Employers

Ever since the pandemic and the tight labor market in its aftermath, employers have shown increased interest in offering paid educational benefits to employees. Under these plans, companies pay for their employees to gain additional education by reimbursing them for the costs of college tuition or other upskilling so that workers can go back to school and earn a high school diploma, certificate, BA, or graduate degree.

Employers have offered education assistance benefits for decades, but historically the percentage of workers taking advantage of them was minimal, languishing in the 1–2% range. Even before the pandemic, there were signs that use of these plans was gaining interest, but that trend has picked up more steam in the past several years. As of 2018, it was estimated that more than 60% of U.S. companies offered financial assistance to employees to further their education,[17] and the nation's employers were spending more than $180 billion a year on educational benefits.[18] Paying for employees to attend college is popular in part because of its favorable treatment under IRS section 127, which allows employers to deduct tuition payments for employees as a business expense and permits employees to exclude from taxable income up to $5,250 annually in eligible education reimbursement.

While it was initially feared that the pandemic would cause employers to cut back on paying for their employees' tuition as a way to trim operating costs, just the opposite happened. In fact, both InStride and Guild, two of the leading private companies helping businesses organize and provide educational benefits to employees, have seen significant growth since the pandemic began, adding new partners on both the educational provider side and on the corporate business side.

   Much of this interest has been spurred by attempts to cope with the reality that millions of Americans left their jobs in 2021 and 2022 in the wake of the pandemic. Whether you call it "The Great Resignation," "The Big Quit," or "The Great Reshuffle," workers in every sector of the economy began to rethink their jobs, their lifestyles, and their values. More than 4.5 million Americans voluntarily left their jobs in November 2021 alone, the highest monthly number in the two decades this figure has been tracked. Labor markets were turned upside down, leaving companies scrambling to find qualified workers. From retail to hospitality, health care to industrials, major companies began offering enhanced benefits, higher wages, and other perks—like paid college tuition—to lure and retain employees in what had quickly become one of the tightest job markets in history.

   The education providers include a range of colleges and universities—public, private, and for-profit—who either partner with an education benefits platform like Guild or InStride or strike their own deals with companies to offer employer-paid educational opportunities to their workers. On the demand side, enrollments have grown dramatically as the number of corporate clients invest in or expand their educational benefits. InStride CEO Vivek Sharma estimates that the take-up rate of educational benefits by employees at companies partnering with his company now runs as high as 20%.[19]

   In addition to early adapters like Starbucks and Uber, dozens of the nation's largest companies now pay all or most of the tuition costs incurred by their employees enrolling in college. Amazon, PNC Bank, Tyson Foods, Macy's, Walmart, Chipotle, Walt Disney, Lowe's, Banfield Pet Hospitals, Herschend Industries, and Prime Communications are just some of the examples. Uber even allows its eligible drivers to transfer their education benefit to a family member. Many employers, like Starbucks, will pay employees' tuition and fees in advance rather than offering reimbursement after they've completed courses, thereby permitting employees who don't have sufficient funds on hand to begin immediately accessing the education options they want to pursue. That strategy has paid off. In 2023, Starbucks and Arizona State University, its educational provider, celebrated the 10,000th college graduate from their Starbucks College Achievement Plan, which pays all tuition for employees earning their baccalaureate degrees.

   Either by becoming part of one of the growing number of educational provider networks or by negotiating contracts with area employers, colleges emerging from exigency should aim to become part of this market. They are in a good position to tailor educational programs to meet employers' and employees' greatest learning needs. Different business sectors prefer different types of programs. Health care has been trying to address a severe shortage of nurses and build greater digital literacy for staffing telehealth operations. In the financial and technology sectors, where many employees already have degrees, the emphasis is on targeted upskilling, making short-term certificate programs a logical priority. In retail and hospitality, there's a focus on improving employee retention by offering high school completion or associate/baccalaureate degrees. Whatever the specifics, this strategy represents life-long learning, which universities have long touted as a virtue, in its most practical form. It can give enterprising Year Zero colleges a chance to turn what's almost become a cliché into a highly functional extension of their academic programs.

IMPROVING DEGREE ATTAINMENT

A student-ready college devotes resources to academic programming that's designed to help students from all backgrounds complete their degrees in a timely fashion. College completion rates have slowly improved over the past two decades. In 2010, the overall 6-year graduation rate for first-time, full-time undergraduate students who began seeking a bachelor's degree at a 4-year school was 58% (56% at public institutions, 65.5% at private nonprofit institutions). Ten years later, in 2020, the overall 6-year graduation rate for the same kind of cohort of undergraduate students who began their studies in fall 2014 had increased to 64% (63% at public institutions, 68% at private nonprofit institutions).[20] That's good progress, but not good enough. Here are four policies that could help increase those rates.

Reform Remedial Education

The problem of students entering college unprepared for college-level work is widespread. Each year, it's estimated that at least one million beginning college students will be forced to take one or more remedial courses in math or English—sometimes both—because they scored too low on standardized entrance or placement exams. Nationally, over half of entering community college students will be told by their institutions they're not ready for college-level math and English courses, and those numbers will be significantly higher for Black and Latino students.

Under the traditional model of remediation, still practiced at many colleges and universities, instead of registering for a credit-bearing course, these students will be placed in prerequisite remedial courses. These are non-credit classes intended to help students with weak academic backgrounds get up to speed so they can succeed in required, credit-bearing courses and ultimately earn a degree. Although remedial courses will not count toward graduation, students still must pay tuition for them, nonetheless.

Remedial coursework is well-intentioned, but it's largely unsuccessful.[21] It's what we've previously called higher education's Hotel California; millions of students enter but they never leave. Among students in remedial courses, significant percentages never finish even one of them. And very few students who start in remediation ever complete the subsequent gateway course. As few as 10% of students in remediation at two-year schools finish their degree in three years; at four-year non-flagship universities, only about a third of students taking a remedial class earn a degree after six years. It's a funnel to failure, and the results are even worse for minority and low-income students.[22]

In 2022, the state of Louisiana adopted a new policy that effectively ended the use of remedial coursework at that state's public universities and colleges.[23] With that decision, Louisiana's higher ed institutions joined a growing number of schools that have abandoned remedial (or what's also called developmental) education in favor of an alternative known as corequisite education.

With a corequisite approach, students entering college who need remediation aren't forced into a no-credit, remedial course. Instead, they register for the gateway math and/or English course while at the same time they receive additional academic support and tutoring to help them pass the class. These students take the for-credit course alongside the extra academic assistance instead of first having to jump over the not-for-credit remedial hurdle.

Louisiana used a grant from the Education Commission of the States to study the effects of using a co-requisite model. Data collected in academic year 2020–21 showed that freshmen participating in corequisite math achieved a pass rate of 55%, compared to 11% for those taking remedial math alone. Those results are consistent with what other states have discovered. In fact, the corequisite model has been found consistently to at least triple the percentage of students who successfully complete gateway math courses and significantly increase the percentage who complete gateway English courses.

A recent report by Complete College America (CCA) analyzed the outcomes of 26,000 college students in Georgia who enrolled in corequisite support.[24] Using the traditional sequence of remedial courses typical of developmental education in the past, only 20% of the Georgia students were able to pass a gateway course in math. With corequisite education the percentage of math gateway completions soared to 66%. The results were similar in English courses. Only 45% of those taking remedial courses in English ultimately passed a gateway English course, but with the corequisite approach, the success rate jumped to 69%.

The positive results of co-requisite remediation are consistent enough that they've shifted the burden for what should become the collegiate standard for remedial education. It's time for colleges that are continuing to use the old prerequisite sequence of remediation to replace that "money for nothing" approach with a co-requisite model. It is particularly important for the colleges we've focused on in this book, which often enroll large numbers of students who need a bit more support to succeed in introductory courses.

Emphasize 15 to Finish

Higher education's completion agenda has featured several policies designed to increase the number of students who complete college and earn a degree. One of its most well-known components has been the "15-to-finish" campaign, the brainchild of Complete College America, a national alliance dedicated to improving college completion rates.[25]

The 15-to-finish initiative encourages students to enroll in 15 credits per semester (or, including summer terms, 30 credits per year). It seeks to change the fact that most college students do not register for at least 15 credits per semester, the minimum course load that would enable them to earn an associate of arts degree in two years or a baccalaureate degree in four years. That pattern also has been reinforced by the federal financial aid definition of a full-time student as one who enrolls for at least 12 credit hours per semester.

In the first year in college, the average full-time student does not attempt or complete enough credits to complete a bachelor's degree even within five years. That's one of the main takeaways from a study by the National Student Clearinghouse (NSC).[26] The NSC researchers analyzed two measures for 905,689 first-time, degree-seeking students (including first-time in college and first-time, transfer students) at 342 colleges and universities. The two measures were first-year credit completion ratio (CCR) and credit accumulation rate (CAR). CCR is the ratio of credits earned to credits attempted. It quantifies students' first-year movement through coursework. CAR identifies the share of students who surpassed specific credit-hour thresholds within a given period. For example, it shows what percentage of students earned 24 or more credits in their first year. It's an early indicator of momentum toward degree completion and reveals where gaps in degree attainment between groups of students are most likely to begin.

The researchers found that in the first year of college, the average full-time student attempted fewer than 27 credits and earned fewer than 22. Only 51% of full-time students earned 24 or more credit hours in their first year. Less than a third (28%) earned 30 or more hours of credit, which would be the pace necessary to complete a BA in four years. On average, students earned about 75% of the credits they attempted. In other words, students earned nine credit hours for every 12 credits attempted.

For undergraduates wanting to earn a BA in four years, the math of completing fewer than 12 credit hours per semester just doesn't add up. Instead, it stretches a four-year degree into five, six or seven years of enrollment, tuition, and greater living expenses. In addition to the extra costs of each additional semester, the odds of "life getting in the way" increase, interfering with—or even preventing—degree completion. By contrast, students who enroll for at least 15 credits per semester earn higher GPAs and are more likely to persist in their enrollment than those taking fewer courses. But unfortunately, regardless of whether it's a two-year or four-year school, the majority of students complete fewer than 30 credits per year

In 2012, the University of Hawaii began an aggressive campaign to inform students about the importance of completing 15 credits per semester if they wanted to graduate in four years and avoid additional years of tuition and the foregone income from not having a full-time job. After just one year, the rate of incoming students at the flagship Manoa campus enrolling for 15 credits per semester jumped from 38% to 64%. Similar increases were achieved on other University of Hawaii campuses.[27]

More than half the states have now implemented some version of the 15-to-finish campaign, involving hundreds of colleges. The findings are encouraging. Here are a few examples. After controlling for high school GPA, students at every level of academic preparation earn better grades and are more likely to be retained if they complete 30 credits per year. Students who enrolled for at least 15 semester credits at Nevada's two-year and four-year colleges were more likely to pass required math courses. When universities combine the push for 15 credits with more early and intensive advising, students earn more credits that count toward degree requirements.[28]

Like most strategies aimed at improving college completion, 15-to-finish should not be introduced as a stand-alone policy. It's most likely to succeed when it's:

- Embedded in a campus culture where degree completion is consistently emphasized.
- Supported by faculty and staff advisors who counsel students about the advantages of 15-credit-hour loads.
- Guided by curricular maps that chart the specific courses students need to take and when they need to take them to earn a degree on time.
- Accompanied by course scheduling that guarantees that required classes are offered when needed.
- Aligned with incentives like banded tuition (charging students who take 15 or more credits the same tuition as students who enroll for 12) that encourage completing 30 credits per year.

Serve Part-Time Students Better

As advisable as it might be, 15-to-finish is just not possible for every student, who, because of family duties, financial limitations, work obligations, or other realities are precluded from regularly taking that many credits. When 12, 15, or more credits per semester are not feasible, colleges must provide alternatives that keep part-time students on track to degree completion. Students who cannot take a full load of courses in each semester—which is often the case for working adults returning to college—cannot be ignored or neglected. They need schedules, financial aid, and advising that addresses their unique circumstances and helps them earn a degree in the timeliest manner possible.

A review by Complete College America found that more than half (55%) of students ages 20–24 and almost two-thirds (64%) of students 25 and older attend college part time, meaning they're enrolled for fewer than 12 credits per semester for some portion of their attendance. Part-time students are more likely to be Black or Latino and come from lower-income backgrounds. They are also more likely to attend community colleges and non-flagship public universities, which also happen to be the kinds of institutions most likely to be suffering financial struggles.[29] Regardless of where they attend, part-time students are much less likely than full-time students to finish their degrees. According to Complete College America's analysis, among first-time students attending all kinds of institutions, 46% attending full-time finished their degree in eight years compared to just 18% of part-timers. Among transfer students, twice as many full-time students completed their degrees in eight years (51%) versus only 25% of part-timers.

The implications are clear. In order to serve all students well, colleges must develop programming for the part-time students who make up a large percentage of their enrollment. Included in that programming should be:

- Scheduling more classes in the evenings and weekends, outside of traditional working hours.
- Offering shorter, more intense courses that run for eight weeks or less, allowing part-time students to focus on one class at a time while still completing multiple classes in a semester.
- Providing credit for previously demonstrated competencies and content mastery so that students do not have to spend additional time on material they've already learned.
- Adding just-in-time, wraparound supports such as emergency financial aid, food pantries, childcare, and other social supports to meet the basic needs felt by many part-time students.

• Tailoring advising to help part-time students meet the obligations they face outside of college and still complete as many credits as possible given those commitments.

Award College Completion Grants

College completion grants are small, just-in-time awards that help students who are on the brink of dropping out of college despite being tantalizingly close to finishing their degree. This target group is not small. As many as 15% of students who've completed three-quarters of their required courses leave college without earning a degree. Often, the main culprit is a financial burden that finally breaks a student's back, causing them to drop out.

In many instances, the financial need is not that large. A student may need just a course or two to finish a degree but lack the money to pay the tuition. In other cases, money is still owed for a prior semester's charges, and the student's registration is blocked. Lower-income students often help support their parents and must abandon their education to pay for family emergencies that arise. Sometimes the obstacle may be as small as unpaid parking tickets or a fine for overdue library books. The goal of completion grants is not to forgive major student debts or to pay off large fund balances they owe. As we saw in Chapter 2, that strategy can help create a financial crisis at a tuition-dependent institution. Rather, the aim is to remove relatively small, but still difficult, financial obstacles to student persistence.

Recognizing such problems, the University of Missouri-St. Louis (UMSL) developed a solution called the Finish Your Degree scholarship. It's for students who are within 15 credits of graduation but who've exhausted all financial aid and therefore cannot remain enrolled. These scholarships are expected to not exceed $1,500, although exceptions allowing larger grants are occasionally allowed. In the first three years of the program, led by a gift from UMSL alum Patrick Gadell, $70,000 in scholarships was awarded, with an average award of only $573. The graduation rate for the more than 100 recipients of those scholarships was 95%.[30]

The former Indiana University-Purdue University Indianapolis offered a Home Stretch grant to students within one year of earning their degree. Under this program, eligible students received an institutional loan that was fully forgiven if they graduated within one year. To receive the grant, students had to demonstrate financial need, have earned a minimum of 80 credit hours, have at least a 2.0 cumulative GPA. and enroll full-time. Of an early cohort of 150 recipients, 75% completed their degree within one year.

Several years ago, the Association of Public and Land-Grant Universities and the Coalition of Urban Serving Universities teamed up with several universities to study completion grants and evaluate their effectiveness. A recent review of completion grants summarized the results of that project: The grants generally varied between $500 and $1500. The typical eligibility requirements were that students had to be within 30 credit hours or less from completion and they had to have "genuine unmet financial need and an unpaid university balance." Administrators identified 75,206 seniors, 59% of whom had unmet financial need. Eventually just over 1,200 grants were distributed to eligible students, and 93% of the recipients were either retained or completed their degrees within one year of receiving an award.[31]

The key to successful completion grants is to combine technology that identifies and tracks eligible students with a personal touch that offers support and encouragement for students to persevere to graduation. Five principles are important:

1. Using predictive analytics to identify eligible students. Universities can turn their AI capacity to this task, using student data to find at-risk students, chart curricular maps aimed at degree completion, and monitor students' progress on a frequent basis.
2. Embedding completion grants in a culture of completion. Completion grants will not succeed as a stand-alone effort. They must be integrated into an overall strategy for improving student completion involving multi-year financial aid packages, intrusive academic advising, enhanced student support services and prioritization by university leadership.
3. Requiring academic and student support staff to communicate frequently with students. Academic advisors, student affairs staff, faculty mentors, and financial aid officers need to develop personal relationships with students that keep them focused on completion. A steady hand, a sympathetic ear, a push here, a pull there—continuing, caring connections with struggling students are essential to success.
4. Securing a student commitment to completion. Recipients of completion need to take personal ownership of the completion goal. An effective means to put student skin-in-the-game is to have them sign a contract that specifies the terms and requirements of their grants.
5. Cultivating private donors to underwrite the grants. Colleges coming out of financial exigency will usually not have the institutional funds to create much of this type of aid. However, at an average of $1,000–2,000 per grant, completion scholarships create an ideal opportunity for annual giving by donors. In addition to the financial gift, donors can be paired with recipients, adding another layer of support and encouragement for students.

Completion grants are a smart addition to the arsenal for any college trying to increase the number of students who finish their degrees. For colleges that have just gone through exigency, two factors will determine the extent to which they can be used. First, can enough private donors be persuaded to underwrite them? And second, because the student support personnel at these institutions is already stretched very thin, can the grants be designed in such a way to minimize the administrative burdens associated with determining student eligibility and making awards?

DEGREES THAT WORK

The single most important contribution that colleges can make to the success of their students is to offer high-quality academic programs that prepare them for effective citizenship and equip them with the knowledge and skills needed for successful careers. The standard higher education formula for this preparation has been to give students a solid grounding in the liberal arts and sciences that lays the groundwork for greater specialization in a major. The success of this traditional curriculum as measured by an increase in student

Table 8.1. Proportions of employers and students saying they/recent college graduates are well prepared in each area*

	Employers	Students
Working with others in teams	37%	64%
Staying current on technologies	37%	46%
Ethical judgment and decision-making	30%	62%
Locating, organizing, evaluating information	29%	64%
Oral communication	28%	62%
Working with numbers/ statistics	28%	55%
Written communication	27%	65%
Critical/analytical thinking	26%	66%
Being innovative/ creative	25%	57%
Analyzing/solving complex problems	24%	59%
Applying knowledge/ skills to real world	23%	59%
Awareness/experience of diverse cultures in US	21%	48%
Staying current on developments in science	21%	44%
Working w/ people from different backgrounds	18%	55%
Staying current on global developments	18%	43%
Proficient in other language	16%	34%
Awareness/experience of diverse cultures outside US	15%	42%

*8–10 ratings on a zero-to-ten scale

Source: Hart Research Associates, "Optimistic about the future: But how well prepared? College students' views on College Learning and Career Success," April 29, 2015. http://www.aacu.org/sites/default/files/LEAP/2015StudentSurveyReport.pdf/

learning is a matter of debate, but there are reasons to be concerned that too many students learn too little from their years in college, particularly when assessed by standardized testing.[32]

One common finding is that compared to the opinions of faculty or students themselves, employers find college graduates to be less well-prepared in a wide range of job skills. In a 2015 study, the Association of American Colleges and Universities (AAC&U) surveyed 400 private- and public-sector employers about the academic preparation of recent college graduates.[33] The results were discouraging. Employers gave college graduates relatively low scores on a range of cognitive abilities, including those judged to be most important for successful careers. As part of the study, college seniors and soon-to-graduate community college students were also surveyed about their own assessment of these same abilities. Consistent with a frequently replicated pattern, students were much more sanguine than employers about their level of preparation. As Table 8.1 shows, on each of 17 measures, the students held substantially more generous opinions about their preparation than did the employers.

A more recent AAC&U survey found strong support among employers for a college education to be grounded in the liberal arts and sciences.[34] Nine in 10 employers said it was important for students to achieve the learning outcomes that define contemporary liberal education. However, the same percentage said they would be more likely to hire a job applicant who had participated in at least one of those "high-impact practices" we described in Chapter 7—experiences like internships, apprenticeships, capstones, and project-based learning.

Employers are looking for an educational sweet spot that mixes breadth with depth. They want the broad abilities of critical thinking, effective communication, and cultural competence that a liberal education nurtures, but they also want practical experiences and specific applied skills that are often best learned outside of the traditional curriculum. According to the AAC&U survey, most employers think there's a gap between that sweet spot and the capabilities of today's college graduates. Only six in 10 employers believe that recent graduates possess the knowledge and skills needed for success in entry-level positions at their companies or organizations. As a result, one of three of the employer respondents said they had "very little" or only "some" confidence in higher education. What does this mean for a college trying to reimagine itself? What are some practical, cost-effective steps colleges can take to increase the economic value of their degrees? Here are two promising options.

Embed Short-Term Certificates in the Curriculum

A certificate is a credential that's awarded for completion of a set of specific, typically occupationally oriented courses. Certificate programs vary in length, but many require around 15 credits, which sometimes can be completed in a year or less. Certificates appeal to both students and employers because they help students acquire the practical skills expected in many beginning positions, increasing their prospects for landing and succeeding at a good job, which remains the number one motive students and their families give for attending college.

A recent survey commissioned by Coursera, the online learning platform and a pioneer of Massive Open Online Courses (MOOCS), revealed that large majorities of employers and students view short-term, industry-related certificates as a worthwhile addition to a college degree and a valuable credential in the hiring and job-seeking process. This interest in what are sometimes referred to as micro-credentials has come at a time when many major, national companies—including the likes of Accenture, IBM, Google, Bank of America—are no longer requiring college degrees for many entry-level jobs. Nonetheless, almost all employers view the combination of a certificate and a college degree as a competitive advantage.

When Coursera surveyed 3,600 students and employers across eight countries—Australia, India, France, Germany, Mexico, Turkey, the UK, and the United States—it found that 89% of students across the globe agreed or strongly agreed that earning an entry-level professional certificate would help them stand out to employers and secure jobs after they graduate. In addition, 75% of students said that including professional certificates in a traditional academic program would make them more likely to enroll in that program. Among U.S. students, 81% believed that micro-credentials would help them succeed in their job, and 74% said the chance to earn micro-credentials would influence their choice of a degree program at their university. Among U.S. employers, 86% agreed that earning an industry micro-credential strengthened a candidate's job application. In choosing between two degreed candidates, 63% said the presence of an industry micro-credential would positively influence a hiring decision, and 39% said they had hired at least one candidate with a micro-credential.[35]

Sub-baccalaureate certificates are now awarded in many content areas, typically developed by a company or industry group, often in consultation with a college or university. Information technology, health care, web development, business management, artificial intelligence, human resource management, cybersecurity, hospitality management, and software engineering are particularly popular subjects.

We believe it's important to recognize that while adding short-term certificates to standard curricula has been on the upswing, existing research has
not consistently demonstrated their long-term economic value. The increase
in earnings associated with short-term credentials tends to fall in the 10–20%
range, but that increase also appears to fade over time. The economic returns
from certificates also vary considerably by student characteristics and the
kinds of occupations linked to the certificates.[36]

Nonetheless, the advantages of pairing a certificate with a BA appear to
outweigh any disadvantages. By adding professional certificates to their academic offerings, higher education institutions can fill gaps in their existing
curricula, meet students' demand for skill-based learning, and improve their
competitive standing—and potentially their enrollments—in the process.
Employers are continuing to endorse the certificate+degree combo as well
because it increases their confidence that new graduates who've earned both
will enter the workforce better prepared with the skills necessary to perform
their jobs well.

All things considered, we think embedding certificates in a BA curriculum
is a smart strategy for colleges trying to boost their appeal to prospective
students, but we also acknowledge there will be obstacles to overcome.
Deciding which certificates to add and identifying the right instructors to staff
the courses will require careful consideration of institutional strengths and
market needs. And overcoming resistance by the faculty to what many will
see as an undesirable intrusion by non-academics into the curriculum is probably the highest hurdle of all. Including faculty on the ground floor when the
certificate curricula are designed is the best way to gain their buy-in.

Increase Internships, Apprenticeships, and Other Competency-Based Experiences

As we discussed in the prior chapter, "high-impact" practices are intense
educational experiences that take place out of traditional classrooms, require
sustained student effort, and involve extended interactions with faculty and
other supervisors as well as with other students. They are forms of active
learning that have been linked to several positive outcomes including greater
student satisfaction with their education, better retention, and increased
graduation rates.

The ability to arrange such high-impact experiences is reinforced by the
enormous growth in digital content and the technology necessary to distrib-
ute that content. When the pandemic brought study abroad to a near total
halt, students still could be zoomed to a study group in Madrid or join an
ongoing project with students in New Delhi. Augmented reality and virtual
reality technologies now make it possible for students to practice health-care

procedures in an immersive environment. Tech-enabled simulations are creating new learning opportunities for students in subjects ranging from art to zoology, botany to world history. Virtual internships have become common as have visits to the world's great museums and rarest habitats. Welcome to the *metaversity.*[37]

The previously described AAC&U survey found that more than four in five employers would be either "somewhat more likely" or "much more likely" to consider hiring recent college graduates if they had completed an active or applied experience in college. Internships and apprenticeships topped the preferred experience list, followed by working in community settings with diverse community partners. Employers also valued work-study experiences and student portfolios, along with global learning and mentored experiences. The common theme was an emphasis on learning and practicing competencies in real-world settings.

We believe that internships are an especially important activity for greater development. The college internship has long been regarded as one of the most beneficial forms of student engagement, valued as a high-impact experience that immerses students in environments where they learn and practice the crucial soft skills of employability. Internships have served as one of college's most practical rites of passage, a frequent steppingstone for graduates into their first job.

Internships vary in quality and availability. Many of the best and most coveted ones are difficult to access. The application process is lengthy and highly competitive, particularly for internships at major tech companies and financial institutions, two of the most preferred sectors for college interns. And many of the best internship opportunities are dominated by students from prestigious colleges and major research universities. Students from less well-known schools are often shut out. That pattern also results in students of color, first-generation-to-college students, and those from lower-income backgrounds to be underrepresented among college internships, particularly those that are paid. These students frequently lack the insider connections and alumni networks that help students secure the best internships. As an example, one recent estimate was that 59.5% of Black students and 53.3% of Latino students participated in internships, compared to 68.2% of White students.[38]

One solution to this problem is for institutions to create their own internship placement program, partnering with companies and agencies to increase opportunities for their students to land internships. An example is Bowie State University, an HBCU in Bowie, Maryland, which customized an internship placement process for its computer science students. The Bowie State program matches students directly with employers seeking interns. It provides training for students on interview skills and workshops on the topics that companies emphasize when selecting interns, and it sets up its own on-campus internships to get students ready for those placements in the private sector.

According to a *New York Time*'s description of the Bowie State program, participating employers come frequently to Bowie State "to get to know, mentor, interview and directly recruit students for internships in a process that is more intimate than the one-off information sessions that tech companies often arrange with university career centers. And the Bowie process does not typically involve high-stress technical tests. That has spared many students, some of whom have part-time jobs, from spending dozens of unpaid hours on applying for Silicon Valley internship programs."[39]

In 2022, with the new program up and running, 60 Bowie State students interned with companies like Deloitte, federal agencies including NASA, and some local start-ups. In 2023, Bowie State began an internship program with Adobe[40] where about a dozen Bowie State students worked that summer as cybersecurity interns, increasing their chances of receiving job offers from the company following their graduation.

Bowie State is not a wealthy institution. It's had to cope with financial crunches over the years, most recently in FY 2021 when its budget was cut by about $3.9 million, requiring it to implement a temporary reduction in salaries. Its internship initiative is an excellent example of how chronically under-resourced colleges can make smart investments in programs that enable all students to earn degrees that are affordable and are better aligned with modern, high-demand workforce needs.

A RECAP AND A LOOK FORWARD

If colleges don't fundamentally change the way they operate, it's unreasonable to think that they can substantially change their costs or their outcomes. In this book, we've highlighted the strong headwinds that higher education institutions of all kinds are facing, and we've discussed several changes that financially distressed institutions will need to make to survive these headwinds and ultimately emerge as better colleges.

The process begins with a thorough financial reckoning where an institution takes a full, clear-eyed accounting of what it costs to offer its educational and student services in addition to all its other activities. Key to this reckoning is the fundamental question—what does it cost to offer our degree programs. At what we believe will be an increasing number of schools, this accounting will show that the institution is offering more academic programs, employing more administrators, faculty, and staff, and spending more money on a range of student activities, including intercollegiate athletics, than it can afford.

Their revenues and expenditures are unbalanced and headed in the wrong direction. In some cases, more careful attention to cost containment, a deferral of new capital projects, a refinancing of debt, and a modest administrative and academic restructuring will be sufficient to achieve the necessary financial realignment. Fiscal problems have not yet reached a crisis at these schools, and drastic solutions will not be required.

In other instances, the money crunch is more severe. Enrollment is eroding, net tuition revenue has declined (often because the institution has spent far too much of its own funds on tuition scholarships), appropriations from the state have stagnated, and returns from the endowment have taken a hard hit. At these institutions, more extreme measures will be required to right the ship. Staff furloughs, hiring freezes, the elimination of some academic programs, cutbacks in athletics and other sponsored activities, the downsizing of the workforce through incentivized retirements and non-replacements of vacant positions, and additional austerity measures will probably be needed.

Then there's the group of colleges we've focused on in the previous chapters. In addition to all the financial problems above, they're carrying huge amounts of debt, most alternative streams of revenue have run dry, and prior attempts to pull their budgets out of the red have proved to be too little, too late. Their financial outlook is so bleak that nothing short of emergency institution-wide measures will sustain them. They're our colleges on the brink.

We described the process of invoking financial exigency that these colleges must confront, involving the ultimate cost-reduction measure—the termination of faculty contracts, including the retrenchment of tenured faculty. We identified the key elements of financial exigency—a modified cash budget, an academic productivity portfolio, attention to student success measures, and a strategic resource allocation model—and we outlined the timeline for how an exigency might proceed.

To weather its financial exigency, a college needs strong leadership, but to be successful in the long run, that leadership also requires the support and backing of its governing board and key external policy makers. Only then will it be positioned to ask the key questions that should inform its strategy for recovery: What are our program strengths? How can we best serve our students? How do we organize for the future?

We emphasized the personal trauma and emotional grief associated with financial exigency, experienced in different ways for nearly everyone at an institution that goes through the experience. Financial exigency is probably the next-to-the-worst experience any college will endure. It's second only to the outcome it's meant to prevent—a college's collapse and closure.

We identified the key steps that a college emerging from financial exigency must take in what we called Year Zero. A successful Year Zero transition should be guided by five principles: continuing to adhere to a modified cash budget, putting students first, developing positive communications for both the campus and external audiences, relying on an academic productivity portfolio to guide program and faculty investments, and forging new educational partnerships with other organizations.

After Year Zero, a college that's able once again to stand on a firm financial floor should focus on redesigning itself around three fundamental priorities: increased access to higher education, better student outcomes in terms of retention and graduation, and improved student learning that prepares graduates for success in life and work. These three objectives define the "student-ready" framework that colleges need to build if they are to educate and serve students well. Figure 8.1 summarizes some of the key features involved in the re-imagined college that has emerged from financial exigency and contrasts them with the business-as-usual approach of many colleges that are on the brink.

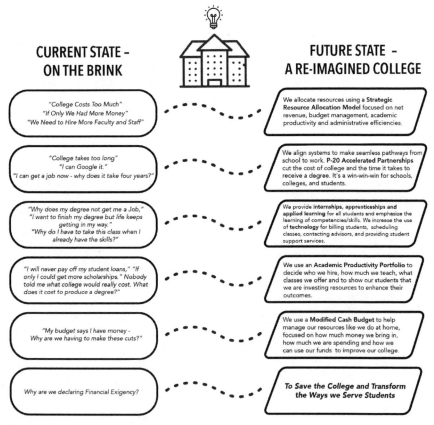

Figure 8.1.   Institutional Re-Imagining

American colleges have proven to be remarkably resilient across the centuries. They've thrived throughout a largely prosperous history, but they've also learned to adapt and survive during hard times. Recently, many colleges have found themselves in various states of financial precarity, threatened by economic uncertainties, a prolonged period of sinking enrollments, a public increasingly skeptical of their value, a global pandemic, and their own tendencies to overbuild and overspend.

The challenge these colleges now face is to build their road back from that perilous position—the brink—and become better colleges that are leaner, more financially stable, and ready to provide the education that students and society need. For those colleges most at risk, financial exigency offers one road back, a rocky one to be sure, but, as we've tried to document in these pages, one that is navigable by the dedicated and resourceful colleges and universities that continue to remain one of America's greatest assets.

NOTES

1. https://www.insidehighered.com/news/business/cost-cutting/2023/05/03/slimming-down-stay-afloat

2. Dual enrollment is sometimes confused with other early colleges opportunities, such as dual credit courses and Advanced Placement (AP) courses, both of which can also enable high schoolers to earn college credits. Dual credit refers to college level courses that are taught by a qualified high school instructor and that allow students to earn both high school and college credit simultaneously. AP courses are college level courses created by the College Board and offered at high schools. Students who score high enough on AP exams associated with the courses can earn college credits. Dual enrollment courses are taught by college faculty and allow a high school student to earn credits that count both in high school and college.

3. https://ies.ed.gov/ncee/wwc/EvidenceSnapshot/671

4. https://www.forbes.com/sites/michaeltnietzel/2022/06/02/how-the-national-education-equity-lab-is-closing-the-college-opportunity-gap/?sh=3a3d92855979

5. https://www.harvardmagazine.com/2020/03/jhj-harvard-credit-for-hs

6. https://www.ucmo.edu/about/locations/ucm-lees-summit-campus/missouri-innovation-campus/

7. https://www.insidehighered.com/admissions/article/2022/07/18/direct-admissions-takes-individual-colleges

8. https://www.highereddive.com/news/direct-admissions-show-early-success-boosting-enrollment-in-idaho/618374/

9. https://www.commonapp.org/blog/common-app-launches-third-round-direct-admissions-pilot-14-colleges-and-universities

10. https://www.tuitionrewards.com/newsroom/news/323/direct-admissions-takes-off

11. https://www.insidehighered.com/admissions/article/2022/11/14/niche-enters-direct-admissions-market

12. https://nscresearchcenter.org/transfer-and-progress/

13. https://nscresearchcenter.org/current-term-enrollment-estimates/

14. https://www.insidehighered.com/admissions/article/2023/04/03/u-california-proposes-guaranteed-transfer-plan

15. https://www.studentclearinghouse.org/nscblog/credit-when-its-due-initiative-leads-to-15000-more-associate-degrees-nationwide-via-reverse-credit-transfer/

16. https://www.ihep.org/publication/lighting-the-path-degrees-when-due/

17. https://www.accessmasterstour.com/articles/view/employer-education-assistance-on-the-rise-globally

18. https://www.forbes.com/sites/michaeltnietzel/2022/02/20/instride-ceo-vivek-sharma-on-the-great-retention/?sh=6410bb344236

19. https://www.forbes.com/sites/michaeltnietzel/2022/02/20/instride-ceo-vivek-sharma-on-the-great-retention/?sh=5a635b354236

20. https://nces.ed.gov/fastfacts/display.asp?id=40

21. https://completecollege.org/wp-content/uploads/2021/04/CCA_NoRoomForDoubt_CorequisiteSupport.pdf

22. https://www.luminafoundation.org/wp-content/uploads/2017/08/time-is-the-enemy.pdf

23. https://regents.la.gov/032322release/

24. https://completecollege.org/resource/corequisite-works/

25. https://completecollege.org

26. https://nscresearchcenter.org/wp-content/uploads/PDPInsightsReport.pdf

27. https://www.forbes.com/sites/michaeltnietzel/2019/03/04/the-15-to-finish-campaign-putting-the-four-year-back-in-four-year-degrees/?sh=73e43a534d6b

28. https://eab.com/insights/blogs/student-success/why-even-c-students-should-consider-taking-15-credits-their-first-semester/

29. https://completecollege.org/wp-content/uploads/2022/07/CCA-Part-Time-Brief-07252022.pdf

30. https://www.forbes.com/sites/michaeltnietzel/2019/01/01/college-completion-grants-the-financial-aid-every-college-should-offer/?sh=331f8b21377b

31. https://ir.library.louisville.edu/cgi/viewcontent.cgi?article=1719&context=jsfa

32. See *Academically Adrift* by Richard Arum and Josipa Roksa, https://press.uchicago.edu/ucp/books/book/chicago/A/bo10327226.html. Also see evaluations of student learning conducted by the Council for Aid to Education. https://cae.org/evidence/

33. https://www.slideshare.net/aacu_/2015-studentsurveyreport

34. https://www.aacu.org/research/how-college-contributes-to-workforce-success

35. https://www.forbes.com/sites/michaeltnietzel/2022/09/27/new-coursera-survey-industry-certificates-hold-strong-appeal-for-college-students-and-employers/?sh=50ff9cebf2e2

36. https://www.luminafoundation.org/wp-content/uploads/2021/05/the-short-term-credentials-landscape.pdf

37. https://www.insidehighered.com/news/2022/08/03/college-metaverse-here-higher-ed-ready

38. https://www.thebalancemoney.com/internship-opportunities-for-students-of-color-5070956#citation-2

39. https://www.nytimes.com/2023/04/05/technology/bowie-hbcu-tech-intern-pipeline.html

40. https://bowiestate.edu/academics/colleges/college-of-arts-and-sciences/departments/computer-science/center-for-cyber-security-and-emerging-technologies/bsu-adobe-internship.png

Index

About the Authors

Charles M. Ambrose is a senior higher education strategist with the law firm of Husch Blackwell. For the past twenty-five years, he has served as a University President, Chancellor and Non-Profit CEO at Pfeiffer University (1998–2010); University of Central Missouri (2010–2018); the KnowledgeWorks Foundation (2018–2021); and, Henderson State University (2021–2023). He also served in senior administrative positions at Carson-Newman College, Western Carolina University, and the American Association of State Colleges and Universities. He has held national leadership positions with the Missouri Council on Public Higher Education, the National Collegiate Athletic Association; Midwestern Higher Education Compact, and the Association of Governing Boards. He also serves as a member of the Furman University's Board of Trustees and as a journal reviewer for Innovations in Higher Education.

Michael T. Nietzel is the retired president of Missouri State University. Prior to his time at Missouri State University, he was at the University of Kentucky from 1973 to 2005, where he served in various leadership roles, including Dean of the Graduate School and Provost. After his retirement from Missouri State, Nietzel served as senior policy advisor to Missouri Governor Jay Nixon and was later the Deputy Director of the Missouri Department of Mental Health. Since 2019, he has been a Senior Contributor to Forbes online, writing about higher education.

Made in the USA
Columbia, SC
25 October 2024

45066280R00143